Join

the millions of American women who have made home sewing their favorite—and most rewarding!—hobby. Using this new approach to home sewing, with today's new methods and new equipment, every woman can easily master the basic steps and become an expert.

Here is the first book completely devoted to the new ways in sewing today. Simple, easy-to-follow directions will teach you how to choose your pattern, pick the proper needle, finish details, do alterations, add designer details. You will learn how foolproof tools take the guesswork out of such important steps as buttonhole making, seam ripping and pattern cutting. You will discover how to reduce the time needed to perform essential steps, and still get perfect results every time!

DRITZ GUIDE TO
Modern Sewing

JULIA McCOMBS

Illustrations by

FRANCES BURGER

JOHN DRITZ AND SONS • NEW YORK, N.Y.

DRITZ GUIDE TO MODERN SEWING

First printing, April 1964
Second printing, July 1964

SPECIAL EDITION

*Printed by arrangement with Pyramid Publications, Inc.,
444 Madison Avenue, New York 22, New York, U.S.A.*

Acknowledgements

My first grateful acknowledgement goes to that dedicated developer of sewing techniques, Mrs. Edna Bryte Bishop. It has been a great privilege to have had the advantage of her friendship, advice, encouragement and instruction for many years. It was this grand lady who revolutionized the whole approach to home sewing and made it a delightful and popular pastime instead of a dreary duty.

Particularly special thanks go to friends in the pattern industry at Vogue-Butterick Company, McCall Corporation, Simplicity Pattern Company and Advance Patterns. Helpful contributions from the fiber-fabric field have come from Dow Chemical Company, Owens Corning Fiberglas Corporation, Armo Woven Interfacing, Milium Division of Deering Milliken and Keybak Division of Chicopee Mills, Inc. Singer Sewing Machine Company generously provided the machine on our cover and other special material. Greist Manufacturing Company gave us fine and detailed sewing machine attachment illustrations and information. Thanks to Proctor-Silex Corporation for the steam-spray iron and adjustable ironing table illustrations. Coats and Clark, Inc., were generous in providing special sewing illustrations and thread information. Talon Educational Service contributed helpful material on zipper applications.

We are also indebted for help from: Rite Dress Form Mfg., Co., Belding-Corticelli, Celanese Corp., Curtain and Drapery Magazine, Lily Mills, Eastman Chemical Products, Inc., Stanley-Judd, White Sewing Machine Co., Famous Features Syndicate, House Beautiful, Dupont Co., Necchi-Elna, Reader Mail Service, Pellon Corp., American Cyanamid Co., Better Homes and Gardens, Courtaulds North America, Inc., Kirsch Co., Inc., Modes Royale Patterns, Good Housekeeping Magazine, Pfaff Sewing Machine Co., Spadea Fashions, American Home Magazine, Conso Products, Inc.

For very helpful impartial product information and analysis

I am indebted to Consumer Reports published by Consumers Union, Mount Vernon, New York. Also, much valuable data was given with permission to use by United States Agriculture Bulletin Service, Washington, D. C.

Julia C. McCombs

Dedication

This book is lovingly dedicated to Mr. John Dritz, who has been far more than a good employer to me. His understanding, encouragement and steadfast confidence, through dark days and bright, have made him a very special person in my experience.

Contents

INTRODUCTION

Possibly you and I have met sometime when our mutual interest in home sewing has brought us together. I have met literally thousands of women and girls all over this country in department stores, at schools, or at Home Bureau meetings since I began to work for John Dritz and Sons, Inc. It may have been even before that when I was a stylist with a pattern company or a zipper organization. We have discussed all kinds of sewing problems and their solutions.

I have found my position with Dritz particularly fascinating while they have been developing so many new sewing aids. I truly believe these new tools have helped greatly to change sewing methods and to make home sewing the American woman's favorite hobby.

New streamlined sewing methods and this new equipment, so essential to these methods, have revolutionized the needle arts for the amateur. Used together properly, they cut hours from what was once a laborious task. The better results these tools make possible have done much to give the most smartly dressed women pride in saying, "I made it myself," when once she kept this fact a great secret, even as I did.

Often I have been asked how I found such interesting work. I'm tempted to answer, "What WORK?," because I have always loved to sew. That is, almost always. The only time I ever took a dim view of sewing was when my grandmother used to insist that I sew two quilt blocks together before I could go out to play, yet how many times I have blessed her for teaching me so early how to hold that tiny needle in my fingers. How often I have watched, with sympathy, young and old alike grapple with a needle as though it were a crowbar.

Yes, the hand needle was the first tool we learned to

1

use. Do you realize how it has been replaced by the beautiful, accurate, electric sewing machine which now can do basting and many other stitches? Of course, it is nice to be able to do fine hand finishing when you become a real sewing addict. But, being clumsy with a hand needle, today, need not discourage beginning sewing efforts.

In this book I bring to you a nice blending of the new and conventional methods of sewing, and instruction in how to use the right tool, in the right place, at the right time, as it has never been done before.

When we first began developing new sewing aids, I did not start out testing them with a professional point of view. I was just an average amateur sewer who liked to sew. As an amateur (who was left-handed, to boot) I had experienced all the frustrations and made all the mistakes that anyone ever had. I felt that if I could improve my sewing by using some of the new techniques and tools, every other amateur could find them helpful, too. So, you see, I hope the trials and successes which make up the experience of another amateur will help you sew easier and with more confidence and a lot more fun.

JULIA C. McCOMBS

New York, 1964

CHAPTER 1

New and Old Tools

The standard list of necessary sewing implements and accessories always included (and still includes) these items for the beginning home sewer:

Needles	Tape measure	Fastenings
Pins	Yardstick	(buttons, hooks
Thread	Skirt marker	and eyes, snaps)
Thimble	Tailor's chalk	Seam and hem
Emery (to sharpen	Dress form	bindings
needles)	Sewing machine	Beltings
Scissors	Pressing supplies	Cutting board
Cutting shears	Patterns	Full-length mirror
Buttonhole scissors		

Today, new things have happened in almost every one of these classifications of sewing accessories. Of course, the beginning sewer does not need to acquire everything at once. In this chapter I will define the essential tools and show what may be added as you go along. But, let us now look at some of the changes that have been made in sewing habits since these new tools have been added to lighten the labor of sewing.

▶ **Needles**

Hand needles are made of steel. Never try to get along with one needle for everything. They come in sizes and types for different uses and different weights of fabric. Consult the needle and thread chart (Fig. I-1) in this chapter. *Sharps* are

FABRIC, THREAD, NEEDLE AND STITCH LENGTH CHART

TYPES OF FABRICS	THREAD SIZES	NEEDLE SIZES	MACHINE STITCH SETTING FOR STRAIGHT SEWING		HAND NEEDLES
			INSIDE SEAMS	TOP STITCHING	
Filmy materials comparable to Net, Marquisette, Chiffon, Silk and Chiffon Velvets, Voiles, Ninon	50 Embroidery 100 Cotton Synthetic Thread	9	15 to 20	15 to 20	10
Sheer materials comparable to Lawn, Dimity, Synthetic Sheers, Paper Taffetas, Pure Silks, Gossamer Silks, Silk or Synthetic Tricots, Synthetic Velvets, Satins	50 Embroidery 80 to 100 Cotton A Silk Synthetic Thread	11	12 to 15	15 to 20	9
Lightweight materials comparable to Gingham, Chambray, Pique, Poplin, Percale, Cretonne, Chintz, Faille, Bengaline, Wool Flannel, Wool Jersey, Wool Crepe, Cotton Velvets and Velveteens, Lightweight Suitings	50 Mercerized 60 to 80 Cotton A Silk	14 or 16	12	15 to 18	8
Medium heavy materials comparable to Corduroy, Crash, Gabardine, Rep, Heavy Suitings and Coatings	Heavy Duty Mer. 40 to 60 Cotton Synthetic Thread	16	10	12	6
Heavy materials comparable to Sailcloth, Denim, Ticking, Overcoatings	30 to 40 Cotton Thread	18	8	10	4
Plastic materials	50 Embroidery Synthetic Thread 50 Mercerized	11 or 14	10	12	—

Fig. I-1 Fabric, Thread, Needle, and Stitch Length Chart

medium length. *Betweens* are shorter for fine stitching on heavy fabric. *Milliners* are longer than either of the others, good for millinery and basting. All of these have short eyes. *Crewel* (embroidery) needles have a long eye. *Chanille* (sharp point) and *tapestry* (blunt point) are short and thick with a very long eye. The newest thing that has happened to ordinary sewing needles is a self-threading needle called the *Calyx-eyed sharp.*

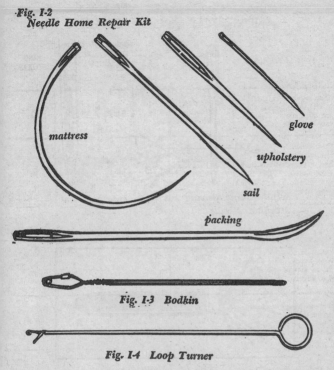

·Fig. I-2
Needle Home Repair Kit

mattress

glove

upholstery

sail

packing

Fig. I-3 Bodkin

Fig. I-4 Loop Turner

Also, there's a *Needle Home Repair Kit* (Fig. I-2), which includes some oddly shaped needles for special tasks that home sewers formerly did not attempt. This kit contains two curved *mattress* needles, a *sail* needle, an *upholstery pin*, a *packing* needle, and a *glove* needle.

In the category of needles comes the new type of *bodkin* which is a combination dull bodkin and safety pin (Fig. I-3). It is 6″ long, and the safety-pin eye may be attached to ribbons or lacings as you pull them through the casing tops of pajamas and such.

Another new tool which seems to fit among needle-type instruments is the *loop turner* (Fig. I-4). It is used when the bodkin is too coarse for turning narrow bias tubing like "spaghetti" trimming. It is 10″ long and has a latch-hook eye, which firmly grips the material that has to be turned inside-out in a very narrow space.

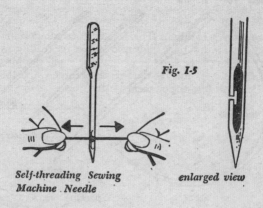

Fig. I-5

Self-threading Sewing
Machine Needle

enlarged view

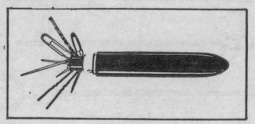

Fig. I-6 Magnet

Sewing machine needles were long the stumbling block in the development of sewing machines because they could not be made to behave as hand needles do in the hand. It was not until the eye was put in the point, instead of in the blunt end, that the problem was solved. Once you had to ask for sewing machine needles to fit a particular make of machine. Now, needles have been developed that will fit several makes of machines. Refer to the package and you will know whether they fit yours. These are made of a special high-quality, polished and nickel-plated steel and have extra sharp points.

Sewing machine needles also come in a self-threading model (Fig. I-5). This is certainly a boon to those always on the hunt for that tiny, elusive hole. There is an almost imperceptible slot into which the thread slips easily as you slide it against the needle's shank.

▶ *Pins*

Pins are made of brass or steel. I prefer steel pins because they are sharper and finer. This is particularly important when working on fabrics that show pin marks as readily as does satin or taffeta. But, whether of brass or steel, the pins must be smooth, sharp, fine, and of first quality. Once they get rusty, bent, or dull, throw them out!

Fig. I-7 Wrist Pin Cushion

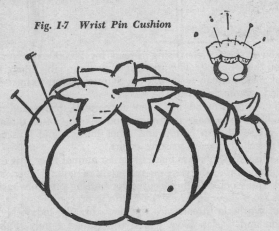

Fig. I-8 Tomato-shaped Pin Cushion with Emery

▶ *Magnet*

Maybe I like steel pins best because I prefer picking them up with my *magnet* (Fig. I-6). It is encased in a handle to which I tie a string so that I can drag it around the floor and not have to bend down. My magnet also fishes steel bobbins, small sewing machine attachments, safety pins, etc., from the depths of the sewing machine drawer.

▶ *Pin Cushion and Emery*

Since a *pin cushion* adds to the convenience of using pins, we might whimsically call it a pin accessory. They say the first highly embellished ones appeared during the reign of Good Queen Bess. I bless whoever invented the *wrist pin cushion* (Fig. I-7) which keeps pins "on hand," yet leaves both hands free. There are gaily colored washable foam rubber ones and cloth-covered, sand-filled ones, both very inexpensive and mighty convenient.

The standard tomato-shaped pin cushion with a strawberry-shaped *emery* attached (Fig. I-8) provides one of the essentials named in my first list. The emery is for keeping steel needles rust-free. It's not just rust that affects needles; they get sticky from hand perspiration. By running the needle through the emery now and then, you sharpen the point and clean the needle.

▶ *Thread*

We sewers have been using thread for 25,000 years; what do you think of that? The first thread was probably linen. But, it took an American woman, Mrs. Samuel Slater, to introduce spooled cotton thread to the world.

Now cotton thread has been mercerized, pre-waxed, and made lint-free to make it stronger and silkier. Cotton thread is used for sewing on cotton and other fabrics, and it is carefully matched to each season's colors.

Because silk thread is made from an animal fiber it is especially appropriate for use on materials of animal fiber, such as silk and wool. Silk thread used for basting prevents basting marks from showing when the fabric is pressed.

The synthetic threads are the new threads, today. Nylon, Dacron and Taslan have joined the thread family. Fabrics containing these fibers should only be sewn with these threads because they wash and clean the same way.

A special *nylon elastic thread* should be mentioned here. This is for shirr-stitching whenever you wish an elasticized shirring. It has a strong elastic core wound in durable nylon so it takes a lot of strain and stretching. You wind it on the sewing machine bobbin and use the regular thread on top, and sew with a large stitch.

Thread accessories are important to home sewers because we accumulate so many spools. There is nothing more annoying than having threads get all tangled up in one's sewing basket or thread box. Now, there are *thread locks* (Fig. I-9), little plastic plugs for the top of a spool that hold the thread and prevent it from unwinding. You wind the loose end around the plug and then push the plug firmly into the spool.

Thread and bobbin boxes hold each spool on its own spindle or in a niche. The transparent *thread box* (Fig. I-10) that holds all sizes of spools is most practical because thread comes

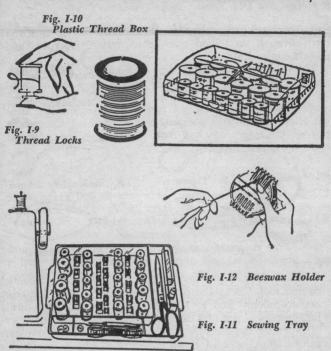

Fig. I-10
Plastic Thread Box

Fig. I-9
Thread Locks

Fig. I-12 Beeswax Holder

Fig. I-11 Sewing Tray

on large and small spools for many different purposes. There is also a *sewing tray* (Fig. I-11) that holds thread spool and sewing machine bobbin side by side. The tray has partitions for shears, small tools, and thimbles. This tray is especially convenient to keep near you as you sew.

Another convenient thread accessory is beeswax, which now comes in a clear plastic case to keep it clean (Fig. I-12). You pull the doubled strand of basting or button thread through the slots in the plastic case so they are waxed together, tangle-free and strong. If you have lost your patience as often as I have while sewing on buttons, because the thread tangles and snaps, you will bless the lowly beeswax.

▶ Cutting Tools

When your cutting is done correctly, half the home sewing battle is won.

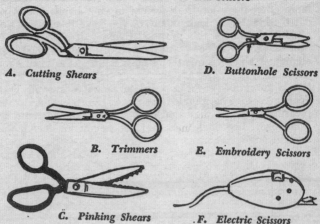

Fig. I-13   Shears and Scissors

A. Cutting Shears

D. Buttonhole Scissors

B. Trimmers

E. Embroidery Scissors

C. Pinking Shears

F. Electric Scissors

Shears (Fig. I-13)—good, sharp shears—are the essential cutting tool. Cheap shears that soon lose their cutting edge are no economy. And, for heaven's sake, keep your good shears for sewing and don't let the whole family use them for everything under the sun. Dressmaking shears usually have one handle large enough for two fingers; the other is smaller for the thumb. The handle is bent so the blade may be rested on the table (Fig. I-13A). Seven-, seven-and-a-half, and eight-inch shears are best for cutting out a garment. Because I am left-handed, shears were always backwards for me and my two fingers had to be squeezed into the thumb hole. Now special shears for "southpaws" are available.

Electric scissors (Fig. I-13F) are the most modern type of the cutting shears. They do the work much more quickly and accurately. The cut line is continuous, exact, never chopped. Electric scissors will cut anything from lace to leather with the same ease. You should see how beautifully they cut my fleece coat, two thicknesses at once, this winter! Furthermore, I had no aching, dented, blistered fingers, after I had finished. Actually, the mild vibration of the electric scissors in your palm rests and relaxes your hand. Best of all, you have never cut out anything so swiftly in all your life! Also, they are completely safe!

Pinking shears (Fig. I-13C) and scalloping shears are finishing shears that give seam edges a ravel-resistant finish. It is best not to use them for cutting out your garment because, more often than not, their weight in your hands makes you cut inaccurately. I know many of you have been using your pinking shears for this purpose, thinking it saves time. No professional ever does! Remember, the saw-toothed edge eliminates almost a quarter of an inch from the seam allowance. If you allow for this, your piece is likely to be too large. Pinking shears give an angular zig-zag finish. Scallopers give a rounded, scalloped finish which is very pleasing. Both of these finishing shears come in large and small sizes. The small ones are light weight for finer fabrics, and the large ones are for heavy fabrics.

Scissors (Fig. I-13B) are small shears with a blade less than six inches long. Both handles are usually the same size and the blades are straight. When small clipping and cutting is to be done it is too awkward to use shears. A dainty pair of *embroidery scissors* (Fig. I-13E), four to six inches long, is necessary. They, too, must be kept sharp, particularly at the points.

Buttonhole scissors (Fig. I-13D) have a little gap in the blade so the cut just goes in the middle of a buttonhole where it belongs. They are a good cutting accessory to own if you make a lot of the stitched-type buttonholes. However, they do not seem to be stressed in modern sewing as much as they were once.

Fig. I-14   Seam Ripper

The seam ripper (Fig I-14) is a handy little tool that works better than buttonhole scissors. It is completely safe to use because the cutting edge is at the center of the curve and is protected by a small red ball on the short side. It's an inexpensive, good quality tool, which has eliminated that menace in sewing, the razor blade. It accomplishes a multitude of other tasks besides piercing buttonhole centers. As its name implies, it is useful for ripping out seams when a mistake has been made. And that's only a small part of what it does for me. Whenever I need a small point to push the fabric into the corner of a buckle I am making, or to poke out a corner, or to slash the welt piece on a buttonhole, my seam ripper is ready.

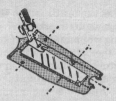

Fig. I-15 Bound Buttonhole Maker

Speaking of buttonholes, I used to avoid making bound buttonholes until the bound buttonhole maker (Fig. I-15) came my way, and now I brag about them. This device makes bound buttonholes easier than the buttonhole scissors ever did. It is not a sewing machine attachment. It is a small bronze plate which holds the fabric welt in place while you machine-stitch over the marked buttonhole area. It helps you make bound buttonholes accurately in any size from ½" to 2".

Another most recent innovation in the bound buttonhole is the decorative three-cornered, or triangular, buttonhole. It may be made with the help of a triangular plastic pattern template to give you the right size and shape. There are directions for finishing these smartly shaped buttonholes that accompany the template.

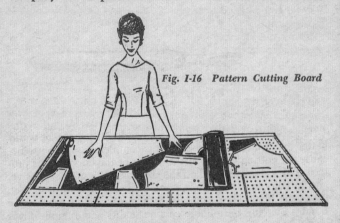

Fig. I-16 Pattern Cutting Board

▶ *Pattern Cutting Board*

To my mind the pattern cutting board (Fig. 1-16) is the best thing that has happened in the cutting department since shears. The board folds so that it is easy to store out of sight when you are not using it. Unfolded it is 40″ wide by 72″ long. The entire surface is marked off in inches in both directions. By pinning your fabric selvage and crosswise ends to the markings on the cutting board, you can be sure that the fabric is perfectly straight when you pin on the pattern pieces. By using a cutting board you save the top of a good table from pin scratches. Also, it makes a wonderful cutting space when placed on a reasonably high bed, without danger to the bedspread.

► *Tape Measures*

Accuracy is the most important consideration in any measuring device. My favorite tape measure story is about the engineer who wouldn't trust his wife to measure for the draperies she was going to make for their new house. He measured meticulously with the tape measure she gave him. When she had finished her sewing, all the draperies were 5″ too short! Imagine the poor man's ire when he discovered this was because his wife had first washed the tape measure and it had shrunk. She would have been much better off to have bought a new tape measure for such a very important undertaking, don't you think? Certainly anyone who is that serious a sewer could afford to have a good, guaranteed-not-to-shrink tape measure.

Your tape measure should be a good one which will not tear, tangle or stretch. (Fig. I-17). Make sure that it starts from number 1 at both ends. The kind that rolls up on a reel is less messy in your mending basket, and there is a bright colored one which is easy to find wherever it is. Some tapes are made of washable oilcloth. There is one with wires woven through it, which was originally invented for surveyors, who cannot afford to have their measurements stretch no matter how tightly they pull the tape measure. There is also a brand-new one, guaranteed for life, which is made of fiber glass.

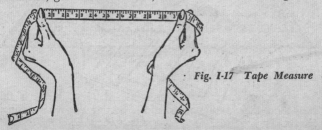

Fig. I-17 Tape Measure

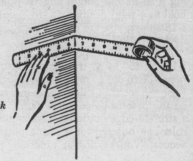

Fig. I-18 Roll-up Yardstick

▶ Yardsticks

The standard yardstick is made of natural-colored hard wood that will not warp and is metal-tipped at both ends. It has a multitude of uses about the house for other things besides sewing. Actually, I don't think that engineer should blame his wife for the short draperies. He should have used a yardstick in the first place.

The roll-up yardstick (Fig. I-18), which is made of flexible metal is a brand new invention. It can be made rigid by roll-

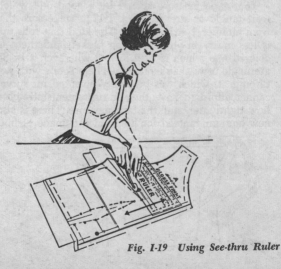

Fig. I-19 Using See-thru Ruler

ing it to its full length and snapping the ends. Or, it can be held in a rigid position at any point along the roll. As Figure I-18 shows, you are able to measure around corners with this new yardstick.

A real multi-purpose sewing aid is the *see-thru ruler* (Fig. I-19), a 15" by 4" transparent T-square. It is almost as indispensable to me as my cutting board and I use them together. I use the see-thru ruler to measure from the grain-line marking on the pattern piece to the fabric selvage. It is also useful as a straight-edge guide for a tracing wheel, and the slots on the ruler can be used for marking pleats, tucks, and bias and for accurately measuring and marking pattern alterations.

▶ Skirt Markers

There is a lovely old-fashioned painting of grandpa down on his knees with pins in his mouth, measuring the hem of grandma's skirt with a yardstick. Of course, he's very bent over because grandma wore ankle-length skirts. This is not so overdrawn, as many a man and boy will attest, because the skirt marker, as we know it, was not invented until nearly the Second World War. This handy device has gone through quite an evolution since its inception. Now any sewer can be quite independent of another's help if she uses the blow-type or chalk-type *skirt marker* (Fig. I-20), which she can control herself before a full-length mirror. There is one kind that even

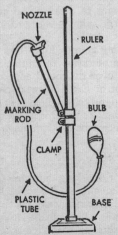

NOZZLE
RULER
MARKING ROD
BULB
CLAMP
PLASTIC TUBE
BASE

Fig. I-20   Chalk Type Skirt Marker

grasps the hem and marks automatically with the mere squeeze of the attached bulb.

Apparently, another thing that once meant "skirt marker" was a notched piece of cardboard which a woman had to make for herself. Now, a six-inch metal gauge (Fig. I-21), with an adjustable pointed staff that may be set at any desired spot along the rule, is much more accurate and flexible. This device is used to measure the width of a hem. It has spaced holes on one edge for use in measuring and marking circles, scallops, and curves.

A similar tool, which may be had in several gay colors of plastic, is called a tailorette (Fig. I-22). In addition to the adjustable gauge there is a small piece of tailor's chalk attached to one end so you can mark as you measure. If the chalk gives out, you can get refills.

Almost as new as this book is a *transparent scalloper* (Fig. I-23), which is a rule on one edge but is shaped in various sizes of scallops on the other edge. The half circles around which you measure your scallop size vary from one half inch all the way up to two inches. This device is slotted so that you can wind your tape measure around it, as a convenient way of storing it.

All of these little tools are far more helpful for correctly adjusting hem lengths and widths than that "by-guess-and-by-gosh" piece of cardboard with only one notch. How complicated the hem-marking process was without any tools! It's no wonder that many women, exposed to the methods of the "good old days," sent all their hems to a tailor and advised their daughters to do the same. Yet, what a waste of money, when it's so easy with good modern tools.

The latest tool is the hem pressing gauge (Fig. I-24) which is used to press the hem over, after marking. You turn the hem back on the chalk line and press over the metal edge of this gauge. You use either the straight or flared edge, depending upon the shape of your hem. The depth of the hem may be cut according to the second line on the gauge. This gauge is also a special joy for turning curtain hems before stitching.

▶ Tailor's Chalk and Marking

Tailor's chalk has been used for marking adjustments on fabric and pattern since time immemorial. It should be the "chalky" and not the "waxy" kind, because waxy chalk stains the modern highly-finished fabrics. But, chalk, used frequently, as it inevitably is, gets slick and won't mark. So, a

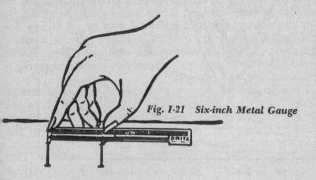

Fig. I-21   Six-inch Metal Gauge

Fig. I-22   Tailorette

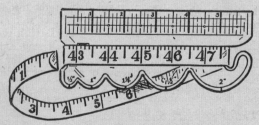

Fig. I-23   Transparent Scalloper

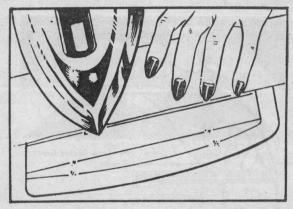

Fig. I-24   Hem Pressing Gauge

great innovation is the tailor's chalk holder (Fig. I-25). This little plastic case has a sharpener on one end to keep the chalk sharpened thin and powdery on the edge. The chalk comes in small white, blue or red squares which fit the holder when the first piece wears out.

▶ Tracing Wheel and Paper

A great new-old discovery makes modern sewing a lot more accurate, simpler, and more fun to do. It is the adoption of an old method, almost forgotten for a while, called a tracing wheel. But, it was so sharp it bit right through the fabric. The new tracing wheel has been designed so that it will not cut the most delicate fabrics. Yet, it marks with precision with the aid of tracing paper (Fig. I-26). Of course, tracing paper has to be used with common sense, because the darker colors particularly do not clean out of all fabrics readily. Try to use the white paper wherever you can, and the dark only when no other shade shows up. Tracing paper is always placed against the wrong side of the fabric.

▶ Dress Forms

Dress forms have been used by amateurs and professionals alike for a long time. There are those made to standard sizes which may be padded to your measurements. Or, you can get

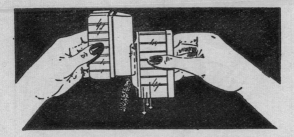

Fig. I-25   *Tailor's Chalk Holder with Sharpener*

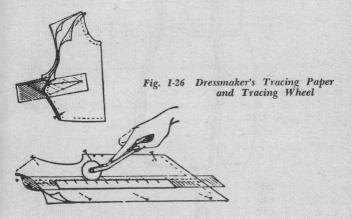

Fig. I-26   *Dressmaker's Tracing Paper
and Tracing Wheel*

an adjustable rigid form (Fig. I-27) that may be changed in
length and width at bust, waist, and hips. Mine has sixteen
sections and adjusts exactly to my figure. Just be careful you
get one designed to modern figure measurements. Women's
figures have changed somewhat since 1890. So, grandma's
dummy in the attic is hardly for you, nor are those forms still
planned to measurement standards of her day. The only dress
form which may be molded on the figure is one made of
pliable wire mesh. The advantage of using a dress form is that
your garment may be tried on it, during the assembly, saving
you from having to dress and undress too often.

The primary reason for working with a dress form is so
that you fit the lines of your garment as it should look on your
figure. There is another way to learn where your adjustments

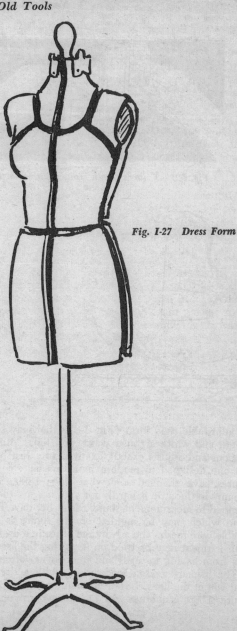

Fig. I-27 Dress Form

should be made, and probably it is the most accurate because it teaches you how and where to adjust each pattern before cutting it out. All pattern companies now make a basic pattern. I don't mean you have to make up a basic pattern of every brand you use. Since pattern manufacturers worked out standardized measurements with the National Bureau of Standards in Washington, D. C., all are the same. So, what you do with one basic pattern will apply to any other brand. After studying out your figure type and choosing the best one for you, make up this basic pattern by cutting it out of a sturdy fabric. I will discuss figure types in the next chapter. Carefully fit your basic cloth pattern on your own figure and make all changes on it. Then, every time you buy a pattern, compare it with the basic pattern and make the same alterations in the new, before cutting out your garment.

▶ *Sewing Machines*

So many changes and improvements are being made in sewing machines that it is hard to keep up with them. Now that the modern sewing machine is so exact and easy to operate, a lot of hand operations have become unnecessary. Let your sewing machine baste for you, gauge your stitch size, make zig-zag finishes, darn, and mend for you. At the push of a button it sews forward and back or locks the stitch and it also embroiders. I am devoting a whole chapter to how you may take advantage of all this new sewing freedom. Also, we will talk about all those marvelous attachments, new and old.

Here I will mention one special accessory that is not included with a sewing machine. Many beginners, even many who sew well, have trouble sewing in a straight line. There is a device called a sew-straight plate (Fig. I-28) to help you

Fig. I-28 Sew-straight Plate

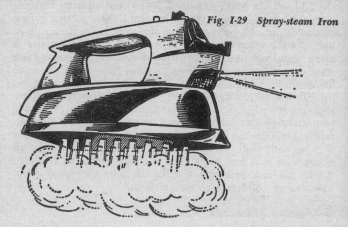

Fig. I-29 Spray-steam Iron

Courtesy Proctor Silex Co.

here. It is a rigid plastic plate that fits in front of the needle and fastens to the machine bed. You hold your finger over your work on a ridge that corresponds to the width of seam you want. This guides your sewing in a straight line.

▶ Pressing Supplies

"Press as you sew!" is more of a command than ever. Once, a whole garment was completed before it was pressed. Then, it was pressed on the wrong side only. But, with new steam-spray irons, adjustable flip-top ironing tables, and all the other tailors' pressing equipment newly adapted for home sewing, everyone can press as she sews and have completely professional results.

Electric steam irons are improving all the time. I have just acquired a new one that sprays as well as steams (Fig. I-29). It is about half the weight of its ten-year-old predecessor, which was the last word in steam irons in its day. It is twice as effective for professional pressing.

A good sturdy ironing board or table is especially important. Remember, sometimes in tailoring you need to pound collar and lapel edges flat with a lot of force. You can't work on a rickety ironing board then. It is mighty nice, too, if you can sit down while you work. I like to keep my adjustable ironing table (Fig. I-30) at the same level as my sewing machine,

Fig. I-30   Adjustable Ironing Table

Fig. I-31   Pressing Hams: (left): seam roll; (middle): tailor's ham; (right): dressmaker's ham

near enough so that I can turn easily from one to the other—sew and press—press and sew. My ironing table has a double flip-top which accommodates pieces of different sizes with a minimum of manipulation. It may be pushed around easily on the wheels under the rear leg.

Some of the oldest professional pressing supplies were only very recently made available to home sewers. These are the tailor's cushions or pressing hams (Fig. I-31). Three sizes are available. There is a seam roll for pressing inside sleeves, zipper plackets, and long, narrow curved seams; a medium dressmaker's ham for dressmaking details, such as pressing the curve under a bust dart, or shrinking the top of a set-in sleeve cap; and a large tailors' ham for tailoring details, such as pressing the proper roll in a collar or lapel. These pressing hams are packed with dry, hardwood sawdust and covered with wool so the steam penetrates the fabric more readily. Also, wool against wool helps to avoid unwanted shine.

A tailor gets that thin, elegantly turned edge to an interfaced collar or lapel by first bringing the steam through the fabric, then clapping it soundly with a heavy wooden block. But the shallow groove around the edge of that block was always so hard to hang on to. So, this clapper, or pounding block, has been combined with the *point presser* as its handle (Fig. I-32).

Fig. I-32
Point Presser and Pounding Block

Fig. I-33 *Velvet Board*

When turning a point on a collar or lapel, first press into the corners of seams over the point presser on the wrong side to get seams flat before trimming them. Use the collar point turner, a 1″ by 4″ plastic rule with a sharp pointed angle at one end shaped to turn out a point just right. The two oval slots in the handle of this tool can also be used for sewing on buttons to give them a proper thread shank. In fact, the full name of the tool is the collar point turner and button gauge (*see* Fig. IX-38).

I think a lot of women have had the mistaken impression that no pressing cloth is needed with a steam iron. Nothing is further from the fact, particularly in sewing. Now, "top pressing" is as important as "under pressing." Top pressing is done on the right side of the fabric. Here's where you must use press cloths to keep from producing a shine on the fabric surface. A treated drill cloth is used for pressing heavy woolens and other sturdy fabrics. I like another light-weight press cloth that I can see through, about the firmness of permanent finish organdy. Also, a length of cheese cloth is useful because it can be moistened and wrung out almost dry, unlike any other fabric or sponge.

A padded press mitt that will slip on over the hand is good to have for pressing hard-to-get-at areas and construction details.

A sleeve board, for turning out a neatly turned sleeve and for many other small pressing jobs is essential for the home sewer.

If you like to work with velvet, velveteen, corduroy, fur fabrics or other pile fabrics, it is good to know that there is a velvet board (Fig. I-33). It looks like a miniature torture mat. The foundation is canvas, into which tiny wire needles have been set upright, very close together. This prevents the pile from being flattened by the pressure of your iron.

CHAPTER 2

Basic Notions

In addition to the new and old tools discussed in the previous chapter, the efficient home sewer should be familiar with, and have a supply of, the notions (or findings, as they are often called) which are described in this chapter.

▶ *Fastenings*

Probably Eve fastened her fig leaves together with thorns, which later evolved into pins. Pins were the only form of fastenings down through many centuries until someone discovered that eyelets and lacing would hold garments together better against chill winds. Yes, eyelets came before buttons, so we'll talk first about eyelets.

Metal eyelets (Fig. II-1) are available to the modern home sewer in two sizes. The small eyelet is now mainly a belt fastening. A larger size is used at tops of shower curtains, or for holding drawstrings at tops of bags. These may be applied to fabric with inexpensive punching and setting tools which are packaged with them. Or, there are pliers which will set both sizes. The pliers will punch a hole and set an eyelet at the same time.

The awl, or stilleto (Fig. II-3), is used for punching holes, too, usually for making hand embroidered eyelets (Fig. II-2). This lethal little weapon comes sheathed in a protective shield.

Buttons have a fabulous history. Since the thirteenth century, when someone slit his cloth and poked a round object through it, buttons have monopolized the fashion stage among fasteners. Making beautiful buttons became such a fine art that they were handed down with the family jewels. King Francis I of France wore 13,600 on a court costume, and

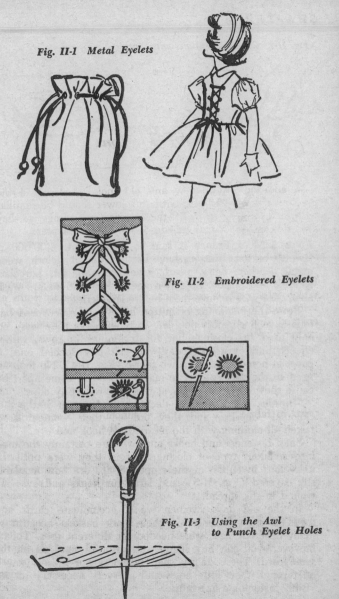

Fig. II-1 Metal Eyelets

Fig. II-2 Embroidered Eyelets

Fig. II-3 Using the Awl
to Punch Eyelet Holes

Fig. II-4 Covering Buttons with Fabric

Fig. II-5 Silk Covered Snap

Louis XIV of France is said to have spent $600,000 on jeweled buttons. Buttons have been made from cloth, wood, metal, leather, ivory, pearl, jewels, crystal, jet, porcelain, ceramic and plastic. Be sure your modern buttons are washable, otherwise remove them before laundering.

From the beginning of button history, fabric-covered buttons have been most popular. In olden days they were not only used for closings but for trimmings in rows, tufting effects, and clusters. Today you can buy special ones to cover at home with your own fabric (Fig. II-4). No tools are needed; they are so easy to make, and never come apart because they're held together at the back with tiny clips.

"Buttons are a vanity" decreed the Puritan Fathers of Colonial America, and they ordered their womenfolk to fasten all clothing with the inexpensive hook and eye.

Snap fasteners and hooks and eyes are certainly the most inconspicuous type of closing; that is, they were until the marvelous invention of the zipper. Snaps are now available silk covered (Fig. II-5), and large fur hooks and eyes are wound in silk thread.

In the old days, women would accumulate cards and cards of snap fasteners in their work baskets because so many different sizes were needed for different uses. Today, however, you can buy snaps with assorted sizes all on the same card. These dainty snap fasteners are always sewed on through their little holes and are very necessary for invisibly fastening a fine fabric.

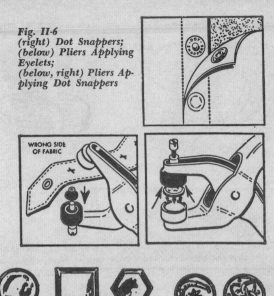

Fig. II-6
(right) Dot Snappers;
(below) Pliers Applying
Eyelets;
(below, right) Pliers Applying Dot Snappers

Fig. II-7   Decorative Dot Snaps

Dot snappers are permanently hammered onto the fabric or applied with pliers (Fig. II-6). In fact, there are double-purpose pliers which apply both the snappers and the eyelets by simply adjusting the head of the tool. These snappers, once affixed to a garment, stay on for the life of the garment. They have saved many a mother hours of sewing on buttons, especially when used on the crotch of youngsters' overalls and fronts of pajamas. Of course, plain ring snappers look strictly utilitarian. But, there are also pearl- and decorative-topped ones that are used on sport shirts, nurses' uniforms, and Western-style play clothes (Fig. II-7).

Hooks and eyes haven't changed. They still have either a U-shaped eye or a long flat eye. A flat heavy hook and eye is used at the top of men's trousers instead of a button because it stays on better and wears longer. Now women have adopted this sturdy type for the belt closing of a skirt (Fig. II-8). It is good, too, for the under closing on a wrap-around skirt. This heavy type can be sewed on, or it can be applied with mechanics pliers.

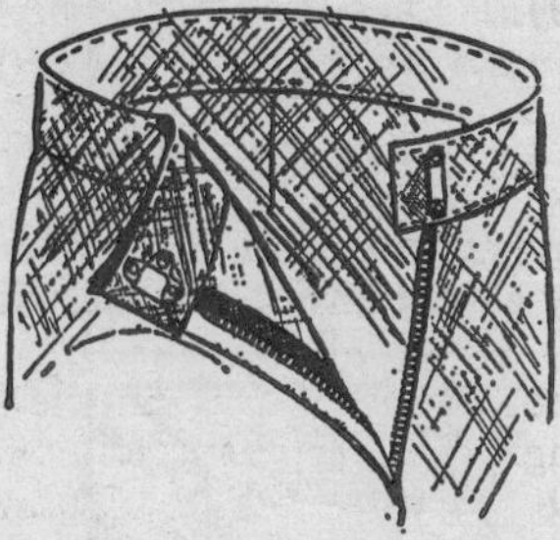

Fig. II-8 Flat Hook and Eye 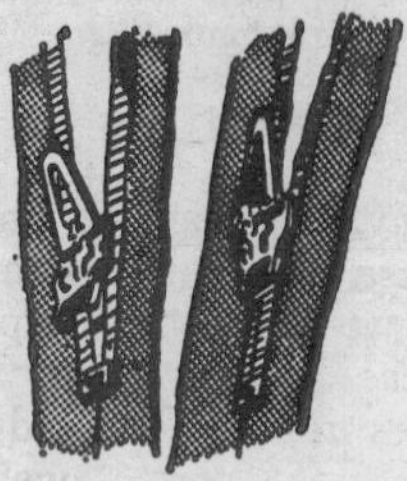   **Fig. II-9 Repairing Zipper**

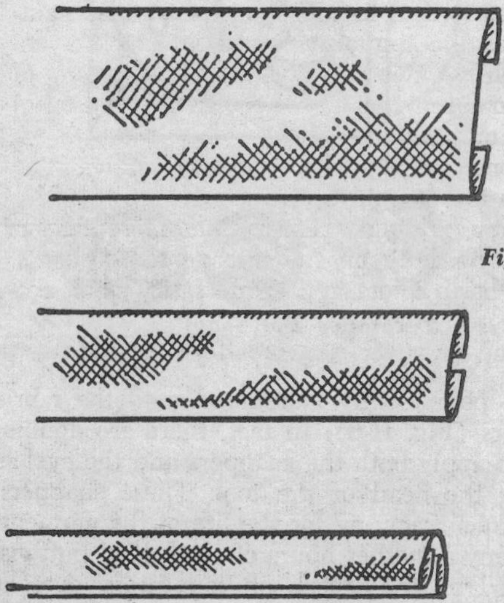

Fig. II-10 Bias Binding

Zippers were originally bulky and made of metal. The home sewer was hesitant to use this slide fastener on fine materials. But now the zipper has come into its own in the fashion field! It can be bought in all lengths and in a variety of colors to match almost any fabric. For work clothes, such as overalls, for children's sturdy play clothes, or for sports jackets, the heavier metal zipper is required; but for fine sewing, use the new seam-thin plastic type which is delicate, yet highly practical, and gives good wear. Follow pressing instructions for this plastic type most meticulously.

In a later chapter I will discuss repair and mending aids;

but I mention here that there is a Zipper Repair Kit, which includes a replaceable slider, should one get lost from an otherwise good zipper (Fig. II-9).

▶ *Bindings*

Today, it is hard to imagine having to cut all the bindings we use because you can now buy almost any shade you wish, in a wide variety of types.

Bias binding (Fig. II-10), both percale and fine lawn, comes in a finished width ½", single fold. You can get a wide variety of colors as well as some stripes, checks, and prints, all washable. The percale binding comes ¼" double fold, too. There is also a 1" bias fold in nainsook and a 2" bias nainsook skirt facing. Bias binding also comes in a ½" rayon. The seam tape which we use for finishing the bottom of hems is ½" wide, rayon and nylon, and is cut on the straight of the goods rather than on the bias.

Blanket binding comes in 2" and 3" acetate satin and in 2" nylon, both cut on the straight of the goods.

Sometimes we want a binding which is much more elegant for use as edging or finishing on the outside of garments. You can usually find basic colors in ½"-wide satin, wool, cotton, and rayon.

Pipings, which come narrower, are in satin, poplin, velvet, and even leather.

An edging, which is inserted in a seam, comes in satin and leather, and there's a ⅜" rayon cording.

Twill tape is used for binding sturdy fabrics for utilitarian purposes. It comes in black and white. It is woven in a twill pattern which gives it that name. You can get it ¼", ⅜", ½", ⅝", ¾", ⅞", and 1". I recommended using twill tape for supporting Dot Snapper applications.

▶ *Beltings*

We usually think of belting as a stiffening which goes on inside of a belt. This may be bought in black and white, ¾", 1", 1¼", 1½", and 2" wide. There is also a 1¼" belting for use inside skirt and trouser tops, which grips a blouse or shirt and holds it in place.

A special kind of belting is made to stiffen the inside of belts you make to match your dresses. It is sold by the

Fig. II-11   Belt

Fig. II-12   Ready-pleated Stiffening

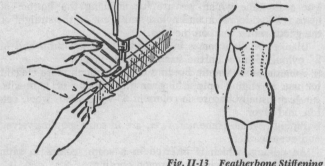

Fig. II-13   Featherbone Stiffening

yard or packaged in kits with buckles (Fig. II-11). Belting is available in ½″, ¾″, 1″, 1¼″, 1½″, 2″, 2½″ and 3″ wide, in black and white, and it can be washed or dry cleaned. Kits also come with a crushable, pellon-lined belting, 2½″ and 3″ wide only.

The popular contour-shaped belt also may be had in a kit so you can make these from your fabric. It includes a type of belting which is washable, dry cleanable and withstands hottest iron temperature.

Did you know it's well-nigh impossible to get a new patent in the fashion accessory field? I'm so proud of my inventive boss for having been granted a patent on a new buckle pattern material. Previously, all buckle patterns were made of a gummed paper similar to masking tape. After the belts had been made, the buckle looked a different color than the belt. The new buckle pattern is made of mylar, a thin plastic that will stretch in all directions with the fabric, as paper never would. One side is white and the other dark. Use the white under thin fabrics so the color is not changed.

Another new device is a clear plastic non-slip strip to hold the belt under the buckle without eyelets. The belt can't slip loose and out of the buckle.

Ready-pleated stiffening (Fig. II-12) is a skirt heading at the waistline, the first function of which is to make painless the calculation of unpressed pleats. It has always been such a chore to figure out ½" pleats so they are all even. This 1" stiffening comes already folded in ½" pleats. You pull away a little tape which holds the pleats together, unpleat, then sew the strip flat to your fabric. Then you pick up the fabric with the pleat, and fold each pleat as you stitch on the ready-folded crease in the stiffening. When used for top of a skirt, this pleating forms a stiffened belt area, which is covered with the belt piece of your fabric.

The *apron clip* comes under the belting category. This stiff, hoop-like circle of unbreakable plastic is made to go around the waist, encircling it like a bracelet. For a quick apron without strings, simply fold back a 1"-wide top hem and stitch a casing to house the apron clip.

▶ Stay Materials

Here is a category that hasn't been included in sewing books since the crinoline days. As you home sewers have become more demanding of modiste-type findings, they have been made available to the market again.

Whalebone was used at one time, but it gave way to feather-bone which was ingeniously braided turkey feather quills. The newest boning is lightweight and as unbendable, but it is made of nylon plastic. This boning is used as a support for the bodice of strapless gowns and bathing suits, as well as in foundation garments. It comes by the yard or in packages in clear only. It is encased in cotton-taped covering and is easy to sew.

Pattern companies sometimes buy finished Paris models, and from them they learn the greatest French couturiers' construction secrets. One secret they learned was the use of a stay material more flexible than featherbone. Zig-zag wires (Fig. II-14), once used for high choker collars, have put in a new appearance. If you watch your pattern instructions

Fig. II-14   Zig-zag Wire

Fig. II-15   Hoop Skirt Stiffening

you'll know when they are best to use. These silk-covered piano wires are bent in a zig-zag manner so that you may stretch, compress, or bend them to mold a curve. They are available in lengths of 3", 6", or 8" in black and white.

If the area down the side bodice of your gown is only 4", 5", or 6" long, you need not finish off the ends. You can use special cushion-tipped spiral bones, like those used in fine French gowns.

Featherboning is sometimes used in a hoop skirt. But, it may tend to bend more than is desirable. There is a kit for making a 96" hoop skirt stiffening (Fig. II-15) which never buckles or loses its completely rigid contour.

Sometimes you want to keep very filmy fabric from clinging and aid its floating quality. Also, heavy satins or silks must be kept mobile at hem edges. Here you use horsehair braid which comes packaged ½" and 1" wide, in black and white. In some trimming departments it is sold by the yard in wider widths. Now, it is made of nylon.

Lead weights give shape to a garment in a slightly different way; they anchor or weigh down fabric. Sometimes front coat corners have a tendency to flop, or back jacket hems ride up. Weights are sewn on to stay these tendencies. They come ¾", ⅞", 1⅛", 1¼" and 2" in diameter. Some are covered; the plain ones you cover yourself before attaching them at the desired spot. They are made of very soft lead and may be cut in two with shears. There is also a gilt and silver chain weighting which comes heavier for suits and coats and lighter for dresses. It is used to keep hem lines even.

▶ *Ready-Made Trimmings*

Before you leave this corner of the notion department, notice the bolts or racks of lovely decorative trimmings for your sewing. There is packaged lace in cotton and nylon in all widths of beading, insertion and edgings. There are eyelet embroidery trims shirred and straight in many widths. There are so many beautiful gay-colored peasant braids. Rick-rack comes in every size from miniature to jumbo, in colors and metallics, or colored with metallic edges. Also, there are woven metallic trimmings in great variety—gilt, silver, and copper. Some of it is on white or colored backgrounds, some tone-on-tone. The satin embroidery trimmings and ribbons are so lovely, and, incidentally, they make exquisite covered belts and buttons.

CHAPTER 3

Order in the Sewing Room

So that you may find much pleasure as well as profit in using the new sewing equipment now on the market, it is well to provide yourself with an efficient sewing area. A sewing machine drawer used to be all that was necessary for the home sewer, before she was blessed with all the new aids which are now available. Even more important is the new concept that sewing can only be done smartly in a logical sequence of motion without wasting time. Time and motion can only be saved in uncluttered space. And, you know how much clutter the simplest sewing project can make.

Gone are the days when the home sewer kept the sewing machine in the upstairs bedroom and ran down to the kitchen to press when everything was half made. Now, we press as we sew. We no longer cut on top of a soft bed or a slippery table. Keeping fabric grain perfect is most important. To save time the new small sewing aids have to be kept right at hand when you need them. So, let us consider in their logical sequence the things that you do when sewing. Then, whether you have a sewing basket to keep in order, or a sewing room, your work will be organized.

What is that sewing sequence which is the key to orderly work? Knowing the sequence will help you plan whatever sewing area you decide to devise. The first steps require considerable space. First you spread out your pattern to study its markings. Possibly then you will find that some of the pattern pieces have to be altered, and that, too, requires plenty of room. After that you have to lay out the fabric and proceed with the cutting and marking.

Now, the equipment you have just used should be put away before you bring out the sewing machine, iron and

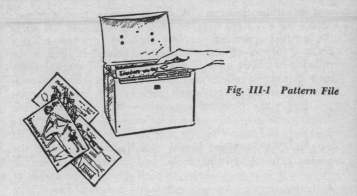

Fig. III-1   Pattern File

ironing board, and other pressing equipment. If possible, you should put the ironing board close enough to the sewing machine so that you can turn easily from one to the other. As you progress in your sewing, the small tools must be so near at hand that you can reach out and pick them up and put them away again without ever having to hunt for one (*see* Fig. I-11). It is ideal if you can work in a room with a full-length mirror. Your skirt marker should be placed right in front of the mirror in readiness for hemming. If you have a dress form, it should be easy to turn to without having to hop up every time.

After you have gone through the sewing routine of cutting out your pattern on the cutting board and transferred all the essential markings, your pattern should be neatly folded back into the envelope. Then it must be filed away in its rightful classification in an orderly manner. Here's where your pattern file becomes an organizer.

These pattern files (Fig. III-1), complete with handle, are gaily colored, plastic-covered boxes which hold more than twenty-five patterns, if all tissue pieces are folded up neatly. Index cards are included for various classifications, such as dresses, suits, coats, and children's clothes. Anyone who keeps more than twenty-five patterns at once should start weeding out the oldies. There are always those favorites which are especially becoming. My newest shantung dress is made from one pattern I have made up three times in different fabrics. Now, I have discarded it because too many alterations were necessary to adapt the style to this season's lines.

When I mentioned having a sewing room, I can imagine

you might be thinking, "Who can have a sewing room?" That's the way I felt once, but now I have one, in just about the smallest apartment in New York. My apartment has a 5′ by 6′ alcove off the diminutive kitchen. It used to be called a breakfast nook. I have planned and utilized every inch, thanks to a collection of ideas from several home decoration magazines. If you watch your favorite magazine, you will find many practical suggestions that may make your dream come true. In one article from my collection dad's workshop and mom's sewing machine are shown cozily side by side in a basement hobby area. In another article the sewing machine, cutting table, and ironing board are all spread out in nice proximity to each other in one corner of a laundry. In two other articles, unused corners of rooms have been turned into sewing areas, with all equipment accounted for. In one of these the folding doors hide the area from the rest of the room.

Some of the areas shown are no bigger than a cupboard; some take up much more space. Some have cabinets and specially built tables that can be folded out of the way when not in use.

Even if you are not ready to make many alterations to provide a better place for sewing order, there is always a bureau drawer or a closet. At least, there is the corner of the room where you keep your sewing machine. Convert an old screen into a sewing catch-all as shown on our cover. The amount of room you have to spare will determine the kind of sewing area you will devise.

▶ Closet Sewing Area

Here is the way I utilized space in a closet in a one-room apartment. In the notion department of a store I found a "jumbo" closet chest, which fit neatly under the shelves. There was plenty of room in the chest for pieces of fabric, long transparent rulers, patterns, and other bulky sewing equipment I had accumulated. I also bought single-tiered closet shoe boxes and arranged them horizontally on the two upper shelves. The old patterns I didn't want to discard were separated according to types of garments and kept in one of these. Into the others went lace, elastic, zippers, and binding.

By this careful arrangement, there was sufficient room left

in the closet for a large clothes bag for suits, and two smaller bags to hold dresses and skirts.

My cutting board stood up neatly in the back of the closet, behind the clothes, without catching into the hanging garments.

My portable sewing machine took up little space in the closet depth.

▶ *How to Use a Sewing Screen*

If you do not have a deep closet, or an empty bureau drawer, you could use a sewing screen catch-all (Fig. III-2).

This screen can make a sewing center in any room. One side is decorative to face into the room, the other side has a peg-board and shelves to take care of all your sewing accessories. When you want to sew, turn the screen peg-board side out, and everything you need is within arms' reach—so handy, you don't need to lose a minute after you start your sewing project. When you are not sewing, no one has to know what is behind the screen. A list of sewing materials you can accommodate behind it could include: fabrics in a box, patterns, sewing aids, scissors, skirt marker, pattern cutting board, sewing machine, ironing board and iron, pressing hams, and spool and bobbin boxes (Fig. III-3).

The screen pictured on the cover was an old plasticized leather one which was converted. The front of it was papered with scenic wall paper. Peg-board was cut the same size as the two side panels and attached to the back surfaces. A sheet of plywood was added to the back of the center panel and a door-size mirror was hung there.

You might paper the front of the screen in the same wall paper used in the room, or with a contrasting decorative design. Or paint the screen and the peg-board back any color to fit the room decor.

There is a great variety of shapes and sizes in peg-board brackets that will hold anything you want to hang up. In our photograph the scissors, small tools, and flat pieces were hung on simple hooks. Shelf brackets and supporting rods hold larger pieces, such as the pattern cutting board, and racks hold literature and patterns.

▶ *Mending Basket*

The efficient sewer should have a separate basket in which she keeps her mending equipment. Do not snarl up the basket

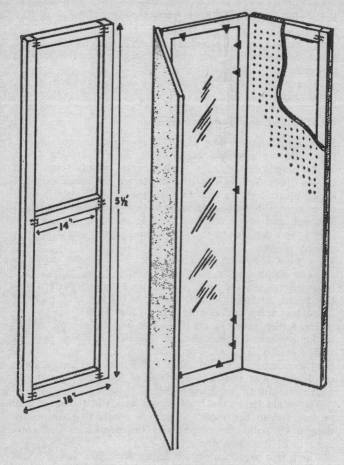

Fig. III-2 Construction of Sewing Screen

with unneeded threads. Just keep in it a spool of black thread, white thread, and a few basic colors (depending on your wardrobe) of mending cotton thread. Then plug the spools with thread locks to prevent tangling.

Get a multi-colored hank of mercerized threads for occasional stitch-in-times and another multi-color hank of light-weight mending wools. A straw basket with a good broad

Fig. III-3   View of Sewing Screen in Use

handle across the top, about 11" by 7" by 5½", is about right to tote around the house. In the plastic tray you can store your seam ripper, button gauge, beeswax and tailor's chalk.

Stick a few pins, good-sized darning needles and medium sharps in a pin cushion with emery attached.

Include a roll-up tape measure, a 6" metal sewing gauge and a few packages of snaps and hooks-and-eyes.

There's a good two-tone sock and glove darner for showing up holes in various colored socks and gloves.

You may want to add a small assortment of buttons, some lingerie straps, safety pins, and narrow elastic. Don't forget your scissors.

▶ *Good Lighting*

An important aspect of enjoyable sewing is good lighting. If you have to squirm every time you need to thread a needle or pin a seam, it is bad for your posture and harmful to your eyesight. The room in which you sew should be bathed in light, with no sharp contrasts. If the room is dim except for one bright light over your sewing machine or table, it is faultily lit. When you look up from your sewing your eyes will meet the contrast of the darker room areas. So be sure to have the sewing area well lighted. There should be no glare from an exposed bulb shining into your eyes. If possible, have the walls painted pastel colors so they won't absorb too much light. In addition, it is also wise to have the sewing machine cabinet, the top of the table on which you work, and even the chairs painted in a light color with a dull finish.

▶ *Scrap Traps*

Have several of these around to catch little scraps of fabric, basting threads, and trimmed edges. You can make these scrap traps by pinning a paper bag to the edge of your ironing board and placing another waste container by your sewing machine or chair.

CHAPTER 4

How to Use All Patterns

I do not think of myself as a professional dressmaker because I have never earned my living sewing for others. But, through my many contacts with home sewers all over the country, I have heard every kind of sewing problem.

When I first decided on a career in fashion I came to the city of New York to study designing. But, by the time I had gone through the pattern drafting and sketching classes, I was pretty sure that my talents were not original enough to make me a designer. However, I did learn how to drape fabric on a dress form and how to draft a pattern. You will learn something about this when you make a basic pattern to fit yourself and when you use your dress form. They both teach you that first essential in fitting, which is the way the fabric falls on grain over the lines of the figure.

Naturally, I have acquired a lot of sewing books because I have never been able to decide where my hobby leaves off and my job begins. But, believe me, this is not going to be a rehash of anyone else's theories. I have learned a great deal from studying under leading sewing authorities and, of course, they have influenced my way of sewing to a marked degree. However, this compilation is about my own experiences—trials and errors, and trials and successes. I have had to originate some sewing short cuts by developing methods of using new tools.

It was a most valuable experience for me to work as a pattern stylist. The most helpful thing I learned is how a commercial pattern is made. Did you know that it is a dress (or other garment) before it is a pattern? Yes, the designer has just a sketch of his idea to go by. He drapes the muslin (the term for "practice" fabric) on a dress form until it looks

43

like the sketch, just as I learned to do at design school. His new creation is then sewn. The belt and buckle shape are chosen, buttons and other trimmings are selected and applied, the kind of interfacing or staying is selected—everything is there in the original. Then, the garment is put on a live model who has all the measurements of the figure type for which it was planned. The fashion department then looks it over and considers what kinds of fabric are best to use to make it and all the other details that go into a successful fashion.

After the design has been approved the designer takes the muslin and cuts it down the center front and back. One half is ripped apart into its separate pieces and becomes the master pattern. The other half is sent to the instruction writers, who work out the best way to put that particular dress together and to write directions in simple terms. Every pattern instruction sheet is the sewing lesson for that particular garment. That is why, if you follow your instruction sheet step by step, you can learn to sew without my help or anyone else's. I still follow my pattern instructions, word for word.

I know what you are thinking—"It's all very well for an experienced person like her, but I still can't figure those things out." Perhaps I can help you learn to read the pattern guides, as I have learned from continued use of them. You probably try to read the whole thing at once and it becomes too intricate.

We'll discuss the layout and cutting guide page of your pattern instruction sheet in the next chapter. But I am talking here about the actual sewing instructions. Let me tell you my easy way to follow the sewing instructions: Read what it says to do up to the first punctuation mark and stick a pin there. Do what you've read. Now, go on to the next punctuation mark, move the pin, do what it says, and so on. Watch the diagrams as you go, because they make the instructions easier to understand.

Another thing, you miss so much if you don't learn to use all the different kinds of patterns. Once there may have been a difference in the way they fit, but not any more. Unlike the ready-to-wear manufacturers, the pattern industry got together with the National Bureau of Standards a few years ago and made all their measurements uniform. In all patterns a size 12 is 32 bust, a size 14 is 34 bust, and a size 16 is 36 bust. So, forget the ready-to-wear sizes you buy and purchase your patterns by bust measurement. The reason the bust measurement is the final determining factor is because it is the area hardest to fit and adjust.

Here, I should like to say something that not everyone I know will agree with. All the pattern companies give you a selection of "Easy-to-Make" styles. Usually, beginning sewers are encouraged to start out with these. I say do that only if you are the impatient type and can't wait to get that first dress finished. I will always remember a fine teacher of sewing who said, "Many of my girls never learned to baste." I looked at her in perfect wonderment and asked, "But how can they sew?" Her answer was that if someone learned to sew without basting they didn't need it as a crutch. So, as I unlearned my habit of much basting, I began to understand what she meant. Don't make a crutch of your inexperience! Dive in and choose for your first pattern the style you will be happy making, instead of limiting yourself to the easiest ones. None of them are so complicated that you need be afraid to tackle them. If there are a few more pattern pieces in a "higher style" design it only means that it takes a little more time to put them together, that's about all. By following my rule of making your pattern instruction sheet your sewing lesson, step by step, you will come out all right.

Patterns are sold in shops as well as through newspaper columns by mail. The major pattern companies make printed patterns. Others make perforated patterns. Whichever brand you purchase, let me repeat that you buy it according to bust measurement, excepting slacks and skirts which you buy by waist and hip measurement.

Many of you, who have been sewing for some time, liked the perforated pattern. You always marked through the perforations with tailor tacks. So often, during my cutting demonstrations in stores, women have said to me that they wished they did not have to cut off the paper margin on printed patterns. It isn't necessary to do so before you cut out your fabric. I never do, except when I have to make some kind of alteration. It is easier to cut accurately through a heavy line than along the edge of a pattern.

Doubtless, you have wasted much time pouring through counter catalogues in stores. Now, you can pick up a home catalogue at the pattern counter or at your favorite newsstand and make your selection while relaxing at home. Most department stores carry several brands, and some patterns have been available through dime stores for a long time. The pattern companies encourage the idea of picking up your zipper, seam binding, thread, and other findings at the same time you get the pattern and fabric. Whatever is needed for each design is listed on the back of each envelope. In the pattern catalogues, in many fashion magazines, and in mail order catalogues, you'll find photographs of styles made up in actual fabrics. This is done to help you relate fabric and fashion so you can visualize what the envelope sketch looks like. In fact, most of the envelope sketches picture actual fabric designs that you will see in stores. I watch these things very carefully. If I'm going to sew something in a plaid or stripe, I choose a pattern made up in such fabric in the drawing or photograph.

Did you know that some newspapers bring out pattern books, which they tell you about in their pattern columns, twice a year? The whole home sewing industry is trying in every way it can to help make your sewing more interesting, more professional-looking, and a lot more fun.

▶ *What Pattern Size and Type Are You?*

Your figure and your curves are a distinctly individual matter. No two of us are exactly alike. Actually, there are as many figure types as there are women in the world. But we do fall into general figure types which are not necessarily age groups. Formerly, figure types were divided into five categories: average, short, tall, top-heavy, and hippy. However, if you look through the pattern books you will see many more figure types, and these are not age groups so much as size groups (Figs. IV-1A, B & C). There seems very little variation between some of the size ranges. Yet, one could be just right for you with very few, if any, alterations necessary. This doesn't mean that you have to pick the same type all the time; it just means that this type will need the least altering and will more consistently feel right when you wear it. Personally, I can make up a half-size pattern without a single change and wear it, but if I like the style of a misses size better, I've learned the alterations I must make to correct the difference. I hate being limited to one classification.

Study your figure honestly in front of a full-length mirror before you determine your figure type. Your individuality is what you are dressing. The safest rule I know is to think of what you wear as a frame with yourself as the picture. I would rather have people say to me, "How lovely you look" than, "That's a stunning dress you're wearing." Let them think

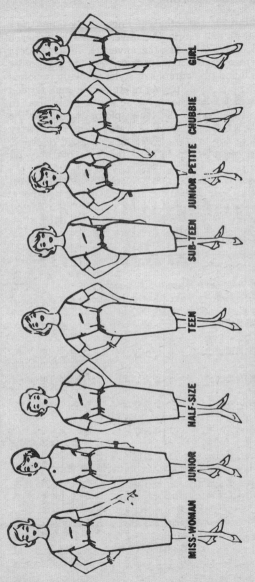

Body Measurement Chart

Approved by the Measurement Standard Committee of the Pattern Industry

Pattern sizes are based on actual body measurements. To determine what pattern size you need, take your body measurements and compare them with the measurements listed on the chart.

Courtesy of Simplicity Pattern Co.

Fig. IV-1A

Sizes for Dresses, Blouses, Suits, Coats: Select size by bust measurement.

Misses and Women

Size	10	12	14	16	18	20	40	42	44	46	48	
Bust	31	32	34	36	38	40	42	44	46	48	50	Ins.
Waist	24	25	26	28	30	32	34	36	38½	41	43½	Ins.
Hip	33	34	36	38	40	42	44	46	48	50	52	Ins.
Back Waist Length	15¾	16	16¼	16½	16¾	17	17⅛	17¼	17⅜	17½	17⅝	Ins.

Half-Sizes

Size	12½	14½	16½	18½	20½	22½	24½	
Bust	33	35	37	39	41	43	45	Ins.
Waist	27	29	31	33	35	37½	40	Ins.
Hip	37	39	41	43	45	47	49	Ins.
Back Waist Length	15¼	15½	15¾	16	16¼	16½	16¾	Ins.

Junior Petites

Size	3JP	5JP	7JP	9JP	11JP	
Bust	31	31½	32	32½	33	Ins.
Waist	22½	23	23½	24	24½	Ins.
Hip	32½	33	33½	34	34½	Ins.
Back Waist Length	14	14¼	14½	14¾	15	Ins.

Junior Miss

Size	9	11	13	15	17	
Bust	30½	31½	33	35	37	Ins.
Waist	23½	24½	25½	27	28½	Ins.
Hip	32½	33½	35	37	39	Ins.
Back Waist Length	15	15¼	15½	15¾	16	Ins.

Teens

Size	10	12	14	16	
Bust	30	32	34	36	Ins.
Waist	24	25	26	28	Ins.
Hip	32	34	36	38	Ins.
Back Waist Length	14¾	15	15¼	15½	Ins.

Fig. IV-1B

Sub-Teens

Size	8s	10s	12s	14s	
Bust	28	29	31	33	Ins.
Waist	23	24	25	26	Ins.
Hip	31	32	34	36	Ins.
Back Waist Length	13½	13¾	14	14¼	Ins.

Girls

Size	7	8	10	12	14	
Breast	25	26	28	30	32	Ins.
Waist	22½	23	24	25	26	Ins.
Hip	27	28	30	32½	35	Ins.
Back Waist Length	11	11½	12½	13	13¾	Ins.

Chubbies

Size	8½c	10½c	12½c	14½c	
Breast	30	31½	33	34½	Ins.
Waist	28	29	30	31	Ins.
Hip	33	34½	36	37½	Ins.
Back Waist Length	12	12½	13	14¼	Ins.

Sizes for Skirts, Slacks and Shorts: Select size by waist measurement.

If hips are much larger in proportion to waist, select size by hip measurement.

Junior Miss, Misses and Women

Waist	23½	24	25	26	27	28	30	32	34	36	38½	Ins.
Hip	32½	33	34	36	37	38	40	42	44	46	48	Ins.

Sub-Teens

Waist	23	24	25	26	Ins.
Hip	31	32	34	36	Ins.

Teens

Waist	24	25	26	28	Ins.
Hip	32	34	36	38	Ins.

Girls

Waist	22½	23	24	25	26	Ins.
Hip	27	28	30	32½	35	Ins.

Fig. IV-IC

you are looking your prettiest, then your dress is a real success.

I never, by the wildest stretch of the imagination, could consider myself a beautiful woman, but I knew that I could be smart looking. So, I learned early to do my best to camouflage my figure faults: too narrow shoulders, too short neck, too flat bust, too wide hips, too short waist, and too heavy legs. At least my legs were long, my waist was small, my hands and arms were well proportioned. I could learn to stand straight and walk tall. Suits look better on me than dresses broken at the waist. If I make a dress it has a narrow self-color belt. I never break the color line from head to toe, if I can avoid it. You see, I'd rather dwell on my shortcomings than point up yours. However, I think you catch the drift of my thinking.

A complete figure and pattern piece measurement chart is shown in Figs. IV-2A, B & C. But, for the purpose of choosing your pattern size and type, four measurements (or six are even better) are enough for now. Jot them down where indicated on the chart and fill in the rest of your measurements later.

Please don't take your own measurements! Let someone else do it for you accurately with a good tape measure. Put on your best girdle and bra or foundation garment and wear medium heels as you stand firm and straight. Tie a piece of tape around your exact waistline. Now measure:

1a. Your *Full Bust,* around fullest part under armpits, across shoulder blades in back.

1b. *High Bust,* high under armpits, across back above shoulder blades, over swell of bust across chest.

2. Your *Waist,* where tape has been tied, with two fingers under end of tape measure.

3a. Your *Hips,* 7″ below waistline. Stand straight, heels together.

3b. *Full Hips,* 9″ or more below waistline.

4. Your *Center Back Neck to Waist.* Feel out prominent bone at base of neck. From bone, measure down center back to waist.

If, on the figure type and size charts (Figs. IV-1A, B & C), you find one with all measurements the same as yours, this is your figure type and you are lucky; no alterations are necessary for you. As you study them, you will find sizes 12, 14, and 16 in "Misses and Women" and "Teens." The measurements for both are alike in bust, waist, and hips, the back neck to waist length is different. Think about the description of the figure types in comparison with yours, and this back neck to waist length may be the deciding factor. If you cannot quite decide, after this, which figure type you are, select from the new proportioned patterns, which include instructions for making three different heights in one-size pattern.

If three of the measurements for one type are the same as yours, but the fourth is different, note this on the figure and pattern piece measurement chart. This will help you when you alter that fourth area. If there is more disagreement between your measurements and any of the figure types, get the nearest pattern size to your upper bust measurement. The bust measurement is the determining factor because the bust is the area hardest to fit. If still doubtful about your best size, experiment with combining two sizes. Sometimes a figure is larger in front than back or *vice versa*. Use the best fitting piece from each pattern.

You look much plumper when you wear clothes that are too tight. The garment which bursts out at the seams across the shoulders, or cups under the derriere, does not fit. Folds of fabric under armpits and bulges around bust line are all wrong. That balloon that rides up above the waist at the back of a jacket needn't be. A skirt should not fold across the upper thigh when you stand or sit.

▶ Individual Style and Taste

The word "fit" also implies something that is suitable. This means choosing your wardrobe to suit the functions of your life. You wouldn't wear a dress meant for a garden party to town or market, nor would you go sightseeing on Fifth Avenue in slacks.

You can have style without being in the latest fashion. "Fashion," according to *Webster's Dictionary,* "is the accepted usage at a given time by those who wish to be regarded as up-to-date." "Style," it goes on to say, "is the distinctive fashion adopted by those who have wealth or taste." Well, you can certainly have taste without wealth. Those we admire most and consider style-setters usually dress to their own taste and figure types and care little about the current trends. Taste is the prime ingredient. And, what is taste? According to the dictionary, "The power of discerning and appreciating fitness, beauty, order, or whatever constitutes excellence." Taste means choosing the right colors and fabrics for your pattern style, for your figure type, and for your social requirements. Be sure all your clothes belong together and belong to you.

► *Enhancing Your Figure Type*

If you have an average figure you can wear almost any style. But if not, play down the defects.

If you are short, do everything to look tall; don't cut yourself up with horizontal lines.

If you are tall and thin, crosswise lines cut height and add width.

If you have a "pouter pigeon" figure, end your sleeves either above or below the elbow, have an easy fit in the bodice, avoid frills, and show off your slimmer hips.

If you are pear-shaped, wear flared or easy-fitting skirts and keep the decorative interest at the top of your figure.

If you are flat-chested or small-busted in proportion to your hips, don't be too proud to pad.

If you are thick in the middle, keep your belts narrow and always the same color as the dress.

A V-neck or wider neckline will make a short neck look less chunky. Keep away from fluffy, frilly collars.

Frous and stand-up collars make a long neck look graceful.

Break the line of a broad shoulder, and pad a narrow shoulder ever so slightly (whether pads are fashionable or not).

If you're a "baby blimp," do not choose fabrics with a large floral pattern. Instead, wear subdued colors and muted, small prints until you've reduced to satisfactory proportions.

If you are maturing, you can look gracious, wise, and alluring, even stunning—but not in baby blue or pink teen fashions.

Now that you have more or less settled on your figure type, it is time to fill in the rest of your measurements. Don't forget to wear a good girdle when measuring. If you have a dress which fits well, you can take your measurements over it to help locate seams at the armhole, neckline, waist, shoulder and side. If measurements are taken over a slip, tie a tape around neck and armholes as well as waistline to get the proper position. Using chalk, mark on your skin the top, front, back, and bottom of armhole, allowing for comfortable depth.

After you have once taken your body measurements completely and written them down, they need to be checked

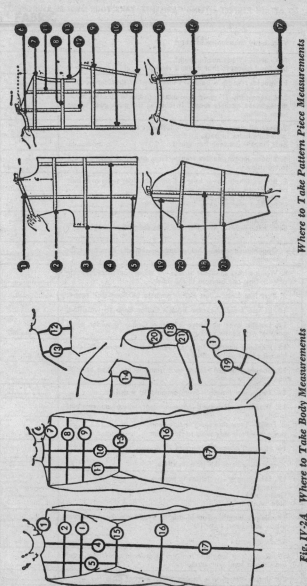

Where to Take Pattern Piece Measurements

Fig. IV-2A Where to Take Body Measurements

TO ATTAIN PERFECT FITTING GARMENTS, TAKE YOUR OWN MEASUREMENTS

Your body measurement chart	
Take SNUGLY but not too tight. Use tape measure that doesn't stretch.	
1. Shoulder width — Base of neck to top of shoulder bone.	....
2. Chest width—6" down from shoulder seam at neckline measure between armhole seams. If taken in slip mark body where seam comes.	
3. Bust all around — Around fullest part under armpits across shoulder blades in back. **Bust Front** — Between side seams.	....
4. Blouse length, center front — From center of base of neck to waistline.	....
5. Blouse length, over bust — Center shoulder seam over bust parallel with center front to waist. a. Shoulder to point of bust .... b. Point of bust to waist	....
6. Neck all around Back neck seam — At collar line from seam to seam.	....
7. Upper Back width—Across back at shoulder from one armhole edge to other.	....
8. Width across shoulder blades—7" down from shoulder seam at neck from one armhole to the other.	....
9. Bust line back — Just below armhole between side seams.	....
10. Blouse length, center back — Collar bone to waistline.	....
11. Length over shoulder blades — Center shoulder seam parallel with center back to waistline.	....
12. Armhole depth — Tie cord around chest at armhole level. Measure from neck to cord.	....
13. Shoulder height—Down back from shoulder seam at edge of shoulder to cord.	....
14. Underarm length — From armhole to waistline.	....
15. Waistline all around—Measure snugly where you want belt to be. a. **Front** — From side seam to side seam. .... b. **Back** — From side seam to side seam.	....
16. Hips all around — Measure 7" down. Measure at widest part of hips. Record distance of this from waistline.	....
17. Skirt length — waistline to bottom. Center front Center back Side seams	....
18. Sleeve length — Top of arm at shoulder point down over elbow (arm bent) to wrist. Underarm to elbow .... Elbow to wrist	....
19. Sleeve cap length — Top arm to armhole after tying cord around arm level with armhole.	....
20. Upper arm girth — Around fullest part of arm.	....
21. Elbow — Around elbow with arm bent.	....

Fig. IV-2B

AND MEASURE YOUR PATTERN, FOLLOWING THE INSTRUCTIONS BELOW:

Pattern Measurements	Pattern ease Allowance	Difference
Take with darts pinned in. Between seam allowance markings.	Add these to body measurements	
1. Shoulder width (blouse front) — Plain or darted shoulder between marks. If gathered take on back shoulder.	¼" to ½"	
2. Chest width — 6" down from shoulder seam mark at neckline measure between armhole and center seam marks.		
3. Bust front — 2" below armhole seam marks to center front. Take back half when measuring back pattern piece.	2" to 3"	
4. Blouse length, center front — At center front between marks neck to waistline.	½"	
5. Blouse length, over bust — Center of shoulder seam line straight down over bust dart to waist line.		
a. Shoulder to 1" above bust dart		
b. 1" above bust dart to waist	½"	
6. Back neck seam (blouse back)—Along neck seam allowance marking.		
7. Upper back width—From top shoulder edge seam mark straight across to center back.	½"	
8. Width cross shoulder blade—7" below shoulder seam mark at neck edge from center back to armhole mark.	½" to 1"	
9. Bust line back—2" below armhole side seam mark to center back.	1" to 2"	
10. Blouse length, center back — Between marks back neck to waist.	½"	
11. Length over shoulder blades — Between marks from center shoulder to waistline.	½"	
12. Armhole depth—Shoulder seam mark at neck to bottom of armhole seam line mark.		
13. Shoulder height — From top to bottom of armhole line before curve begins.		
14. Underarm length—Between marks from underarm to waist.		
15. Waistline (all blouse and skirt pieces)		
a. Front — If gored pin together	(skirt 1")	
b. Back — If gored pin together	(skirt 1")	
16. Hips(skirt pieces) Measure 7" down with gores together .... Measure same distance from waist as widest part of hips on body.		
17. Skirt length — Between waist and hem		
Center front		
Center back		
Side seams		
18. Sleeve length(Sleve)—Between top of shoulder and wrist seam marks on grain.		
Underarm to elbow		
Elbow to wrist		
19. Sleeve cap length—Center top of shoulder seam mark straight down to bottom armhole seam.		
20. Upper sleeve width — Between seam marks below arms.	3" to 4"	
21. Elbow — From center fullness to between matching notches on opposite side.		

Fig. IV-2C

only if you gain or lose weight. Also, after the first time you check all pattern pieces, you will know which ones need to be altered each time. The only time when all pieces need be checked again is when there is a radical difference in style, as between a princess line dress and a casual shirtwaist.

▶ *How to Alter Each Pattern Piece Correctly*

Many sewing books give you rules on how to alter your pattern. The best and most thorough treatise I have found on the subject is *Farmers' Bulletin #1968*, which you can order by number for 15¢ from the Superintendent of Documents, U. S. Government Printing Office, Washington 25, D. C. I have used this bulletin, with permission, as the basis for my measurement chart. This chart allows you to compare your body measurements with pattern piece measurements. As you measure each pattern piece, enter all measurements in the second column on the chart (Fig. IV-2C).

Some years ago I met a designer who gave me one new measurement which no one else has suggested, and which I'll pass on to those of you who have to adjust bust darts. Measure the distance between the points of the bust and add this to your chart.

It has always been a practice to pin pattern pieces together, after pinning in all darts, etc., and then trying on the pattern to find out where adjustments may be necessary. With tissue paper, this is a little difficult to judge accurately. If you are accustomed to doing this and have had success with it, by all means, continue. However, one reason I like the government bulletin is that it advocates measuring each pattern piece and comparing body measurements.

Before measuring pattern pieces, press them out with a warm (not hot) iron. Pin in darts, tucks, pleats, or gathers. Be sure to work on an uncluttered, flat surface. Don't try to hold up each separate piece and measure. All measuring is done between seam allowances, either parallel or at right angles to straight-of-goods markings. The chart illustrations indicate the points at which to do your measuring. Only a few measurements are taken around curves. Keep together —and remember the relationship of—all parts of each section of garment, such as fronts and their facings; sleeve pieces and their facings and cuffs; and skirts sections. All related pieces must be altered to correspond with each other.

For most pattern pieces, remember that only half the pattern is being measured. For example: Twice the front pattern measurement (plus ease) should be the same as your bust measurement across front. Also remember that the full bust measurement is estimated after adding back and front pattern piece measurements (plus ease). By measuring each piece separately you learn exactly where any alterations may be needed.

All the patterns have built-in body ease or over-all fullness. If they did not, your clothes would be too tight and you would be unable to move around in them. The ease for fullness has been calculated according to the style of the garment and the weight of the fabric for which the style is best suited. There is little variation among brands of patterns when the style is the same. One column on your chart (Fig. IV-2C) shows the standard amounts of body ease which the pattern companies allow for each piece.

When you have finished measuring all the pattern pieces and entered all the measurements on your chart, add the allowance given and estimate whether there is any difference to be altered, and on which pieces these alterations need be made. Unpin all darts, tucks, etc., lay aside only the pattern pieces which need to be adjusted, and fold the other pieces back into the envelope.

At this point, you need to understand something about how your fabric should fall on your figure, so you know why the pattern alterations must be made before the fabric is cut. Grain line really means the thread line of the fabric. Fabric is made of crosswise and lengthwise thread woven at right angles to each other. Fabric is off grain when it pulls off the thread line, thus stretching and forming ugly folds and bulges. I have indicated below where the threads of fabric should fall on a figure in order to make a garment fit smoothly.

Blouse Front

1. Crosswise thread of fabric comes across chest between armholes, 4″ below shoulder.

2. Crosswise thread runs across the point of bust from underarm seam to underarm seam.

3. Crosswise thread runs across front about 2″ above waistline from seam to seam.

4. Lengthwise fabric thread runs from point on shoulder line about 2½″ from neck, over point of bust, to waist.

Blouse Back

1. Crosswise fabric thread comes 4" below shoulder line from armhole edges.
2. Crosswise thread runs across shoulder blade from underarm to underarm, at same point as bust.
3. Crosswise thread runs across back about 2" above waist from seam to seam.
4. Lengthwise fabric thread comes at shoulder blade from same point at shoulder line to waist.

Sleeve

1. Usually your pattern piece has a marking to indicate top of sleeve. Lengthwise thread must fall from this line straight down to wrist.
2. Crosswise thread must go straight across sleeve cap about 3" down and at right angles to lengthwise thread.

Skirt

1. Lengthwise thread should run straight from waist to hem both center front and back, if there's no seam. If a seam shapes flare, the line is indicated on the pattern piece.
2. Crosswise thread runs straight from seam to seam about 7" below waist, both back and front.

▶ Pattern Alterations

Unless your figure is extremely irregular your alterations will be minor and come under one of the few common changes I shall illustrate here (Figs. IV-3A & B). If you have a more serious problem, you are almost sure to find it and instructions for making corrections in *Farmers' Bulletin #1968*. You will be able to apply the same principles I am about to explain with the help of a bit of simple arithmetic and your see-thru ruler.

All pattern alterations should be made at right angles to the straight-of-goods marking on any pattern piece. The see-thru ruler, called *the sewer's T-square*, makes it easy to find the right angle. There are three ways in which it is used in general pattern alterations. Learn to understand these three simple applications and you will be able to apply the principle to any other alterations that you may find necessary.

The first one is applied when a pattern piece has to be either shortened or lengthened evenly all the way across, as

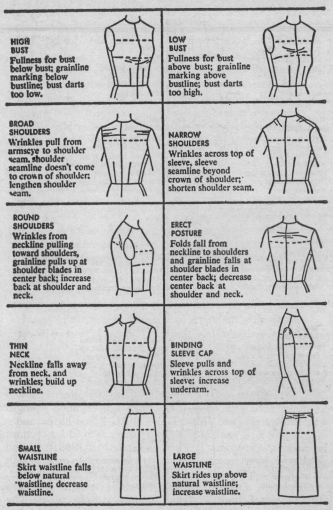

HIGH BUST

Fullness for bust below bust; grainline marking below bustline; bust darts too low.

LOW BUST

Fullness for bust above bust; grainline marking above bustline; bust darts too high.

BROAD SHOULDERS

Wrinkles pull from armscye to shoulder seam, shoulder seamline doesn't come to crown of shoulder; lengthen shoulder seam.

NARROW SHOULDERS

Wrinkles across top of sleeve, sleeve seamline beyond crown of shoulder; shorten shoulder seam.

ROUND SHOULDERS

Wrinkles from neckline pulling toward shoulders, grainline pulls up at shoulder blades in center back; increase back at shoulder and neck.

ERECT POSTURE

Folds fall from neckline to shoulders and grainline falls at shoulder blades in center back; decrease center back at shoulder and neck.

THIN NECK

Neckline falls away from neck, and wrinkles; build up neckline.

BINDING SLEEVE CAP

Sleeve pulls and wrinkles across top of sleeve; increase underarm.

SMALL WAISTLINE

Skirt waistline falls below natural waistline; decrease waistline.

LARGE WAISTLINE

Skirt rides up above natural waistline; increase waistline.

Fig. IV-3A   Courtesy McCall Corporation

in our skirt example (Fig. IV-4). If your skirt needs shortening, don't decide to cut off the bottom. Your pattern has been designed with a given amount of flare and you change the fashion line if you cut off at the hem.

Many times the pattern indicates where the shortening or

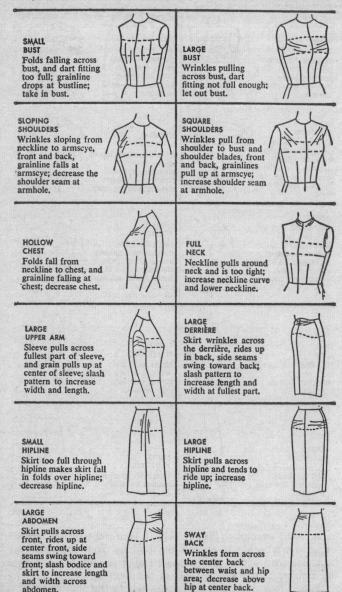

SMALL BUST
Folds falling across bust, and dart fitting too full; grainline drops at bustline; take in bust.

LARGE BUST
Wrinkles pulling across bust, dart fitting not full enough; let out bust.

SLOPING SHOULDERS
Wrinkles sloping from neckline to armscye, front and back, grainline falls at armscye; decrease the shoulder seam at armhole.

SQUARE SHOULDERS
Wrinkles pull from shoulder to bust and shoulder blades, front and back, grainlines pull up at armscye; increase shoulder seam at armhole.

HOLLOW CHEST
Folds fall from neckline to chest, and grainline falling at chest; decrease chest.

FULL NECK
Neckline pulls around neck and is too tight; increase neckline curve and lower neckline.

LARGE UPPER ARM
Sleeve pulls across fullest part of sleeve, and grain pulls up at center of sleeve; slash pattern to increase width and length.

LARGE DERRIÈRE
Skirt wrinkles across the derrière, rides up in back, side seams swing toward back; slash pattern to increase length and width at fullest part.

SMALL HIPLINE
Skirt too full through hipline makes skirt fall in folds over hipline; decrease hipline.

LARGE HIPLINE
Skirt pulls across hipline and tends to ride up; increase hipline.

LARGE ABDOMEN
Skirt pulls across front, rides up at center front, side seams swing toward front; slash bodice and skirt to increase length and width across abdomen.

SWAY BACK
Wrinkles form across the center back between waist and hip area; decrease above hip at center back.

Fig. IV-3B

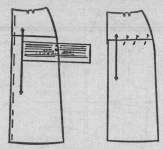

Fig. IV-4 Shortening or Lengthening Straight Across Pattern Piece

lengthening is to be done. However, if there is no line to show where it should be on the pattern piece, draw your own line below the fullest part of the hips, usually 10″ to 12″ below the waist. If you are using a perforated pattern there will be straight-of-goods perforations shown, so connect them with your ruler and a pencil line. On some printed patterns this straight-of-goods marking is very short and must be lengthened. On a skirt, remember to include the hem allowance in your calculations.

To shorten

Place the 4″ end of the see-thru ruler against the straight-of-goods marking so that it is at exact right angles to the line. On a skirt piece the ruler should be about 10″ below the waist. On a bodice piece, it must be decided whether shortening is needed above or below the armhole (Fig. IV-5). Now draw a pencil line the length of the ruler and then continue it the rest of the way across on the other side of the grain line. There is now a straight line across your pattern piece at exact right angles to the grain. How much will you shorten? Let us say 1″. So, 1″ below the first line, draw a second line parallel to it. Now, fold up the first line to meet the second and pin or tape it in place. The fold will be ½″ wide, but because you doubled the paper you have taken out a whole inch.

If the bodice or blouse pattern pieces are too long or too short at both center back and underarm, use this same alteration. The tricky alteration is the one in which the center back is off but the underarm measures as it should. This was one of my problems before I found so many smart styles in half-sizes. We'll learn how to do that after we learn to lengthen a skirt.

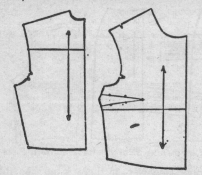

Fig. IV-5

To lengthen

As in the shortening, a line is drawn at the exact right angles to lengthwise grain. But, the second line is not necessary because you will cut across the first line. Then, an extra piece of tissue must be set in. If it's 1" that has to be added, draw two parallel lines 1" apart on a 3" strip of tissue. Insert this 1" of tissue at the point where the pattern piece was cut apart, and pin or tape together.

Underarm normal, front or back too short or too long (Fig. IV-6)

This is the second application of the see-thru ruler for pattern alteration. Check to see whether difference comes between underarm and waist, or above armhole across shoulder. If it is across the shoulder or chest, the line is drawn above the armhole notch. Again the line is drawn on a straight right angle from the crosswise grain. If the line is below the armhole, try to avoid interference with the darts.

Let us assume that the center back needs shortening 1" below the armhole and the line has been drawn, but the darts coming up from the waistline were too long to avoid. Now at center back edge, mark off ½" either side of the straight line. Lay the see-thru ruler with one end at one of these marks, and the other end at an oblique angle which connects the center line at the seam allowance. Draw a line and repeat this process on the other side of the center line from the second ½" mark. In other words, the alteration will be nothing at the underarm, but when the center line has been slashed down to the seam allowance and two pieces of tissue are lapped, 1" has been taken off the center back.

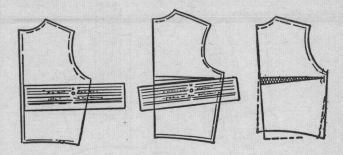

Fig. IV-6

Adjust the dart as in illustration (Fig. IV-7). When you lay the altered pattern piece on the fabric to cut, pin down the edge placed on the fold as far as it is even. Pin the pattern across the bottom, across the shoulder and neck, and around the armhole, and cut out these areas. Now, unpin the alteration and pin the pattern on grain of center back fold, down to cut. The armhole will have shifted back into position where you can finish cutting underarm edge. Mark the darts on the new dart line.

If you lengthen instead of shorten for this alteration, as you might for a very long back, pin in the extra tissue, carefully drawn in proportion.

This use of the see-thru ruler applies whenever more is being taken out at one side of a pattern piece than on the other.

Shoulder too narrow or too wide (Fig. IV-8)

The third application of the see-thru ruler for pattern alterations is used where a new right angle must be created in relation to straight of goods. Here the ruler is first placed at the right angle to lengthwise grain and the line drawn. Then, another right angle is taken from the first.

If the front shoulder shows gathering, alter the back pattern piece only. If the front shoulder is plain, or darted, alter both back and front pieces. Is the alteration at the shoulder only or does it run down through the chest? At a shoulder alteration, the straight-of-goods marking will be parallel to where the alteration comes. Draw a horizontal line at right angles to the grain either above or below the armhole, as the case may be. Midway on the shoulder, draw a vertical line to meet this horizontal, at right angles to it. The altera-

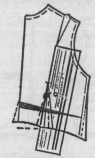

Fig. IV-7 Adjust Dart

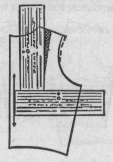

ALTERATION FOR LARGE UPPER ARM

Fig. IV-8

ALTERATION FOR A HOLLOW CHEST

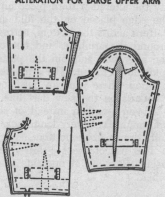

Fig. IV-9A

tion comes on this vertical line. If the amount of alteration is ½″, for example, divide it ¼″ each side of the vertical line. Connect these marks on an oblique angle with the bottom of the vertical line. Here you will lap paper for any shortening or add paper to widen, as in illustrations.

Other common alterations are shown in Figs. IV-9A, B, C & D. If you use your see-thru ruler and work all alterations at exact right angles to the grain, you can follow any of the given diagrams to successful pattern correction.

The best thing to do is to get a basic pattern in your best figure type and size, alter it according to these few simple rules, and make it up with corrections in muslin. This will give you a model by which to check all pattern styles, so

ALTERATION FOR SMALLER THAN AVERAGE BUST

ALTERATION FOR FULLER THAN AVERAGE BUST

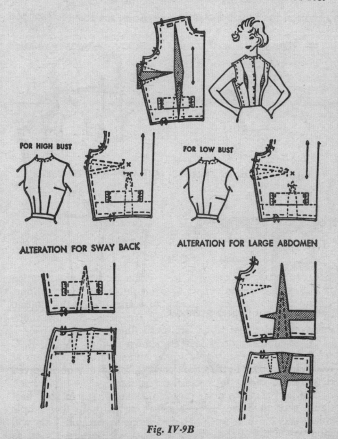

FOR HIGH BUST

FOR LOW BUST

ALTERATION FOR SWAY BACK

ALTERATION FOR LARGE ABDOMEN

Fig. IV-9B

ALTERATION FOR NARROW SHOULDERS **ALTERATION FOR SLOPING SHOULDERS**

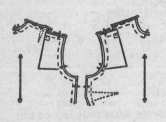

ALTERATION FOR SQUARE SHOULDERS **ALTERATION FOR ROUNDED SHOULDERS**

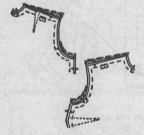

ALTERATION FOR BROAD SHOULDERS **ALTERATION FOR SLEEVE WIDTH**

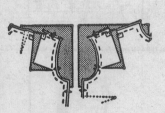
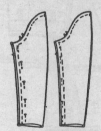

ALTERATION FOR BINDING SLEEVE CAP

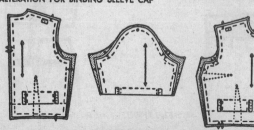

Fig. IV-9C

ALTERATION FOR FULL NECK

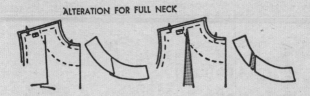

If you have made any alterations on the basic dress be sure to make the same alterations on the neckline facing pieces, and be sure to retain the original width of the facings.

ALTERATION FOR THIN NECK

ALTERATION TO DECREASE WAISTLINE   ALTERATION TO INCREASE WAISTLINE

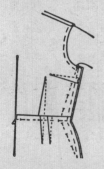
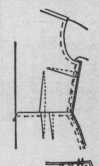

ALTERATION FOR LARGE DERRIERE

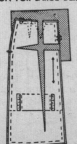

ALTERATION TO TAKE IN HIPLINE

ALTERATION TO LET OUT HIPLINE

Fig. IV-9D

Sizes for Men and Boys: Select Shirt size by neck measurement. Select Jacket and Coat size by chest measurement.

Boys

Size	1	2	3	4	5	6	8	10	12	14	16	
Chest	20	21	22	23	23½	24	26	28	30	32	34	Ins.
Waist	19½	20	20½	21	21½	22	23	24	25½	27	29	Ins.
Neck Base Girth						11½	12	12½	13	13½	14	Ins.

Men

Chest	32	34	36	38	40	42	44	46	48	Ins.
Waist	28	30	32	34	36	38	40	42	44	Ins.
Neck Base Girth	13½	14	14½	15	15½	16	16½	17	17½	Ins.
Shirt Sleeve Length	33	33	33	33	34	34	34	35	35	Ins.

Children

Size	1	2	3	4	5	6	
Breast	20	21	22	23	23½	24	Ins.
Waist	19½	20	20½	21	21½	22	Ins.

Toddlers

Size	½	1	2	3	4	
Breast	19	.20	21	22	23	Ins.
Waist	19	19½	20	20½	21	Ins.

Fig. IV-10

that your clothes which you sew for yourself will always fit perfectly.

By the time you have learned how to alter patterns to make them fit, you will be so expert that you'll know just how to go about it when you want to make something for someone else, such as your children or menfolk. The body measurement charts for them are shown in Fig. IV-10.

CHAPTER 5

Fabrics and How to Cut Them

All pattern companies have fabric departments. Special fabric stylists shop the market of manufacturers who sell their materials over the piece goods counters. These stylists are important members of the fashion staff and are the first to get that new style the designer has created. They decide what material it shall be made in, and they furnish swatches to the artist who makes the finished drawing that appears on the pattern envelope. Yes, the artist actually sketches the fabric from the swatch. On the back of the pattern envelope the stylists suggest other appropriate materials that may be used for that particular style. Of course you want to use that lovely piece of fabric you bought, but be sure the style calls for that kind of material—if you really want it to be a success.

It is really best to buy your pattern first. Then you will not buy too little or too much fabric, or the wrong width for the style you want to make. The back of the envelope tells you what width of fabric to use for the style (Fig. V-1). For instance, your fabric may be 36″, but if this width is not shown on pattern envelope it probably means that the flare of the skirt is too large to fit on this narrow fabric width.

Do not decide that "the pattern companies always allow for extra fabric." They do, but only about ¼ yard, which isn't much. You should see the care with which they calculate your yardage on every single pattern! Experts lay the pattern pieces on large tables, and they plot and scheme to save you ½″ if possible, before they make up the layout. After they've saved every bit of yardage possible and still kept the garment pieces all true to grain, the layout diagrams on

69

Misses' and Women's Dress and Jacket

Sizes FABRIC REQUIRED	MISSES' 12	14	16	18	20	WOMEN'S 40	42	
DRESS ONLY —								
35" Without Nap*	2⅞	2⅞	2⅞	3⅛	3⅛	3½	3⅝	Yds.
45" " "	2¼	2¼	2⅜	2⅝	2⅝	2⅞	2⅞	"
DRESS AND JACKET —								
35" Without Nap*	4⅝	4⅝	4¾	5	5	5¾	5¾	"
45" " "	3½	3½	3⅝	3⅞	3⅞	4⅜	4⅜	"
Jacket Lining — 35" Fabric	1¼	1¼	1¼	1¼	1¼	1½	1½	"
Jacket Lining — 39" Fabric	⅞	⅞	1	1	1¼	1¼	1⅜	"
Jacket Interfacing 35" Woven Interfacing	¾	¾	¾	¾	¾	¾	¾	Yd.
¾" Wide Belt Backing (Optional)	⅞	⅞	1	1	1⅛	1⅛	1¼	Yds.

*WITHOUT NAP means fabric with either way design, or without nap or pile.

Body Measurements	12	14	16	18	20	40	42	
Bust	32	34	36	38	40	42	44	Ins.
Waist	25	26	28	30	32	34	36	"
Hip	34	36	38	40	42	44	46	"
Back waist length	16	16¼	16½	16¾	17	17⅛	17¼	"
Finished Jacket length from back of regular neckline (1⅝ inch hem)	16¾	17	17¼	17½	17¾	18	18⅛	"
Finished Dress length from back of regular neckline (2⅝ inch hem)	43	43½	43¾	44	44¼	46	46⅛	"
Width at lower edge of Dress	61	63	65	67	69	72	74	Ins.

SUGGESTED FABRICS: Shantung, Surah, Tussah, Printed Silk or Cotton, Synthetic Mixtures, Linen, Silk Linen.

NOTE: Not Suitable for Diagonal Prints or Diagonal Weaves.

NOTIONS: Thread; Dress — Seam Binding, 22" Neck-type Zipper, 1 Hook and Eye, Prong-type Buckle for ¾" Wide Belt or Belt and Buckle Kit; Jacket — Two 1⅛" Buttons or Molds to be Covered.

Fig. V-1   Typical Fabric Requirement Chart from Back of Pattern Envelope

your patterns are sketched from the exact pieces they have worked with.

Most cotton fabrics still come only 36" wide. However, more and more of the better cottons are now being loomed in wider widths. So, when you buy 42" or 45" cottons you may pay more per yard, but you will use less yardage because the pattern will lay out on it to better advantage. Fabrics like silk, linen, rayon, and other synthetics come 39", 42", 45" and 50" wide. Woolens are usually 54" to 60" wide. Felts often go up to 72". Many beautiful fabrics imported from lands where weaving is still done by hand are very narrow, 27" wide or less.

I wove my first half-yard of fabric last summer. It certainly gave me respect for the artisans who make lovely hand-loomed silks and cottons in the Orient and woolens, linen and rare fabrics in Europe and Africa. I wish every woman could try her hand at weaving. It's a fascinating hobby and it teaches so much about the way the crosswise (woof) and lengthwise (warp) threads form the grain of the fabric. You also learn what it means to combine different yarns and fibers to get certain textures.

▶ Buying Fabrics

Your favorite store may have an advertised sale of piece goods at fantastic prices. Good brand-name fabrics are well to investigate, but some unidentified fabrics are often mixed with these on the same counter. Examine these carefully if you don't know much about them. Will they be easy to sew? How will they wash, dry clean, and so on? Or, you may go into a fabric shop where they tell you all about the famous couturier whose fabric left-overs they were able to purchase. The fabrics are fabulously beautiful and so reasonable! But, they are often unlabeled so you don't know what they are made of. The fabric bought by couturiers may not be as carefully finished as that which has been made for retail sale. That's because the couturiers are willing to do the finishing themselves to save money.

You are safest when you buy piece goods by brand names. You wouldn't think of buying canned goods without a label. Conscientious manufacturers who make their fabrics just for retail sale are careful to label their fabrics so that you know what they are made of and how to care for them. In fact, since March 1960 there has been a federal law that all piece goods sold over the counter must be labeled. Watch for these labels and read them carefully. You will save yourself an endless amount of time if you do not have to shrink, straighten, and prepare your materials before you cut them out. This is particularly true of so-called wash-and-wear fabrics.

I shall never forget my experience with a beautiful little brown faille suit I made from fabric bought in a bargain shop. I had come away with yards of wonderful buys, including the brown faille. It had been sold to me for all silk and when I finished it, everyone thought it extremely smart. It was made from a pattern style of the company for which I was then a traveling stylist so I wore it on one of my out-of-town safaris. I had it cleaned in a small city and prepared to wear it the morning of a big fashion show I had to give. When I put it on, you can imagine my dismay; it fit like my bathing suit. I took it back to the cleaner and he was as disturbed as I was. He said the wool in it had made it shrink. When I later told the fabric shop about it they told me it was an unlabeled end piece from a couturier collection.

My story is not meant to blame the people who sell us these materials. I'm trying to impress you with the importance of thinking carefully about what you are buying. All the protective measures in the world are not going to help you unless you help yourself. If you are unsure of a fabric's fiber content, test it by washing and ironing a small piece of it before you cut into it. Also, read all you can about the new fibers and finishes so you will know how to care for your garment after it is made. A very fine short book on this subject is a part of the same Pyramid "Royal Series" that the book you are now reading belongs to. It is *Encyclopedia of Clothes Care* by Betsy Wade.

A fiber is a hair-like strand which is twisted into yarn and then woven or knitted into fabric. The four natural fibers are: cotton, linen, silk, and wool. Cotton and linen are vegetable fibers. Silk and wool are animal (protein) fibers. Cotton, linen, and wool are all short fibers compared to silk, which is the only continuous natural fiber. There are man-made fibers of vegetable origin made from wood pulp or cotton linters, such as rayon and acetate. Then there are man-made fibers that are wholly synthetic chemical products from start to finish, such as nylon, orlon, dacron, and Zefran. Some rubber fibers come from natural rubber plants and some are all synthetic. Glass fibers have a mineral origin, as do some of the metallics. Other metallics are wholly synthetic.

The man-made fibers are all continuous. A continuous fiber,

or filament yarn, gives fabric a smooth appearance. The continuous synthetic fibers are also cut into short, or "staple," lengths and spun into yarn to simulate fabrics made from the short natural fibers. These terms may seem very technical but they often appear on the fabric manufacturers' labels and in advertising.

Conscientious fiber developers do not allow their names to be used unless they carefully control the production of fabrics from these fibers. They make sure the right blends are used in the yarns being woven into the finished piece goods. Glass yarns, as yet, are the only ones that do not blend with other yarns.

Many fiber names appear on the labels of fabrics that contain synthetic blends:

rayon	nylon	dynel
Corval	orlon	Verel
Bemberg	Acrilan	fiber glass
acetate	dacron	neoprene
Estron	Kodel	Lurex
Chromspun	Vycron	Zefran
Arnel	Fortrel	

All of these fibers and yarns and blends are being woven into a variety of fabrics so vast that it would take a whole book just to list and describe them. Synthetics are made to look exactly like silk, wool, linen, and cotton. Cotton comes in winter weights that are hard to distinguish from wool, and summer cotton satins are as lovely as silks. Coatings that look like fur may be pure synthetic, and wools have been made washable. You have to develop a sleuth-like perception to tell what is what.

The half yard of fabric that I wove looked dismal indeed until I washed it, stretched it to grain-perfection, and sized it slightly. You wouldn't consider wearing much of the fabric straight from the looms, and it is appropriately called gray goods. Many different finishes are applied to improve the surface appearance. Fabric may be mercerized to make it shine, or de-lustered to make it dull. It may be sized to make it stiffer, or chemically oiled to soften it. It may be Sanforized to keep it from shrinking, or Tebalized to make it crease resistant. It may be treated to make it water repellant. It may be moth- and mildew-proofed. It may be napped, moired, flocked, or embossed. It may be treated with resin to make it wash-and-wear. This last treatment of fabrics is the "greatest textile innovation in recent years" according to *The Good Housekeeping Institute*. I strongly recommend that you send for their booklet on this subject.

As you can see, the whole character of a fabric depends upon the processes through which it passes after it leaves the weaver's loom. For this reason dyeing and printing are very important phases in the finishing of a fabric. The type of dye used depends on the fiber and the use for which the finished fabric is intended. Also, some dyes that color one fiber may have no affinity for another. For example, some wool dyes have no effect on cotton. Many synthetics require a special dye unlike any used on other fibers. Because of the end use of a fabric, the quality of "fastness" of a color has to be considered. Drapery dyes must be fast to sunlight, wash clothes fast to laundering, and linings fast to dry cleaning and perspiration.

Some of the latest dyeing processes in synthetics are done in the chemical solution before the fiber has formed. This makes the resultant fabrics practically impregnable to sun, gas fumes, and other detrimental influences. Fine woolens and worsteds are commonly dyed in the "raw stock" before the yarns are spun. Yarns may be dyed in the skein before being woven into fabrics. The most common method is to dye the fabric after it has been woven into piece goods.

In printing, a pattern is applied to the fabric by means of dye pastes. Most inexpensive prints are directly applied to yards and yards at a time from copper plates on a roller. When a light print is applied to a dark fabric a "discharge" paste is used to remove color in the desired places. Photographic printing gives accurate, beautifully shaded patterns. Screen and block printing are the most expensive methods because they are done with stencils, often by hand. You should avoid buying a fabric that has printed stripes or plaids, anything that has to be matched, because it is almost impossible to keep such a print true to fabric grain.

Some of the fabrics you should learn to identify for fiber content, weight, and weave are:

Cotton type

Batiste, broadcloth, calico, chambray, denim, dimity, dotted swiss, gingham, lawn, madras, mull, nainsook, organdy, percale, piqué, plissé, poplin, seersucker, voile. Read carefully the labels for washing instructions and save them.

Silk type

Shantung, crepe, faille, bengaline, surah, taffeta, satin, brocade, foulard, tie-silk, tussah. If a silk fabric is not labeled washable, it is wise to have it dry cleaned by a professional cleaner.

Wool type

Serge, sharkskin, covert, homespun, cheviot, melton, duvetyn. Learn the difference between woolen and worsted. Woolens are made of short-fibered, soft-twisted yarn. Nap is noticeable and threads indistinct. Tweed is a typical woolen. Worsted is made from long-fibered, hard-twisted yarn. The surface has no nap and is smooth and hard. Gabardine is a typical worsted. You are always safest to have woolens and worsteds dry cleaned. There is a washable woolen on the market, but you should never expect a woolen to launder like cotton. Wool is affected adversely by high temperatures, and wool colors are seldom as resistant to washing as cotton colors.

Napped fabrics

Velvet, velveteen, corduroy, fleece, flannel, duvetyn, cheviot.

▶ Choosing Your Fabric Colors

What is your favorite color? Even though it is the brightest red or yellow, you can enjoy wearing it, if only as a trimming. Sometimes I prefer basic black. At one time I was known as the "brown lady." But mostly, I am all for every woman knowing her best color and wearing it.

Most of us have several becoming colors. Key your wardrobe each season to some color, not necessarily the one that all the shop windows are showing. No matter how few new clothes you can afford, you need not dress in monotones unless you happen to feel most comfortable that way.

My favorite color is purple. Mother said I could say it before I said "Mama." It's a rich color, a royal color, a serene color like twilight. It has every variation of red and blue, because it is a combination of both. Its complement is green, and my eyes are green, so I can wear yellow and blue, too —almost the whole gamut of color. That's pretty flexible.

Recently, I attended a most interesting clothing seminar in which many shades of red fabrics were discussed. The commentator introduced a model who looked very elegant in a red flat wool crepe which seemed to make her extremely slender. Then, she came out in the same dress made up in a shiny red satin which gave off highlights over figure bulges you hadn't noticed before. Next she wore a velvet, same style, which made her figure look thick because of the deep pile. The last dress was a bulky-knit jersey which made her look almost twice the size she was in the original crepe. All the dresses were *exactly the same shade of red*. This demonstration brought out emphatically how careful you must be to choose the right texture of fabric as well as the right color to complement your figure. Even basic black plays the same tricks on you if the texture is wrong.

One season, the pattern company I worked for had a program on choosing colors according to the five types of skin and hair: Blond—Brownette—Brunette—Redhead—Gray.

I'm a brownette and I learned that we in-betweens are not so ill favored by nature, after all. Actually, we have the widest choice of colors of any type. Complement your eyes, no matter how colorless they seem. Mine are about the shade of pea soup and yet I can make them look green or aqua or brown by wearing those colors. My skin is peachy rather than ivory toned. Shades of purple on the red-purple side are most becoming. My hair is brown with a wee bit of red in it, so brown to red-brown is for me.

If you are a blond you can play with the lighter tints of color and can look very dramatic in black and most angelic in white. Usually, you can wear yellows, which so many other people have to shy away from. Of course blue-eyed blonds look divine in blue and pink.

If you are a brunette you can wear most of the startling and vivid shades. You must avoid yellows if your skin has an olive cast. Usually only the intense shades of green, such as Kelly, are good even when your skin is ivory white. Contrasts of black and white together are very becoming to brunettes or graying brunettes.

Why shouldn't the gray-haired woman try some shades of brown if she was once a brownette? Probably she should try a brown on the pinkish side. And a color all her own is blue. If your hair is gray, think of yourself in royal blue, for instance. If your hair is practically white and your skin very fresh, of course you look wonderful in black. But, usually black, unrelieved with another color, makes a gray woman look so much older. Even if you are an older woman, there's no reason why you should not go in for colors. Perhaps, now that your skin tones have softened, you can wear some vivid tones you never wore before.

Some redheads I know simply yen to wear red and are so surprised to hear me say, "Why not?" A kind and ravishing redhead taught me this, years ago. She came into my mother's shop to purchase some yarn. She picked up and toyed with a beautiful shade of American beauty red which has just a suggestion of purple in it. I sprang up with, "Oh! No!" She smiled and chose a lovely aqua blue on the green side. Her skin was ivory white, with almost no color. Her eyes were a luminous red-brown. "Do you like this one for me better?" she asked as she held it under her chin. It was lovely, yet it made her look pale. She switched back to the American beauty red and held it under her chin the same way. There was something about that deep red that made her exceptional beauty vibrate. I was barely in my teens then and ever since have talked my red-haired friends into experimenting with shades of red if they wished. Let me add that a redhead's commonly good colors, such as yellow, tans, copper, orange and green, are often quite unbecoming to other types.

While I was working with this complexion color key I was scheduled to give a fashion talk at Howard University, then an all-Negro college. Of course, I had to throw away my color key geared to white skin and vari-colored eyes and hair. Most Negroes have the same color hair and eyes. But their skin tones have every color in the rainbow in them: red, blue, purple, green, and yellow. Negroes can wear vivid colors because high shades are most becoming, just as they are to brunettes. Contrasts of pure white are most dramatic with ebony skin tones, as are pale blue, pink, and lavender. All the blues are lovely on those with red-purple or purple-blue skin undertones. We found that the one color most Negroes had to avoid was green, particularly a yellowish green.

Of course, when choosing your best color in fabrics, you will come across various in-betweens, such as blue-greens and yellow-reds. You will be wise to hold up the bolt of material to your face, in a light similar to that in which you will wear the garment when it is completed. For instance, fabric for an evening dress should be studied by you in a mirror which is illuminated by electric light; fabric for a costume you will wear in the daytime should be studied next to your face in daylight, not under electric lights in the shop.

The following will help you to get a clearer concept of color. Color has three dimensions:

1. *Hue* is the name of a color.
2. *Value* is the lightness of a color.
   Tint is a light value.
   Shade is a dark value.
3. *Chrome* is the strength of a color, or color intensity.

Because of new discoveries in pure color pigments, the concepts of color have been extended beyond the standard three elementary colors: red, yellow, and blue. There are now *five* elementary colors: red, yellow, green, blue, and purple.

The three secondary colors, once considered combinations of elementary colors, were: orange, green, and purple. Now there are *five* secondary colors: yellow-red, green-yellow, blue-green, purple-blue, and red-purple.

Total the five elementary colors and the five secondary colors, and you now have a choice of *ten* from which to select those most becoming to you.

Many women who are inclined to be too heavy usually minimize their size by sticking to black or navy. What they are doing is choosing the darkest value of a color. They might also choose a dark value of green, often called bottle green or a green-yellow. A dark value of red is sometimes called burgundy or maroon, which is a red-purple. Or, how about darkest purple or brown?

I went off on a color tangent in this fabric chapter because the simplest fabric chosen in the color that becomes you can become a successful garment for you to wear.

▶ *What the Beginning Sewer Should Choose*

I cannot tell, as I think of you, just what point you have reached in sewing. I assume that you have bought this little book because you have done enough sewing to know how helpful good tools can be, and you would like to learn more and better ways of using them to advantage. However, I hope beginners will find my discussion of the use of modern sewing aids as helpful in perfecting their skill as those who sew more than a little.

I know that my theory that all beginners need not, necessarily, start out sewing on cottons is somewhat unorthodox. Cottons, particularly the new wash-and-wear finishes, can sometimes be most difficult and discouraging because it is so hard to straighten to grain perfection before laying the fabric out.

The latest theories for teaching beginners allow them to start on something to wear, which nearly always leads to a skirt first as that needs little fitting. In this case, the easiest fabric to sew on is a good medium weight, pre-shrunk wool crepe of firm weave. I know it is more expensive. But, if a sizable investment has been made, you may be more cautious and do things correctly the first time. I would rather see a first skirt a success to be proud of than something you hate every time you put it on just to wear it out. The pattern should be a suitable "Simple-to-Make." Many begin with a shirred skirt that needs no zipper and no pattern at all. But, so often the shirring string breaks halfway through a waistline fitting. This could be avoided by beginning with a pleated skirt that needs no zipper and which can now be made by stitching on the new pleat-as-you-sew stiffening.

I do not agree that a beginner can start out with a suit or coat. Tailoring details take the skill acquired with experience. An investment in this much material is too great for the disappointment that could come with amateur results. Certainly, I would avoid plaids or stripes, corduroys, velvets, jersey, satin, chiffon, stubborn synthetics, and some of the new laminates and stretch fabrics until your sewing techniques are somewhat perfected. But don't put off working with the harder-to-sew fabrics forever or you will miss a lot of the fun of new sewing adventures.

▶ *Linings, Interlinings, Facings*

I see the Fashion Group import collections of fabulous fashions twice a year as soon as they arrive in New York. The last one I saw gave me the feeling that if a model stepped out of a garment and walked away, it would not fall in a limp heap, but would almost stand by itself. This is because today's fine clothes are all thoroughly interfaced and innerlined with inner supporting fabrics and boning to help them keep their beautiful shape.

These are the clothes we home sewers should be copying rather than cheap ready-to-wear garments that you can buy less expensively than you can make them. So, these supporting fabrics are also among the things you should know how to select. Don't shudder at the thought of learning to use two fabrics together. Often a supporting fabric helps to make a contrary outer fabric sew together much easier.

Interfacing and innerlining are two separate processes and require different fabric for each purpose (Fig. V-2). When all parts of a bodice and skirt or coat are mounted on another under fabric, this is called innerlining. Collars, lapels, revers, front closings, cuffs, and jacket hems are the areas of a garment which need to be supported, reinforced, shaped, or molded, and this is done by interfacing. Lining is done in those areas where unfinished seams need covering, such as inside jacket or coat or inside a panel that may fly free from a garment in movement. Interlining is when a third fabric is inserted between outer and lining fabrics for warmth.

Interfacing was once done only in very tailored coats and suits, and a special "hair canvas" or "French canvas," then only made in France, was used. This was known about only by experienced tailors and dressmakers. If some of the more knowing home sewers tried to interface they attempted to duplicate the professional work by using an old sheet or unbleached muslin. However, this type of material does not have the proper resilience and moldability. After American manufacturers began to duplicate, and even surpass, the quality of the imported materials, they saw a growing trend in home sewing toward professionalism. They suddenly deluged the fabric counters with more than thirty kinds of interfacings, innerlinings, linings, and other underpinnings.

There are special hair canvas interfacings in all weights. There are innerlinings in woven and non-woven fabrics. The latest addition to this category of fabrics is a press-on support fabric, both woven and non-woven, for small areas such as buttonholes, welts, and seaming points. This material, which is pressed on with a hot iron, should never be used for full interfacings or innerlinings.

If your garment is made of washable fabric and will be laundered frequently, be sure your interfacing and innerlining is also of a washable quality.

Nothing makes a collar roll and hold its shape as well as hair canvas. Use the coat weight for a coat, the suit weight for a suit, and the dress weight for a dress. I have tried using innerlining throughout as an interfacing, but I am always sorry after the garment has been washed or cleaned a few times. It is worth the extra effort to learn how to attach interfacing to innerlining in the right areas.

Fig. V-2 *Points of Garment Construction Where Interfacing and Innerlining are Used*

Courtesy Chicopee Mills, Inc.

Specially woven innerlining comes in soft, super-soft, and firm. A new silky weight comes in soft and firm, too, and is much superior to old fashioned china silk. Marquisette, china silk and nylon organdy are used for innerlining under very sheer fabrics. Choose your innerlining so that it is pliable and never heavier than the fabric it supports. Try a piece of your outer fabric over that innerlining or interfacing before you buy it.

For collars and lapels, woven interfacings produce a well-tailored result.

The non-woven or felted type of interfacing is unsurpassed when a bouffant effect is to be created. This type of underpinning comes in interfacing and innerlining weights both on straight line or bias that stretches in all directions. It has a flat felted texture and may have a porous look. The non-woven interfacings are wonderful for making soft and packable hats and bags and many other items too numerous to mention.

The filmiest weight non-woven press-on interfacing is perfect for supporting buttonhole areas and welts on soft fabrics. However, the press-on interfacing should never be used throughout to interface a lapel or collar.

Interfacing takes considerable tailoring skill. Innerlining means twice as much cutting for the home sewer and is cut from the same pattern pieces as the ones it supports.

There are special lining satins and crepes to be had in most fabric colors. Or, you can line a suit jacket or coat with the same fabric as a blouse or dress which is being made to go with it.

Interlining is usually done for extra warmth, and there are special materials for this third layer. However, it has been something that so many home sewers have tackled with dread that now there are several interesting "warmth without weight" linings, which combine the luxury look of satin with a warm backing. One of these is wool and silk woven as one piece of fabric, with a satin outer surface and napped woolen inner surface. Then there is a satin with a luminous coated back that is incredibly cozy considering the weight of the material. This luminous lining has recently had a very thin coating of foam rubber added for even more warmth. Other foam rubber laminates come in lining and outer-wear fabrics. Also, there are beautifully quilted fabrics for both these purposes.

► *Cutting Fabrics*

Many fabrics have a right and wrong side. Napped fabrics with a piled or fuzzy surface on the right side, like corduroy or velveteen, often have an up-and-down which must be cut all in one direction. When preparing to cut fabrics in double thickness, the right sides are turned inside and the wrong sides outside.

There are several ways of telling the right from the wrong side of flatter fabrics, sometimes by the way they are rolled or folded. Linen and cotton frequently come folded right side out. Silk and wool are often folded right side in. If the fabric comes on a long roll, the right side is usually turned in. If one side of a fabric is shinier than the other, the more lustrous is the right side except where a shiny design is woven into a dull background. A twill weave runs from lower right to upper left on the wrong side. Ribbed or corded weaves always predominate on the face. Selvage edges are usually smoother on the right side. Printed fabrics are brighter on the right side. If the right side is hard to determine, choose the side with fewest flaws and rough spots. Of course, some fabrics are the same on both sides.

All woven fabrics have three different grains: crosswise, lengthwise and bias. Lengthwise grain is parallel with the selvage edge. Crosswise grain crosses the lengthwise grain at a right angle. Bias grain falls on the diagonal. If you fold a piece of fabric with the selvage parallel to the crosswise threads, the fold is a true bias.

For complete accuracy in cutting any fabric use a pattern cutting board made of a special material soft enough to hold pins. It is marked off every inch in both directions with rows of various shaped characters. These markings are not all alike because repetition of the same marks has a tendency to dazzle the eye on so large a surface. If the creases in the board hump when you first unfold it, crease one section back against the next in the opposite direction and it will lie perfectly flat.

The pattern cutting board is much more than protection for a table top or other convenient cutting surface. Because you may pin fabric down to the surface it never slips out of position while you are affixing pattern pieces. Lay the board out on a long table or extend the length of a short table under it by using your adjustable ironing board at right height. You can fold one or two sections of the board behind a short table and cut on less space, as I must in my small apartment. A high bed or a game table are good cutting places, too. When the cutting is finished refold the board and store it. If you are unable to finish all your cutting at once, fold your pinned-on fabric inside the board and store away together until the next time. Your fabric will be as straight and fresh as when you left off, without having to be laid out all over again.

Before laying out fabric decide which view of the pattern style you will use (Figs. V-3A, B & C). Take out all pattern pieces and examine them to be sure they pertain to that view. Fold up all the paper pieces you will not use and return them to the envelope. Press with a warm iron the pieces to be cut. Examine the various layout charts and find the one showing your size and fabric width. Draw a circle around the chart so as not to confuse it with the others while laying out the pattern pieces on the fabric.

The pattern layout is your blueprint. I am giving here some general rules for using the pattern cutting board; however, always study your layout in relation to your particular style and fabric. Recently, I cut out five garments from different fabrics, and out of the five, not unusual fashions, no two were cut the same way.

Be sure your fabric is well pressed and straight. If your material does not tear readily, you can straighten the crosswise edge by pulling a thread and cutting along it. If the selvage edge is not perfectly flat, snip it with scissors about every 12″. Examine your pattern layout and determine whether fabric is to be on a lengthwise or crosswise fold. Sometimes part of it will be laid out one way, part the other; or one edge will be folded towards the center; or perhaps both edges folded towards the center. In any case, pin crosswise grain ends together, and pin selvages together or on straight lengthwise grain (*see* Fig. I-16).

If the fabric will not smooth out grain perfect and flat, it will have to be stretched or shrunk so that it will. Sometimes this can be done with a steam iron while the material is pinned out on the cutting board. While you are steaming, a gentle pulling on the diagonal from corner to corner may help. If material still does not lie grain perfect, you will have to unpin it from the cutting board and go in for some more serious shrinking.

You may have a good tailor who will shrink and straighten your woolen fabric for you, at little expense. Otherwise, using

35" FABRIC

SIZES 9-10-11-12

SIZES 13-14

IMPORTANT—FOR NAP FABRIC

FOR LAYOUTS MARKED "OPEN DOUBLE FABRIC" PLACE ONE LAYER OVER THE OTHER, RIGHT SIDES TOGETHER, WITH NAP RUNNING IN ONE DIRECTION.

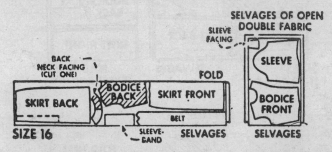

Fig. V-3A   Typical Fabric Layout in Various Widths

your sewing machine, baste the crosswise edges together and then the lengthwise edges together. Spread a piece of plastic (perhaps an old shower curtain) over a large table or on the floor. Wet a doubled bed sheet and roll your fabric up in it, carefully straightening it as much as you can while you roll.

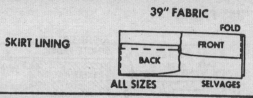

SKIRT LINING

45" FABRIC

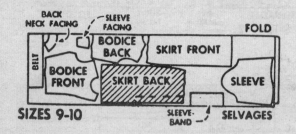

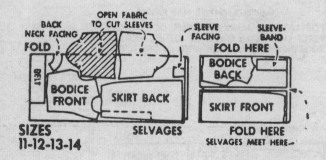

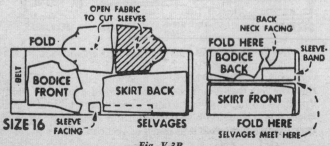

Fig. V-3B

52" FABRIC

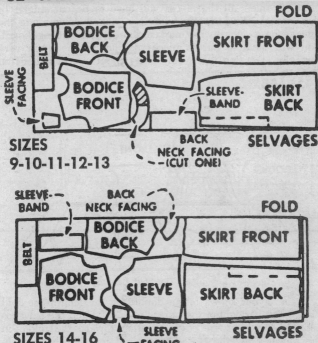

Fig. V-3C

If you are working with washable cottons, follow the same procedure of basting selvages and crosswise ends together. But, cottons can be wet directly instead of rolled up in dampened sheets. Then, you press the material dry, straightening as you press.

Some of the wash-and-wear cottons, as well as other fabrics that have been permanently pulled off grain by one of the many new finishes, are impossible to straighten. The selvage edges will come together nicely, but, pull as you will, the crosswise grain will be uneven. Here the cutting board may save the day because, if the off-grain tendency is very slight, it is possible to pin the selvage edges together very carefully along a lengthwise marked line and cut out a double thickness of fabric on a perfectly even grain. When it is utterly impossible to get identical straight-of-grain when cutting two pieces at once, all the pieces will have to be cut singly. In this case, the single layer of fabric is pinned down along the selvage on a lengthwise marked line of the cutting board. You will have to fit the pieces parallel to the grain very carefully, working out your own layout so that not too much fabric is wasted.

Fig. V-4   Layout on Doubled Lengthwise Fold

If the layout shows fabric double on the lengthwise fold (Fig. V-4), straighten the crosswise end. Match the selvages and pin the crosswise edges together toward the fold. Pin the selvages together for the required length. Then, begin pinning the double fabric down to the board where the first crosswise and lengthwise rows of inch marks meet inside the yardage ruled line. First pin down the crosswise ends towards the fold across the board. Then, pin the doubled selvages along the first lengthwise row of inch marks, as far as you can. If the layout indicates all pattern pieces are being cut lengthwise of the fabric, extra length may be left over at the farther end of the board. Fold this excess material at the other end of the board in a neat roll. Smooth the fabric away from the pinned lines in every direction until both layers are perfectly flat and the fold lies parallel to a lengthwise row of inch marks. Then, pin on all pattern pieces possible up to the roll, according to the layout.

Some pattern pieces are marked "to be laid against the fold." All other pieces are marked with a straight-of-goods line somewhere on them. Often this line is not parallel with the edges of the pattern piece. The pieces must be placed on

the fabric according to the layout with the straight-of-goods
length at the selvage along lengthwise edge of cutting board,
marking in the right relation to the selvage or crosswise edge.
Check them exactly with your see-thru ruler or tape measure,
and pin the straight-of-goods line down to the straight grain of
fabric first. Then pin all around the edges of the pattern piece,
placing pins with the grain of fabric. You must lay out all pattern pieces according to the pattern layout before you start to
cut to be sure you have enough fabric. Don't try to make
them fit in somewhere by changing the direction of the layout or fabric grain, because the piece thus cut will surely
fit badly when you try to sew it into the garment. If the
layout is longer than the length of the cutting board, leave
all pattern pieces on as they are this far. Unpin the fabric
edges only from the edges of the board and carefully roll
them up inside the fabric. Pull the fabric roll gently towards
the end of board where you began before. Pin the unused
length at the selvage along lengthwise edge of cutting board.
Smooth out the fabric below the roll, being careful to maintain grain perfection on both layers. Continue to pin on the
pattern pieces as before, until all are accounted for.

If the layout shows fabric double on the crosswise fold

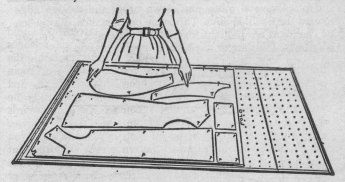

Fig. V-5 Layout on Doubled Crosswise Fold

(Fig. V-5), straighten both crosswise ends and pin them
together. Then, pin the doubled selvages together on each
side. Beginning where the first lengthwise and crosswise rows
of inch marks meet inside the yardage-ruled line, pin down
the doubled crosswise edges all across board on the first row
of lengthwise marks. The crosswise fold will run parallel
with a crosswise row of inch marks. Smooth out the fabric

until both layers are perfectly flat and pin on the pattern pieces according to the layout.

Some layouts show fabric double on both crosswise and lengthwise folds. Here it is wise to lay out the pattern pieces without pinning them down to determine how much fabric is required each way. Then, without any waste of fabric, these pieces may be cut apart and each pinned down to the cutting board separately.

Other layouts of wider doubled fabrics show pieces, often skirt sections, cut on a fold only as wide as that particular pattern piece. Or, sections cut on folds may show a fold on each edge with the selvages meeting at the center. Here it is important to begin to make the fold at the crosswise end. Measure off with the see-thru ruler or tape measure the width that the pattern piece requires. Pin the crosswise fold over this amount, then pin down the crosswise edges along the row of marks on the cutting board, leaving the fold at the lengthwise outside edge. Judge the necessary length for the pattern piece. Measure this distance up the folded edge. Then, parallel to this measurement, check the selvage to be sure it is the same distance from the fold as on the crosswise end. Pin the selvage down so it doesn't slip off grain, and place several other pins down along the selvage edge toward the doubled ends. This same care is taken, also, when two selvages are brought together at the center and the two lengthwise folds are at the outside lengthwise edges.

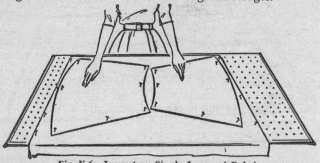

Fig. V-6 Layout on Single Layer of Fabric

If the layout shows single layer of fabric (Fig. V-6), always cut it with the right side up. First pin the single crosswise edge down to the cutting board on the first row on the end where the crosswise and lengthwise rows of inch marks meet. Then, pin down the single selvage edge along the first row of lengthwise marks as far as you can go. In the case of a single fabric which is wider than the board, lay out and pin the pattern pieces grain perfect as far over as possible. Then, unpin the edges from the board and move the other selvage edge to the opposite lengthwise side of the board and pin it down. If you are cutting a very wide single layer of fabric, you may prefer to work with the crosswise of the goods on the lengthwise of the board so as to get all pattern pieces pinned down to the width of fabric at once.

Since the inch marks on the cutting board run perfectly true in all directions, the diagonal intersection of all marks

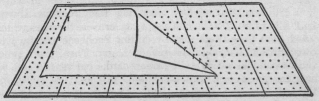

Fig. V-7 Layout on Fabric Bias

are on the true bias (Fig. V-7). In order to cut perfect a bias strip, such as for binding, piping, or welting, pin the fabric down to these intersections on the cutting board. Let us say we are going to cut bias from a straight 18″ piece of fabric. Straighten the crosswise grain on both edges. Pin one single selvage edge down to the first lengthwise marked line on the board. Pin the bottom crosswise grain across where it hits a crosswise marking. At the top crosswise edge begin at the first pin and fold along a bias marking from that point, pinning the fold every 2″ or so, until entire length is folded along the bias intersection markings in a straight line. The first crosswise edge will be turned back so it lies parallel with and on top of the pinned-down selvage. The fold will measure one half again as long as the 18″ length of the piece, or 27″. You are sure now that you have a true bias. At the fold, lay your see-thru ruler, and mark with chalk through the slots for any width bias strip you desire and as many more pieces as you need. On page 197 is a special lesson on using this diagonal line of intersection marks to cut a bias plaid.

▶ *Cut Several Things at Once to Save Time*

While you have your pattern cutting board out, you might as well cut out several things before you set up your sewing machine. This is what I prefer to do, because it saves time in the long run. Then I take all the fabric pieces (and lining and interlining if I have also cut those) and I pin all the related parts together: for instance, cuffs to sleeves; interfacings and facings and fronts; backs and back facings, and skirt pieces, etc. On the wrong side of the cut fabric I mark the fronts with a large "F," the backs with a "B," the sleeves with an "S," etc., using my tailor's chalk. Then I fold the pieces with their matching interfacing or interlining, if any is used, and I place them in a neat pile inside a plastic bag with the instruction sheet which accompanies the pattern. If you desire, you can even pile them in the order in which they will be used, by just consulting the directions. If you do not have any plastic bags, you can convert the ones which come from the dry cleaner by cutting each one into two or three sections (to give you several bags). Then, lay a press cloth over one end of each section of the cut plastic and go over the press cloth with a hot iron. This will seal the ends. Keep the plastic bags in your fabric box or drawer until you are ready to sew.

▶ *Cutting Tools*

The best cutting tools for a beginning sewer to use are good, sharp dressmaker shears, *never* pinking shears, under any circumstances. Of course, I prefer cutting out patterns with electric scissors (Fig. V-8), possibly because I'm left-handed. Also, the cut line is so clean and continuous, never choppy; and my hands are never grooved from the handle pressure, or tired out from manipulating the blades. However, these scissors are expensive and you need to have regular shears for much other cutting.

You can always get left-handed dressmaker shears if you have my problem. They are the ones with the uneven bent handle. You put your thumb through the smaller handle and two fingers through the larger one. The blade rests on its edge against the surface of the cutting board. Never let it tilt at an angle while cutting around pattern pieces. Cut with long, even, sure strokes; never use little fussy, jerky ones. Cut through pattern tissue edge and fabric together, keeping on the outside of the heavy printed line. The paper margin falls away as you work. When you come to a notch, cut *out* around it, *not in* because, if the seam is strained at this point, a notch is the first thing to give way.

Fig. V-8 Electric Scissors Being Used with Cutting Board

If a piece, such as a cuff, has to be cut twice, don't remove the pattern from the first cutting; pin the whole thing down together and cut around the pattern outline again. Always leave fabric pieces pinned to the pattern until marking has been completed. And, do your marking immediately to avoid permanent pin marks in your fabric.

If you are a beginning sewer, you should never try to cut difficult fabrics. Leave plaids, stripes, velveteen, corduroy, heavy woolens, laminates, jersey, chiffon, lace, thin synthetics, satin, and taffeta to more advanced sewers.

CHAPTER 6

Marking and How

Laying out and cutting patterns on the straight of goods and transferring pattern markings to the fabric pieces used to be the hardest things to teach when I was a pattern stylist. Women frustrated me so when they came to me for advice and then said smugly, "Oh, I never bother with those marks!" Perhaps I am more convincing now, because today everyone seems to learn the better, more accurate way to do these things.

Today, most of the patterns are printed and, probably because pattern marks say what they are for, they mean more to you (Fig. VI-1). These lines, darts, tucks, notches, squares, and numbered pattern pieces are the keys to construction of a garment. The reason you must transfer pattern markings is to make those indications, which mean fitting, come exactly where they are intended to come. It is particularly important to get doubled thicknesses marked identically because two sides of a garment which have been cut together must look alike.

Probably most of us disliked marking because we hated making thread tailor's tacks which was, then, the only way we knew. Today there are many ways of transferring pattern marks to fabric. Also, there are now numerous marking aids to help make them more accurate. Markings may be made with pins, thread, chalk, tracing paper and wheel, a stylus-type tailor's tacker, chalk pencil, transparent adhesive tape, or by pressing. Marking aids include a 6″ sewing gauge or a 6″ tailorette with chalk attached which allows you to mark as you measure, a see-thru ruler of clear plastic which is a 15″ sewer's T-square slotted for marking pleats, tucks, bias, etc., a 6″ clear dressmaker's gauge with a scalloped edge of various sizes for marking scallops, an aluminum hem gauge

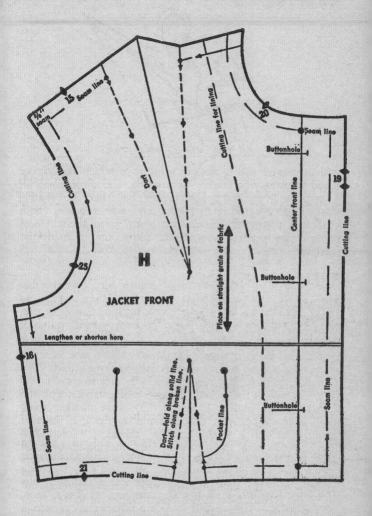

Fig. VI-1 Typical Marking on Pattern Piece

Fig. VI-2   Thread Tailor Tacks

with a curved and a straight edge over which straight or flared hems may be marked by pressing, a chalk holder with a sharpener in one end to keep tailor's chalk sharp and chalky, marking pencils for small places, and skirt markers (both chalk and pin type) for marking hems. Even though most patterns are printed, you should learn how to mark the perforated ones.

► *Tailor Tacks*

Although the thread tailor's tack takes much time, there are occasions when it is the only way to mark; so everyone should know how to make a tailor's tack (Fig. VI-2). Use contrasting color thread, usually white basting cotton. Double a very long thread in your needle. A thread tailor's tack is made wherever a pattern is marked with dots, as along a dart. Take a small stitch through the paper and both thicknesses of fabric (it goes through the hole on a perforated pattern). Pull the thread through until a 1″ end is left. Take another small stitch in the same spot, this time pulling up a 1″ loop of thread. Cut off a second end of thread 1″ long. You now have two ends and a loop 1″ long, sticking up over the mark. Pull this tack right through the hole of a perforation, but cut the center of the double loop if pattern is printed, and carefully pull the pattern piece away without pulling out any of the thread. Now it is necessary, after all tailor's tacks are completed, to separate a double thickness of fabric without disturbing any of the threads. Pull the two thicknesses gently apart until about ½″ of thread shows between them. Being very cautious not to snip the fabric, cut these threads at the center so that a tuft is left in the same place on both pieces.

Keep the tailor's tacks in the fabric until the d... detail has been stitched. Then remove the marks ... out all the threads. Be careful all tailor's tacks are ... before you wear the garment because they have a w... ...r hiding in seams and then showing up at the most embarrassing moment to proclaim "home-made"!

Some patterns show different shaped marks, such as small and large circles, squares, or triangles, to point out various sewing details. To help you remember their purpose, use a different color of thread for each mark.

▶ *Tracing Paper and Wheel*

The quickest and most accurate method of transferring pattern marks to fabric is with tracing paper and wheel. In a time and motion study once made by some teachers, it was found that it took 3½ minutes to mark seven perforations with thread tailor's tacks and 30 seconds to trace the same dart. But, I'll never forget the first time I used tracing paper!

A sewing teacher introduced it to me while I was making a white piqué dress. But, at that time the only colors to be had were red and white. She was hasty in her explanation of how to use it. I spread my white fabric right side down over the full-sized sheet of red carbon paper. I leaned on it to hold it down and my hands became smudged. Results: a mess of fingernail marks, fingerprints and crooked lines that never came out. Besides, it took twice as long as tailor's tacks.

Now, how easy! The package instructions tell you how to use it. Try to do your marking before putting away your cutting board because you should work on such a large, uncluttered surface, and the board is of soft composition. Otherwise, slip the little cardboard which comes in the package under your tracing (Fig. VI-3). It acts as a cushion to the wheel so your pattern pieces aren't cut to ribbons.

There are three tracing wheels, a serrated edge (Fig. VI-4A), a needlepoint wheel (Fig. VI-4B), and a plain edge. For most of your work you will use the first of these. The needlepoint wheel is used by professional pattern makers to transfer lines from their "muslin" to paper. But, the sharp points will cut or score some fabrics. The one time you will find it more useful is when you are trying to make marks on thick woolens.

Some of you may hesitate using tracing paper because you've had bad experiences, as I did. But, you can almost

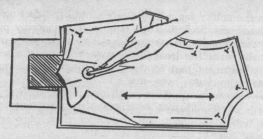

Fig. VI-3 Cardboard Used to Keep from Cutting Up Pattern

(Fig. VI-4A)

(Fig. VI-4B)

always use tracing paper, if you do so with judgment. Remember, you are the only one who has to see that line, and then only long enough to stitch over it. There are five colors in the tracing paper package: white, yellow, orange, red, and blue. White carbon marks always disappear as soon as a hot iron touches them. So, use white whenever you can, and that is more of the time than you think. For instance, mark white organdy or chiffon with it because it shows up through a transparent fabric. When do you need to worry whether or not marks clean out? Only when they show on the right side. It doesn't bother me to see tracing marks inside my garments.

If in doubt as to whether the color will show or press through your fabric, test a sample of it. Naturally, bright red or dark blue used on white or pastels is likely to show through on the right side. Use the color which shows up least but that you can still see, not the greatest contrast. Use the dark colors only when nothing else will do. Of course, when you line a garment and darts, tucks, gathers, and seams are sewn as one, the marking needs to be done only on the lining. If mistakes are made on the right side, naptha soap or tetra-chloride-based cleaning fluid will often remove carbon marks, providing it has not been pressed in with a hot iron. On some fabrics that have an affinity for color the marks simply will not come out. Oh yes, please don't be like a friend of mine who, when my back was turned, used typewriter carbon! *Dressmakers' carbon* is another name for tracing paper, and is specially made for dressmaking only.

Many beginners mark all the lines on their pattern, including seam allowances, and this is a good way of assuring complete accuracy until you feel safer about judging the standard ⅝". Some sewing machines have the sole plates printed with all necessary seam allowance measurements. If yours does not, you can attach the seam guide found in most attachment boxes and adjust it to ⅝". Or, lacking a seam guide, make your own by sticking down a strip of colored adhesive tape ⅝" from the needle. Better still, there is a special sew-straight plate which will fit on any sewing machine, to help you get absolutely straight seam allowances.

Whether or not you mark seam allowance lines, all essential markings must be transferred to fabric pieces accurately. Before removing pattern from fabric examine every piece carefully to be sure you have missed nothing. Study these details and know what they mean, because all the printed information is essential to your knowledge of the garment's construction. Of course, you must mark all darts, pleats, tucks, gathers, buttonholes, and pockets. Mark an extra cross line termination point at the end of all darts and tucks. If the dart does not show a center line for its "take up," or fold, add one. There may be different shaped marks that indicate seam joinings, collar attachment, or fastening details. Mark them with an X in another color to flag them. With the scissors, snip center line at both edges, or mark it in a straight line if the pattern piece so indicates. It is better to mark something that you may not need than to leave something essential out.

You don't have to use the whole large sheet of tracing paper to mark double fabric thicknesses (Fig. VI-5). That's so awkward. These sheets have been folded, sometimes two ways, with the color inside. Cut off a 3"-wide doubled slice of the paper so there is a fold at one end. Unpin the pattern piece only over the area to be marked. Place the bottom layer of folded tracing paper under the bottom layer of fabric, carbon against the wrong side of the material. Slip the top layer of carbon paper under the pattern marking over the wrong side of top layer of fabric. The fabric is thus sandwiched between the carbon paper slice. See how this

Fig. VI-5 *Tracing Paper Used in Strip*

Fig. VI-6 *Use See-Thru Ruler to Guide Tracing Wheel*

slender piece of carbon may be moved about under the pattern without smudging the work or your fingers?

Using your see-thru ruler as a guide over straight lines,

but drawing freehand over curves, mark with the tracing wheel (Fig. VI-6). Press down on the handle of the wheel firmly and trace back and forth several times. But do not bear down with all your strength. Use the serated tracing wheel on most fabrics. However, you have two alternatives (other than using a stronger color) if the tracing does not show up. If you are working on spongy woolens, such as tweeds, the needlepoint tracing wheel will often mark them best. It isn't safe to use this tracing wheel on fabrics which are easily scored or marked. Then, as with pile fabrics which should be cut pile up, reverse the carbon side of the tracing paper. Turn the fold so the paper side is back to back. Sandwich this strip of two-faced carbon between the wrong sides of the fabric under the pattern marking. The color, in this case, must be the strongest and most contrasting. Here you exert as much pressure as possible on the tracing wheel.

If the folded slice of tracing paper is not as long as the line to be marked, unfold it and cut a second 3″ slice of the same color paper. Sandwich the fabric between these two long slices of tracing paper as before, with wrong sides next to the carbon. Move the papers along to finish the line if they are still not long enough (Fig. VI-7). Usually, these longer pieces of carbon paper have to be used when marking pressed pleats all the way down the skirt. Don't forget to mark a crosswise termination line where the stitching ends and the pleat opening begins.

All the markings have to be transferred to a single thickness of fabric (Fig. VI-8), just as on a double thickness. However, a single thickness of fabric is cut with the right side facing the pattern piece, so the carbon side of the tracing paper is placed under the wrong side of the fabric. The tracing is done exactly the same, but without pressing down on the wheel handle so hard.

There is an instrument called a tailor tacker (Fig. VI-9) which is ideal for marking through the holes of perforated patterns. Blue and white strips of tracing paper are supplied in the package with this stylus-type instrument. Stick the point of the tool through the perforation and apply pressure so that it recedes into the handle. Then twist it several times until there is a good solid dot on the fabric. Of course, the carbon paper is inserted over and under the fabric and the perforated area of the pattern piece, as described in working with the tracing wheel. Use this instrument with printed patterns, under dots or other markings, if you wish to indicate

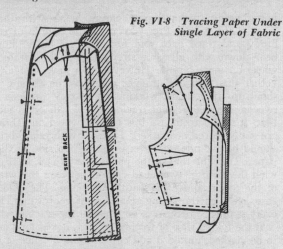

*Fig. VI-8 Tracing Paper Under
Single Layer of Fabric*

Fig. VI-7 Tracing Long Marked Lines

them only slightly instead of marking a whole line (Fig. VI-8).
This stylus-type instrument is also good for transferring embroidery designs. It is simply used as a tracer with the carbon
paper placed under the design which is put over the fabric.

▶ *Tailor's Chalk and See-Thru Ruler*

Tailor's chalk may also be used for transferring pattern markings to fabric, as well as for marking alterations or guide
lines for pleats, tucks, or trimmings. Tailor's chalk comes in
packages of assorted colored squares of white, blue, and red.
Again, use the white wherever possible because the colors
do not clean out readily, and try to make the marks on the
wrong side of the fabric. There is a handy little plastic tailor's
chalk holder, ready with one piece of chalk and a sharpener in
one end of the case. This keeps the chalk whittled sharp and
chalky, and when one piece is used up the squares from the
regular package will fit it.

You may wish to mark with a chalk dot on both sides of
the fabric where a pin goes through two thicknesses. Or, you
can heavily chalk a basting thread and bring it through one
or two thicknesses of fabric to mark them. Tailor's chalk is
usually used to mark alterations after a fitting. Open the seam
allowance and chalk along new line of pins or basting.

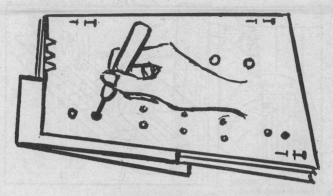

Fig. VI-9   Tailor Tacker

If you are going to add tucking or pleating details to your garment, or if you plan to pleat a skirt all around, this takes extra fabric which must be estimated. If, for instance, you are adding a tucked yoke to a blouse, measure the yoke pattern piece when pleats or tucks are not indicated on it. Then allow enough extra fabric for three times the width. If unpressed pleats are being used from waist down on a skirt, they will take up three times the amount of fabric as the waist measurement. If the whole skirt is being press-pleated, you need three times the hip measurement. Then the pleats from hip to waist have to be fitted into a smaller area in the waistband by lapping them a little more. These pleating details can all be measured and marked with the aid of the see-thru ruler (Fig. VI-10). Or, skirt pleats may be made on the special pre-pleated stiffening shown in Fig. II-12.

The see-thru ruler is slotted in various widths. When you decide the width to make your pleats, you can mark through this width slot with tailor's chalk. You can easily repeat ½″, 1″, or 2″ marks throughout the skirt width as follows: For ½″ markings, begin in the three ½″ slots, and after the first three, place the first slot over the last mark and repeat until all ½″ pleats are marked off. For 1″ markings, begin with the 1″ side of the ruler for the first mark, the second at the 1″ slot, the third at the second ½″ slot, and repeat. For 2″ markings, begin with the 1″ side of the ruler for the first mark, use the center slot on the ruler for the second 2″ mark, and the other outside edge for the third 2″ mark, then repeat.

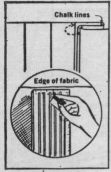

Chalk lines

Edge of fabric

Fig. VI-10 Marking
Pleats and Tucks

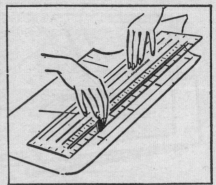

Fig. VI-11 Marking Buttonholes

The see-thru ruler and tailor's chalk, combined with basted thread markings, will insure uniform buttonholes on the straight of the grain (Fig. VI-11). With tracing paper and wheel you have transferred the buttonhole placements from pattern to fabric. But these are only short lines that indicate length and the distance apart, if there are more than one. Sometimes these marks are on the interfacing and sometimes directly on the outer fabric. However, both stitched and bound buttonholes are made on the right side of your work and the marks must be brought through. Thread basting is the only marking that can be taken out afterwards without showing. If your fabric is the kind that will show the needle mark, baste with silk thread by hand. Otherwise, large sewing machine basting is quickest and more exact.

First, connect the front ends of all transferred buttonhole marks with the see-thru ruler and draw a chalk line through them. Make another line through the other ends of all buttonhole marks. Now you have a ladder effect. At the center line of each buttonhole, chalk the rung of the ladder more firmly about 5″ in from the outside edge. If the markings have been made on the interfacing piece, baste it together with the corresponding piece of the outer fabric. Now, baste exactly over the chalked buttonhole ladder to bring the marking through to the right side of the work.

When the time comes to mark your buttonhole facings, the most accurate way is to use a chalk pencil. Pin the attached facing exactly against the wrong side of the finished button-

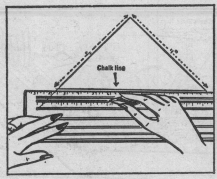

Fig. VI-12 Marking Bias

hole and pin together at each end, placing pins at right angles. Now, mark through the slot of the buttonhole onto the facing with the point of the pencil. On the reverse side, mark the place where the pin comes through for the exact length. You will learn how to complete the facing neatly on page 175.

Often bias strips must be made from scraps of fabric with no even edges. The see-thru ruler and chalk are handy here, too (Fig. VI-12). Examine your largest fabric scrap, find a crosswise grain and straighten here. Place the 4″ end of the ruler on this straight edge, mark a right angle lengthwise down the fabric as far as possible, and straighten. Fold the crosswise straight edge even with the lengthwise, and the fold is your first edge of true bias. Pin or press it in to hold the line. Lay the edge of the ruler on this line, and use the width of slot that corresponds with your desired bias width to mark through. Continue marking through these slots until you have several lengths of bias marked. If you haven't enough fabric for a true bias and the edge to be faced is fairly straight, you may use a "dressmakers' bias." This is marked on the diagonal of the fabric, but not exactly on the true bias. It must be marked very straight.

▶ *Marking Scalloped Edge*

Perhaps you would like to have a scalloped edge which has not been indicated on the pattern. Here you may use the little 6″ see-thru scalloper, a gauge with one straight edge and the other edge scalloped in various sizes from ½″ to 2″ (Fig. VI-13). You will need to allow 1″ for seams and then

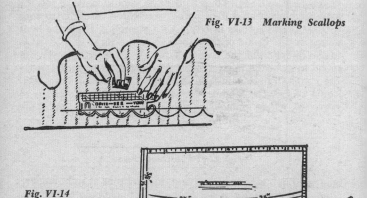

Fig. VI-13 Marking Scallops

Fig. VI-14
Pressing Flared Hem

do a little figuring to decide which size scallop best fits your area. You also have to fit the depth of the scallop in, plus a ½" seam at the top edge. At this distance in from the edge draw a line across on the wrong side of your fabric. Now, allowing a ½" for the side seam, lay the scalloper down on the line at the desired size. Chalk around the scallop shape from corner to corner. Lay the same size scallop down next to the last, so the corners meet and chalk around it again, being careful to hold the line. Continue in this way for the rest of the scallops.

Remember, scallops on anything but felt must be faced, unless you are planning to embroider them. So, you will have to cut a facing piece the same length and width, and mark the scallops on it so that they will both match up.

▶ Hem Pressing Gauge

When you are making a new garment, if you have an even figure and if you have adjusted your pattern length before cutting, you can press hems up without having to chalk-mark them. The aluminum hem pressing gauge is marked in various hem depths on both the straight and the curved edges (Fig. VI-14). Your hem edge should have a row of stay-stitching around it; if flared, stay-stitch carefully so that excess fullness shrinks in easily with steaming. Place the hem gauge on the inside of the fabric with the right shaped edge in the direction of the crease. Turn the fabric edge over the metal to meet the measurement mark of desired width. Hold the gauge firmly against the fold as you press on the grain. You'll be pressing about 8" of hem at a time. Continue to move the gauge along, measuring carefully, until the whole hem line has been firmly crease-marked.

▶ *Skirt Marker*

Everyone making new clothes is not so fortunate as to have such an even figure that she can take up skirt hems without a regular skirt marker. With hem fashions going up and down and sagging out of shape, a skirt marker in the home is an absolute necessity, whether you sew your own clothes or buy them ready-made. It's easy enough to mark your own hems and do them yourself. If you are making a dress, I'll tell you how here. If you are changing the length of a ready-made dress, turn to page 267.

The hem is not marked in a skirt until after the waistband and zipper are fitted and finished. In a dress the waist and skirt must have been attached and the zipper placket completed. Wear the shoes you intend to wear with the costume, as well as the right girdle and bra. Do the marking in front of a full-length mirror. Adjust the marker to the right length. You can mark your own skirt without help when you use the squeeze-bulb type of chalk marker (Fig. VI-15).

Stand very straight with your toe against the base of the skirt marker and let the hem fabric fall between the lip of the chalking device and the measure. The long measuring stick is under your skirt. Begin at the center front and hold the bulb lightly in your hand. Squeeze it firmly until a clear chalk mark appears. The chalk comes in white and pink and is easy enough to change if one color doesn't show up sufficiently. Turn slightly until you can make the next mark about 4" from the first. Continue in this way with the toe against the base of the marker, until you have turned around as far as you can without distorting your posture. You should be able to mark very close to the back. Then, begin 4" from

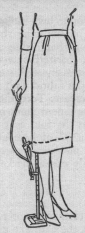

Fig. VI-15   Squeeze-Bulb Type Skirt Marker

the other side of the center mark, and turn in that direction, marking as far as possible. The back marks will usually come near enough together so they can be made to meet evenly in the turn of the hem. However, if you have no self-confidence, have someone else mark your skirt with your skirt marker, using either pins or chalk.

After you have finished with the skirt marker, the chalk marks may be pressed up over the hem gauge, and the edge trimmed even along the measure. Then, stay-stitching will complete the job.

▶ Mark By Pressing

There is another time when press-marking works best. If there are two pointed or curved corners that must look identical, as in a shaped neckline, trace the shape from the pattern onto a thin cardboard, inside the seam allowance. Cut out the shape very accurately in the cardboard. Then, press the seam allowance edges over the template you have just made to get the exact shape on both sides.

Sometimes you may wish to mark lines at the bottom of a skirt for rows of trimming, such as rick-rack or braid. It is important to keep this parallel with the hem line. Your skirt may be straight line or it may be circular. The trimming should be sewn on as flat a piece as possible, probably before the seams are sewn up, certainly before the hem is made. With the see-thru ruler there is no problem getting nice straight, parallel lines on a straight skirt. But, unless the pattern is marked and the markings can be transferred with tracing wheel and paper, the curved lines are more of a problem. You will have to decide how far up from the hem the lines are to be made, measure and mark (about 6″ apart) this distance up from hem, then connect your marks with a line curved approximately the same as the hem.

When you get to the point of tailoring, there is a special marking on the under-collar which is very easy to do with the aid of the see-thru ruler. After the interfacing pieces are cut like the undercollar, find the center back (if no seam) and mark it with a straight line. Then, place your ruler on an angle about 1″ on each side of this line and draw converging lines to meet at a point at the center. Draw a second diagonal set of lines 1″ away from the first, and perhaps a third. If the collar is quite wide, you may want to cross the lines in a diamond design. This will be stitched over the undercollar to hold the two pieces together, and help the neckline turn over gracefully.

CHAPTER 7

The New Sewing Machines and Their Accessories

After I became a travelling pattern stylist, I bought a portable sewing machine which went everywhere with me. Many of the young pattern stylists you meet do this. Never think they talk sewing from theory alone! Most of us in this business are really avid home sewers ourselves. Believe me, that little gem of a sewing machine has seen me through many a pleasantly creative evening when I might otherwise have been very lonely in a strange city.

Only recently I have acquired one of the latest automatic zig-zag models with a slant needle, like the one on the cover of this book. It does almost everything but talk. With it I can make stitched buttonholes, sew on buttons and hooks and eyes, mend and darn, blind-hem and embroider. It adjusts automatically for every weight of fabric.

Fifteen or twenty years ago, even the latest sewing machines had changed very little since electrification. Then, after the Second World War, manufacturers who had been making zig-zag embroidery machines for industrial use adopted them for the home sewing market. Women were utterly delighted with them from the first. Today, so many wonderful improvements are being made very fast in new sewing machines, that it is like buying a car. Within five years this year's model will almost seem obsolete. Also, today, the new home sewer who goes out to buy her first new machine can find one to match her ability and her budget.

If you are just learning to sew, the first thing you must master is how to stitch straight. Of course, if you have a good hand-me-down, straight-stitch machine, use it. There is little new that has been added to straight-stitch machines except the streamlining on the outside.

If you have no sewing machine, you might rent one, or buy a used one. Usually you can apply the rental fee toward the ultimate purchase of the machine, if you decide that sewing is going to be hobby number one. In fact you can buy a brand-new straight-stitch machine relatively inexpensively. In this type of sewing machine the needle just moves straight up and down. It will do all ordinary sewing chores such as mending and making garments, slip-covers, or curtains. You straight-stitch more than anything else, anyway, and this machine is all a novice or an occasional sewer will ever need or use.

▶ Attachments to Machine

Even inexpensive machines of a good brand have a box of attachments that go along with them. Usually the assortment includes a zipper and cording foot, a seam guide, a gatherer, hemmers of different widths, a tucker, a quilter, and a ruffler. Besides, there are separate attachments you may buy later, which will convert a straight-stitch machine so that it can perform many tasks of a zig-zag machine.

Usually the inexpensive machines are portables; but they can be installed in a cabinet or be made a part of a built-in sewing unit later on. The major disadvantage of a portable is that the work space at the left, where most of the work falls, is usually rather inadequate. Your work space should be arranged so that this is taken into consideration.

▶ Zig-Zag Machine Sewing

If you would prefer to start out owning a zig-zag machine, it's practical enough. It is like starting out driving a car with power drive; you can concentrate on the learning. With all the features built into the machine, you save all that time used up in stopping to put on attachments. Also, as you improve your sewing skills, you become more and more aware of the extra finishes given by a zig-zag machine which make for a more professional look.

A zig-zag sewing machine will sew straight, darn, mend, overcast, sew two edges together without overlap, fasten lace, appliqué, sew on buttons, hooks and eyes, and snaps, make buttonholes, embroider and perform many other needlework operations, plain and fancy. One of these machines even embroiders in a circle.

The needle on a zig-zag machine moves up and down for straight stitching, then with a mechanical change it may be made to move from side to side to perform the zig-zag stitch. The basic zig-zag stitch may be varied in many ways. The width may be made broad or narrow, and the length of the stitch may be adjusted for a close-packed satin stitch or an elongated zig-zag. Many women are skillful enough to operate the controls manually so they can make a variety of fancy patterns without using the automatic feature.

Finally, you may become such a sewing addict that you will want the ultimate in sewing equipment, a machine that practically thinks for you. Or, does it? The more a machine is required to do, the more dials there are to understand. The difference between the plain zig-zag machine, the semi-automatic, and the fully automatic, is the variety of stitches with one, two, three, or four needles that may be achieved with a single setting of the controls. After mastering the use of a zig-zag machine you will amaze yourself and your friends by the wealth of embroidery effects you can achieve.

By the time you are ready to take full advantage of the fully automatic zig-zag sewing machine you are no longer a novice but an accomplished home sewer. You can easily turn the right dial, change to the correct cam, and use more than one needle as you enjoy all the intricacies of decorative stitchery.

There are three most important factors to consider when choosing a fully automatic machine: (1) over-all quality, (2) suitability and versatility of embroidery patterns, and (3) simplicity of operation. No two machines make the same set of patterns. So, perhaps the first thing you need to look for is the patterns you like best.

▶ Shopping for Machine

Please shop for your machine—and I mean shop. Pay no attention to those glib salesmen who come to your door with fancy talk about bargains. Be leary of too-sensational sewing machine advertising. Buy a good brand and be sure the dealer has a good reputation for servicing the machine after you have bought it. Be sure you know what guarantee is given, what it means, and how ethical the people are who stand behind that guarantee. The leading manufacturers have built their business on trustworthiness.

Several times when I have visited sewing machine departments, I have overheard zealous salesmen using technical jargon which I did not understand, such as "rotary," "oscillating," and "gear driven." They used these terms to appeal to the menfolk. Like most women, you and I look wise, though we don't have the foggiest notion what these words have to do with a sewing machine. Well, I looked these terms up in the dictionary, then made some inquiries. "Rotary" really means that it takes a whole revolution of the bobbin case hook up to complete one stitch. "Oscillating" means that this mechanism runs half-way in one direction, and back half-way the other, to make one stitch. "Gear driven" means that the mechanism drives the motor without a belt. Remember when we used to have to replace the belt so often because it would stretch out? Now, sewing machine belts are made of rubber or nylon impregnated with fiber, so they last two or three years.

Some of the automatic zig-zag sewing machines operate with interchangeable cams or discs which have the size and kind of stitch printed on the outside. Some machines have built-in cams which are worked with a dial on the front of the machine. Some have built-in cams plus a selection of extra ones to change manually. Some have mechanisms that make it possible to combine patterns, or reverse stitching (the machine backs up during a part of the embroidery cycle). One machine has four dials and a lever which combine the cams in various ways to extend the number of pattern combinations. You always have to think in terms of length of stitch, width of stitch, and either forward or reverse direction. One machine offers these three variations in machine motion in a selection of cams which you insert in three places.

The number of combinations thus available is staggering. You get different patterns if you put a cam in upside down, or give it a half-turn or insert it in different order. Try out several automatic zig-zag machines before you decide on yours. The most awe-inspiring one I have seen is a brand-new one which operates with push buttons, but you can be sure if you get this much versatility there is more than one button to think about.

Before we leave the wonderland of automatic sewing machines, I must call your attention to the fact that several of them come with a "free arm" arrangement which permits slipping on a sleeve or sock so that you can sew or mend in small spaces. This is the only new feature to be found in the bed of machines. However, when you balance all the other features in your selection, this is important to take into your consideration.

Before you buy any sewing machine, sit down and try it yourself. Here are some things to ask questions about: How easy is it to thread? (The slant needle is the easiest to thread and to see the stitching.) Does the needle thread from front to back or side to side? If side to side, from which side and where is the light? Here, let me digress long enough to caution you about getting good sharp needles, the right length for your machine. How easy is the bobbin to get at and thread? Can you sew both forward and back? Can you sew over pins? How do you adjust the foot pressure for different weights of fabric? Does the bobbin winder release automatically when the bobbin is full? How do you control the speed? Can you begin to stitch quite slowly without having to put your hand on the wheel? How much noise and vibration is there? Where is the electricity controlled, by knee or by foot or both? If you are considering an automatic zig-zag machine, which set of designs do you like best and will you want to learn the intricacies of combining them? How important is a "free arm"?

Remember, you will use your sewing machine in proportion to the amount it reminds you that it's there. If you are cramped for space, of course the portable is the only solution (Fig. VII-1). However, a handsome sewing machine cabinet can double for a needed piece of furniture, such as a desk or an end table (Fig. VII-2). But be sure the cabinet has some drawer or storage space in it and is not just a false front. Certainly a console is easier and quicker to set up and gives you more sewing space. For those with a limited budget, a portable may be the only choice for the present. Don't compromise on the working quality of the machine in order to get a fancy cabinet. Be sure to find out exactly what comes with your machine and what is available, including cabinets, as optional extra-cost equipment.

► *Understanding Your Machine*

No matter which sewing machine you decide on, there are certain basic things you need to know whether you do plain or fancy stitching. Remembering these details gives you good sewing machine habits. First, become very familiar with that sewing machine instruction book which comes with the machine. Usually, if something goes wrong while you are sewing,

Fig. VII-1 Portable Sewing Machine

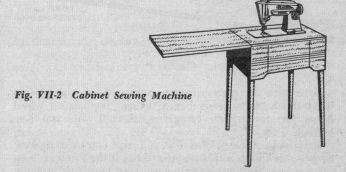

Fig. VII-2 Cabinet Sewing Machine

if you refer to the instruction book on the threading, needle-placement, tension, or pressure, you will find the answer to your particular problem.

Become thoroughly acquainted with names of the parts on your machine and find out on the diagram where they are (Fig. VII-3). Parts you should learn are: throat plate, presser foot, thread guide, tension spring, pressure control screw, needle post, feed dog, bobbin winder, balance wheel, stitch regulator, thread cutter, presser foot lift, thread take-up, seam guide, and zipper foot. Most important, learn how and when to oil your machine.

When you connect your machine to the electric outlet, plug the cord into the socket by holding the plug. *Never* pull the plug out by yanking the cord.

When you are ready to sew on a garment, the first thing

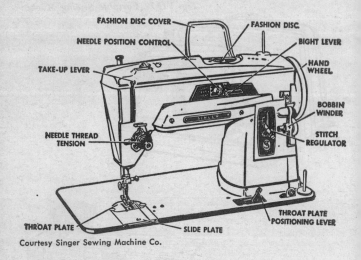

FASHION DISC COVER
FASHION DISC
NEEDLE POSITION CONTROL
BIGHT LEVER
HAND WHEEL
TAKE-UP LEVER
BOBBIN WINDER
NEEDLE THREAD TENSION
STITCH REGULATOR
THROAT PLATE POSITIONING LEVER
THROAT PLATE
SLIDE PLATE

Courtesy Singer Sewing Machine Co.

Fig. VII-3

you have to do, even before threading the machine, is to wind the bobbin. Remember to loosen the balance wheel *before* you start and don't forget to tighten it when you have finished.

Before you can sew, of course, you must know exactly how to thread both top and bottom correctly. If the stitch on both sides of your work is perfectly even, your tension is properly adjusted for the particular type of fabric you are working on (Fig. VII-4A). But, if the thread loops on the under side, your top tension has to be regulated (Fig. VII-4B). If the top thread pulls, it means your bobbin tension must be adjusted (Fig. VII-4C). Never stitch without first putting the foot down with the needle at the highest point, and both threads between the toes of the foot behind the needle. Oh, do remember at the end, when the thread has been broken, to fit the needle bar to its highest point so you are ready to begin your next stitching correctly. This little habit saves many needle re-threadings. Guide your fabric very gently and with the lightest touch of your hands. Be relaxed. The only time you push, pull or hold is when you turn corners or do something like "stay-stitch plus." Don't start out running your sewing machine at top speed. You can regulate it down to one stitch at a time by learning to work with your right hand on the balance wheel.

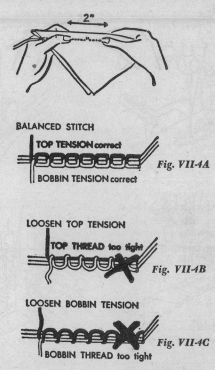

BALANCED STITCH

TOP TENSION correct

Fig. VII-4A

BOBBIN TENSION correct

LOOSEN TOP TENSION

TOP THREAD too tight

Fig. VII-4B

LOOSEN BOBBIN TENSION

Fig. VII-4C

BOBBIN THREAD too tight

Fig. VII-4   Checking Thread Tension

You should learn to vary the size of your stitches for different kinds of fabric, or for certain points in your sewing. Use small stitches over areas which will receive extra strain. The longest stitch on the sewing machine is used for basting. Firmly woven, thin to medium-weight fabrics are usually stitched with a medium-sized stitch, 12 to 15 to the inch. Thick or heavy fabrics are usually stitched with a longer stitch. Sometimes, delicate or dressy fabrics look best when stitched with a fine stitch; but generally, 18 to 20 stitches to the inch are used only to reinforce small areas such as points of collars, or gussets, underarm curves, or troublesome fraying fabrics at places where seams may receive a lot of strain. The stitch regulator on your sewing machine is a most important feature.

Fig. VII-5A
Walking Presser Foot

Fig. VII-5B1
Zipper Cording Foot at Right of Zipper

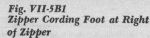

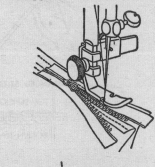

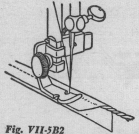

Fig. VII-5B2

Zipper Cording Foot at Left of Zipper

Fig. VII-5D Gathering Foot

Many fabrics, such as velvet, corduroy, velveteen, laminates, jerseys, or synthetics, will act up when you begin to stitch them, no matter how carefully you adjust the tensions. This may be due to the fact that the pressure on the presser foot has to be adjusted or because the needle is the wrong size. Tightly woven, smooth-finished fabrics require more pressure, thicker and spongy fabrics require less.

Always sew with the bulk of your fabric at the left and, if you are using a portable, don't let it drag off the edge and pull away from the needle because this makes you stitch crooked. If you stop your stitching in the middle of a row, to turn a corner or for some other reason, always leave the needle down in the fabric before you raise the presser foot.

Extend your sewing skill by learning to use the extra attachments that usually come with most machines. Too many of us ignore them and laboriously attempt to do the things they help us do easily, just because we are too lazy to turn a screw or use our minds for what they are intended.

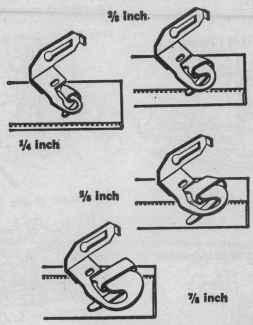

Fig. VII-5C Hemmer Feet

The usual presser foot is called a "walking presser foot" (Fig. VII-5A) because it is hinged and will sew over pins. Use the same gauge throughout your sewing to keep even seam allowances if there are no markings on the plate. In order to sew in a zipper, cord the seam, and make tubular cording and slipcover welting, use the zipper, or cording foot (Figs. VII-5B1 & 2). There is a set of hemmers with which to make narrow hems and ruffle edges, hem seams, and hem with lace (Fig. VII-5C). Another uncomplicated foot is the one used for even gathering (Fig. VII-5D). If you have the zig-zag machine you usually have to change to a special foot for sewing on buttons, snaps, hooks and eyes.

More complicated attachments which come with your machine may take a little more patience to master, but the results are most rewarding. There is a tucker (Fig. VII-5E) which, when properly adjusted for the desired size, will make tucks from ¼" to ¾". It spaces them and keeps them straight,

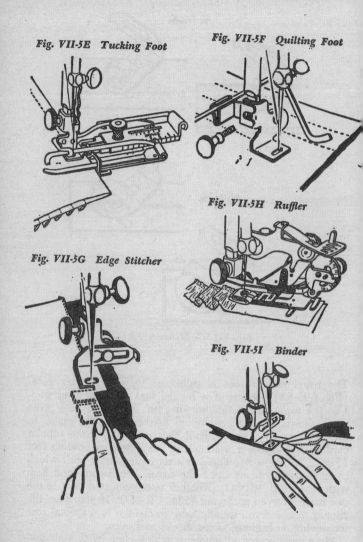

Fig. VII-5E Tucking Foot

Fig. VII-5F Quilting Foot

Fig. VII-5G Edge Stitcher

Fig. VII-5H Ruffler

Fig. VII-5I Binder

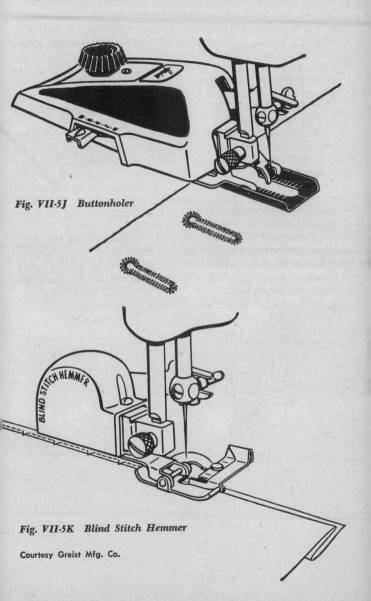

Fig. VII-5J   *Buttonholer*

Fig. VII-5K   *Blind Stitch Hemmer*

Courtesy Greist Mfg. Co.

so you can tuck all in one direction or two ways of the fabric to achieve very expensive effects. With the quilter (Fig. VII-5F) you can make beautiful quilted accessories, robes, and bedspreads. The edgestitcher (Fig. VII-5G) joins single rows of lace or alternate rows of lace and beading and attaches narrow finishes like bindings. The ruffler (Fig. VII-5H) allows you to make the loveliest ruffles in the shortest length of time. The binder (Fig. VII-5I) turns edges and stitches on binding in one operation.

In addition, it is possible, to a limited degree, to convert any straight-stitch sewing machine into one that will do some fancier things. For instance, there is an attachment that does some decorative zig-zagging. Another attachment is the buttonholer (Fig. VII-5J), which makes several sizes of stitched buttonholes. Still another attachment is the blind stitch hemmer (Fig. VII-5K) which helps you put in hems without so much laborious hand work.

Of course, I can't begin to give you instructions for using all these wonderful aids because they work differently on different machines. You need to buy them to fit the brand of sewing machine which you own, and complete instructions come with each one.

CHAPTER 8

Learn the Basic Stitches

Now that you are all prepared to sew efficiently, how about beginning to do just that by improving your technique and letting go of old fashioned habits, such as basting too often. Remember, today's mechanically improved sewing machines can be depended upon to baste for you faster and more accurately than you can do it by hand. Instead of basting everything, use pins to save time and energy (Fig. VIII-1). Eventually, you may become so proficient that you will be able to hold two layers of fabric exactly together and eliminate using pins, as experts do.

I don't mean to imply that you should never baste. Hand basting should only be done when necessary. In fact, I always hand baste and pre-fit satin or taffeta because these fabrics (and some others) show the machine-baste needle marks. Basting is also necessary on intricate tailoring details, when one layer of fabric is fuller than the other and must be eased in, where complicated seaming is involved, or when matching plaids and stripes. So, since such exceptions make knowing how to baste necessary, you must learn to baste if you don't already know how.

Baste with a single thread and a medium needle, most usually in a contrasting color for easy removal when permanent stitching is finished. However, when basting in a zipper, I use the same color thread so that, if the stitching catches it, the fuzzy ends won't pop out and show in wearing.

Even basting is used most often (Fig. VIII-2A). Pin the layers of fabric together, if you can't hold them together evenly. Knot the long end of thread and insert the needle into the edge of the cloth through both thicknesses, making even ½" stitches on both sides over the seam line.

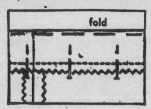

Fig. VIII-1
Sewing Machine Basting

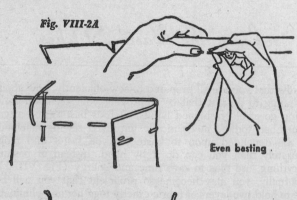

Fig. VIII-2A

Even basting

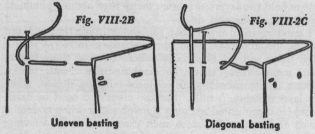

Fig. VIII-2B

Uneven basting

Fig. VIII-2C

Diagonal basting

Fig. VIII-2D

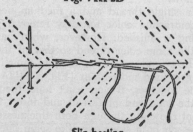

Slip-basting

Fig. VIII-2E Running stitches

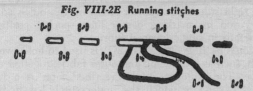

Fig. VIII-2F Back stitching

Fig. VIII-2G Whip-Stitch

Fig. VIII-2H Overcasting Stitch

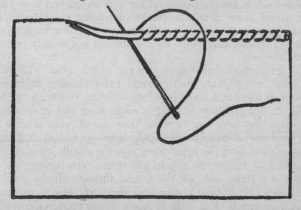

Uneven basting (Fig. VIII-2B) is where a 1″ stitch is made on the right side and a shorter stitch on the other side. It is usually used for marking center lines, pocket positions, or other details in single layer of fabric.

Diagonal basting (Fig. VIII-2C) is used to hold two layers of cloth, such as interfacing and outer fabric, together without slippage. The padding stitch described later is a form of diagonal basting in which the under stitch has to be kept invisible on the top fabric side. To make a diagonal basting, a long diagonal stitch is continued in a straight row, one next to the other, with the diagonal thread on top and a short vertical stitch underneath.

Slip-basting (Fig. VIII-2D) is done on the right side of fabric for intricate matching of designs, lace, plaid, or stripes or when an alteration must be made on the right side. First, fold under the seam allowance of the top layer and press the fold. Then, pin this over the seam allowance on the under layer, matching as you pin. Start the slip baste by taking a small stitch in the fold. Then carefully take the next small stitch in the under piece and keep alternating the stitches.

Sewing machine basting (Fig. VIII-1) is made with a slightly loosened tension and the longest stitch (6 or 7 to the inch). Pin the seam together at the seam allowance or practice with no pinning on a firm fabric. Leave a long end to pull up the gathers with if used for stitch-basting.

All of these stitches are temporary stitches. One of the joys of the new sewing techniques is that hand sewing is not so necessary as it once was. However, some practice along these lines is always beneficial for a more custom look later on. Hand sewn details on better garments are often what raise the price and are the refinements in your sewing repertoire. The following hand sewing stitches are usually permanent stitches.

A *small-stitch basting*, or running stitch (Fig. VIII-2E), is used in mending, quilting, and hand tucking. It is also the basis for the pick-stitch described later. You might gather with it; but machine basting is more even and professional looking. The best way to make these small, even stitches is to hold the fabric in one hand, between thumb and first finger, then with the other hand run the needle through the material ⅛″ to a stitch as you did when even basting, six or eight at a time, and pull the thread through all the stitches at once. This is time-saving and keeps stitches more even.

A *back-stitch* (Fig. VIII-2F) is a strong reinforcing stitch.

Take a ⅛" stitch which produces a ⅛" blank space on top side. Now go back ¹⁄₁₆" (half way of the first stitch) and take another ⅛" stitch forward. One side of work will seem to have a running stitch, the other side will resemble a "locked" machine stitch.

A *whip-stitch* (Fig. VIII-2G) and an *overcasting-stitch* (Fig. VIII-2H) are similar. The first is used to join two fabric edges, as in lining a coat; the other is done over a raw edge to prevent raveling. One of the plus values of a zig-zag sewing machine or attachment is that it will overcast a seam automatically. But, when making either of these two stitches by hand, the needle is brought through the fabric from back to front, then around the edge, and, about ⅛" farther on, brought through again from back to front. An overcast stitch is usually made farther apart than a whip-stitch. A well-made whip-stitch is used for fine hand rolling and hemming as on a scarf or chiffon dress, or when mounting lace.

Hand Hemming Stitches

Everyone should learn to do hand hemming well in spite of the wonderful blind-stitch hemmer attachment. A machine-made hem like a machine-stitched buttonhole is quite acceptable on house dresses and sports and casual wear, but nothing gives a finished custom look on fine dressmaker or hand tailored garments like hand hemming.

There are several hemming stitches like the whip-stitch used on rolled edges. They are done with a fine needle and thread to match fabric.

The finish on a hem often determines the manner of hemming. If a fabric ravels or is too thick to turn and stitch, it is finished with seam binding (Fig. VIII-3A). Firm cottons, which are frequently washed, are best turned and stitched at the edge before hemming (Fig. VIII-3B). If a thick wool, like a tweed, is firmly woven it may be stitched ¼" from the edge, pinked with pinking shears and then catch-stitched (Fig. VIII-3C). Before an edge is rolled and whip-stitched, a line of stitching ⅛" from the edge keeps it from stretching in the hand as you work.

Spread out your garment on a table in front of you so it doesn't drag away. Begin at a seam and hold the hem over your first two fingers, with the bulk held down under the third finger and thumb. The needle in the other hand slants a little as you work. Hem towards you by picking up a thread

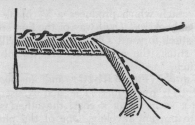

Fig. VIII-3A Seambound Hem

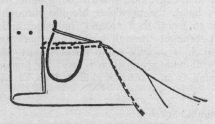

Fig. VIII-3B Hem Turned and Stitched

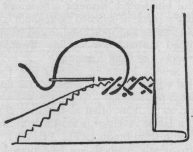

Fig. VIII-3C Catch-Stitched Hem

or two of the outer fabric and taking a small stitch through the turn of the hem or the edge of the binding.

These stitches can be ¼" to ½" apart, depending upon the delicacy of the fabric and the flare of the edge. As your hem gets longer, you may find it faster to anchor the finished portion to a cushioned surface.

The catch-stitch hem over pinked edges (Fig. VIII-3C) is often used at the bottom of a jacket or coat under the lining. It is a criss-cross stitch. Take a stitch in the hem edge below the machine stitching. Cross the thread diagonally to the

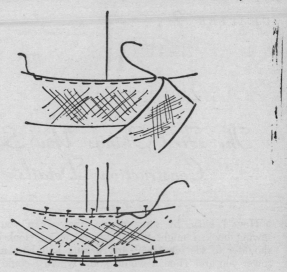

Fig. VIII-3D Horsehair Hem

garment and take up a thread of fabric in a back-stitch. Now cross the thread down for a back-stitch behind the stitching again, with the diagonal going in the other direction. Continue this criss-cross pattern and your hem will lay nice and flat. Never pull the thread taut on any hemming stitch, particularly on the catch-stitch.

When garments are underlined, the underlining fabric is cut at the turn of the hem. Then, the hem edge is turned up over the underlining fabric and is hemmed to it. Be careful not to catch the hemming stitch through the outer fabric.

I should like to mention here a special kind of hem that is made on some filmy fabrics, even some rich luxury fabrics, to give a garment grace. That is hemming with horsehair braid (Fig. VIII-3D). The horsehair is stitched to the bottom edge on the right side of the garment. Turn the braid inside ¼" from the edge and pin in place. If there is a flare to the hem, find the thread on the edge of the horsehair and pull it (gather it) as you would pull a basting until it lies flat against the fabric. Hem the braid to the under side with as invisible stitches as possible. Even though you may have used silk thread throughout the garment, this hemming is more inconspicuous when done with a duller mercerized cotton thread in the same color.

CHAPTER 9

The First Things You Sew— Construction Details

How I wish, by some magic, that when you buy my sewing book, I might follow you home and look over your shoulder to see what you are making and how much of a sewer you are! Then, I would know where I could help you most.

The reason I feel I may be able to contribute something a little extra to your sewing knowledge is because of my intimate experience in helping develop some of the new sewing aids. So, perhaps I can pass on to you a clearer understanding of where and how they can be used to make a home sewer's life simpler.

Up to this point we have gone through the process of pattern and fabric selection, preparation, cutting, and marking. This is the halfway point because, if you have followed the rules of altering the pattern to your correct measurement, cutting on grain, and careful marking all details, the actual sewing can be very easy.

Basically, everyone begins the sewing process the same whether a novice or an experienced sewer. And, it's a common hope we share that this time we will discover an easier way which will give better results. For years I approached sewing as a chore, and was discontented at the results. Now, I enjoy it more every time I make something, and I anticipate good results because I know how to use my sewing tools where they help.

Whether you are a novice or not, you are better off not to stray too far from your pattern instruction sheet when assembling a garment. I first learned to sew from a pattern, and I have found that the pattern companies have always kept up with the latest and best techniques, even developing some new ones of their own if a need arises. The individual instruction sheet enclosed in each pattern envelope is the sewing lesson for that particular style. Whether the pattern pieces are numbered or lettered, the sequence given is the one tested and found best by the designer for the most orderly assembly of the particular pattern.

Sewing theorists (as I am) can only give the general rules most usually applicable to garment assembly. Your pattern instruction sheet gives the specifics for that one style. I will tell you, in addition, when your sewing tools come into play most advantageously. You have already used the pattern instructions for cutting out your fabric. Then check and read over the general rules it gives on details, such as the meaning of the notches, working in units, and other pertinent information. I do this almost every time I make something, often refreshing my memory on some fact I might otherwise overlook.

▶ *Making a Pleated Skirt*

Now that I have convinced you that you should always follow your pattern instructions, my first project will be a skirt that you can make without a pattern. I only hope I've put you in the mood for instruction reading, and that reading mine will be as easy for you. My object is to teach you how to sew a straight seam on something you will wear proudly. It is made from a straight piece of fabric without any shaping. It will be—and here's a complete surprise—a *pleated* skirt (Fig. IX-1)!

There is a new ready-pleated stiffening which is sewed flat at the waistband. Then, on a second straight row of stitching it catches up the fabric into ½" unpressed pleats from the waistband down. To get the right amount of fabric, measure your waistline and multiply by three. In other words, if your waist measures 24", you will need 72" (or 2 yards) for the width. If it's a 36" cotton, get two times the length you like your skirts, plus enough more for a 2" hem. Let's say you wear 25"-long skirts, you will need 54" (or 1½ yards). Or, you may wish to make this skirt of a plain, light weight, firmly-woven wool 54" to 60" wide. If skirt length varies little from 25", one yard is enough and you will make it widthwise of the cloth.

Cut the 36″ cotton in two pieces from selvage to selvage —or, the yard of wider wool through the lengthwise center of the fabric. Now, pin together your first straight side seam ⅝″ from the edge.

Fig. IX-1 Unpressed Pleated Skirt

From the beginning of your sewing, get the habit of always taking up the full-sized seam allowance called for in the pattern instructions, which is now a standard ⅝″ on all patterns, unless otherwise specified. The style has been planned with all the fullness and ease required. You have accurately altered the pieces with your own necessary changes. If you take too shallow seam allowances for fear your garment will not be big enough, you will likely make it too big.

If you are sewing with a late model sewing machine, the ⅝″ seam allowance, as well as all other measurements up to 1″, are probably marked on the plate at the right of the needle, ⅛″ apart. This is the guide you use to keep a completely straight seam. Many of the older machines included a *seam guide* (Fig. IX-2) in the box of attachments which came with the machine. Attach it where there is a screw hole at the right of the needle, according to the instruction book of your machine. You will be able to adjust it on the sewing machine bed exactly ⅝″ from the needle, so that it helps you keep seams all the same width. Another thing you can do, if there's no seam guide among your attachments, is to use two contrasting colored strips of adhesive tape—let's say red and white. Place your see-thru ruler so the sewing machine needle goes through the end of the ⅝″ slot. Lay the white adhesive tape down along the edge of the ruler and stick it down across the bed of the sewing machine for about 3″. Place the ruler over the first strip of adhesive so the needle goes through the ½″ slot. Lap the red tape over the white, ½″ out from needle, so that ⅛″ of white extends beyond the red on the outside. Now you have a ⅝″ seam allowance guide line extending beyond a ½″ guide line for stay-stitching (Fig. IX-3).

There are still some people, otherwise good sewers, who have difficulty keeping a straight seam with all the measurement helps that have been given them. If you are one of these, you will be glad to know about the sew-straight plate (Fig. IX-4). It is a soft, green-colored plastic plate, 5″ across and 6″ long, which may be affixed to the bed of any sewing machine at the same screw hole that holds the seam guide. The 6″ side, which has a ruled-off edge on it, is on the right of the presser foot and needle. This plate has raised grooves on it every ¼″ lengthwise of the plate area. Seven grooves from the left, there is a shallow groove between the two higher ones at the ⅝″ mark. This is intended to come exactly in front of the needle. By starting the seam, and then holding the forefinger lightly on top of the work over any one of

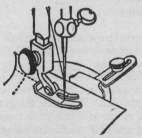

Fig. IX-2 Seam Guide

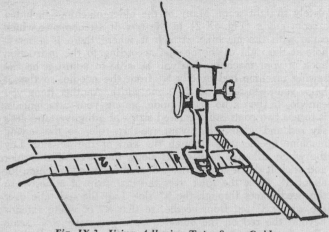

Fig. IX-3 Using Adhesive Tape Seam Guide

Fig. IX-4 Sew Straight Plate

the grooves, your stitching is kept in a perfectly straight line. If you let the outside edge of your seam come 4 grooves from the center line, and hold your finger at the center groove, you will get a straight ⅝″ seam allowance.

▶ Simple Seams

In this chapter on basic sewing we will use only a simple seam. Next chapter, for more advanced sewing we'll discuss some of the other seams.

A seam is where you lap the two pieces of cloth, right sides inside, with edges matched evenly and sew them together in a straight line. The main thing to remember with a simple seam is never to allow it to pucker with too tight tension, and to press each seam flat before finishing it. The best finish for simple seams, after you have completed all the sewing steps between, will depend upon the fabric texture, the article being made, and the place where the seam appears.

If the fabric is firm and doesn't ravel, pink the seam edges with pinking shears or scallop them with scalloping shears. Of course, if the fabric has the slightest tendency to ravel, stay-stitch ¼" from edge before pinking (Fig. IX-5A).

Whenever the garment is medium or light weight and you prefer not to line it, use a turned and stitched seam (Fig. IX-5B). That is, turn under each seam allowance edge ¼" and stitch as close as possible to the edge.

On fabrics that fray only slightly, overcast by hand both seam allowance edges (Fig. IX-5C). You might pink them first and let the overcast thread come between each point. If you have a zig-zag sewing machine, it will overcast much faster than by hand.

When the edges ravel too badly, particularly on heavy fabric, bind each edge of seam with matching bias seam binding (Fig. IX-5D). Pin or baste it on and stitch.

Now, we'll take up where we left off with the first seam made correctly on your skirt. Take out your package of pleated stiffening and cut off a strip, while it is still pleated, the same length as your waistline measures. Then, pull away the narrow tape which holds the pleats together on the wrong side (Fig. IX-6A). Flatten the stiffening out perfectly flat and lay it at the waistline edge on the wrong side of the fabric. Place it ½" in from the edge and 1" in from the open side. This side will be closed later 8" down from waistline as the left hip opening. Here, stop and calculate a little. If you take care at this point to have your pleats turn right, you won't need to worry about applying a zipper in your first skirt because the opening will be hidden under the first and last pleat. Turn a couple of experimental pleats over the stiffening with your fingers. Do they fold to the left on the right side of your fabric? If not, switch to the other end of the stiffening before sewing it down. Then, stitch it flat to the skirt top, about the distance of the presser toe from the edge. (Fig. IX-6B).

The ratio of three times the waist measure for the fabric usually leaves a few inches of cloth over after all the stiffening has been stitched on. Cut off excess cloth and save it to make the waistband. Now begin the pleating. Place the stiffening side up under the sewing machine, and begin stitching over the same place as the last row of stitching

Fig. IX-5A   Pinked Seam

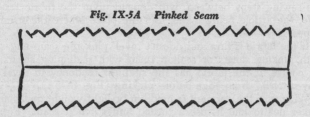

Fig. IX-5B   Seam Edge Turned and Stitched

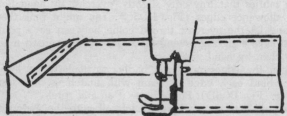

Fig. IX-5C   Seam with Overcast Edges

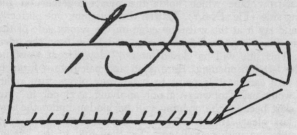

Fig. IX-5D   Seam with Bound Edges

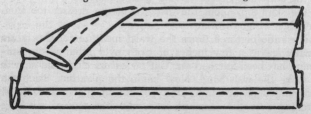

Fig. IX-6B
Stitch Pleating Flat on First Row

Fig. IX-6A
Release Pleats by
Pulling Away Tape

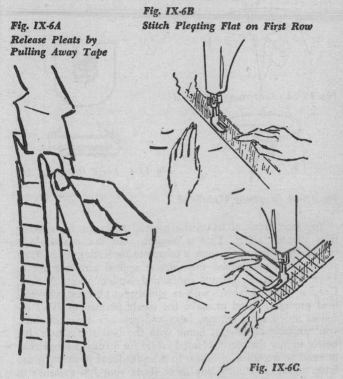

Fig. IX-6C
Fold Pleats as You Stitch Second Row

(Fig. IX-6C). Fold the stiffening where it was creased and you will find that the fabric pulls right into a pleat with it. Begin by stitching over a couple of pleats until you come to the fold of the next one, then fold in one or two more pleats. Stitch across them, and continue in this way until the whole waistline has been pleated. Then seam up the other side leaving that 8″ opening. Press the seam flat.

This first skirt will have ½″ unpressed pleats at the waistline all folding in the same direction. If you are a more experienced sewer, when you become familiar with using the pleated stiffening, you will want to experiment with making all kinds of pleats. You can make box, sunburst, and cluster pleats, and pleats of different widths—any ½″ multiple.

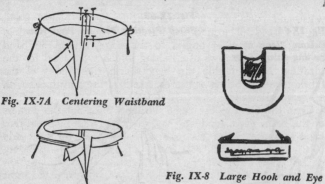

Fig. IX-7A *Centering Waistband*

Fig. IX-8 *Large Hook and Eye*

Fig. IX-7B *Applying Waistband*

You may think of using the pleated stiffening for making fully pleated skirts. This is possible, but not practical. It would mean going through a complete repleating every time you washed or cleaned the skirt or spilled anything on it. Even with Arnel, fabrics containing Kodel, orlon, Acrilan, Creslan, or other fabrics with an affinity for pleating, a special heat process is used to make the pleats permanent. This requires much more intense heat and pressure than anything you can now achieve at home with the best steam iron. It's better to buy the ready-pleated fabric for a fully pleated skirt or send your choice of fabric to a professional pleater. In the latter event, you must buy three times your *hip* measure in any unpleated fabric.

When you are ready to apply the waistband, cut off a strip of the left-over fabric, about 4″ wide, and 4″ longer than your waistline measurement. It will not be necessary to interline this waistband because the stiffness of the pleating has enough firmness. Pin the open side seam of the skirt together at the waist. Fold it over to meet the other side seam, find the center front and center back at the two folds, and mark them both (Fig. IX-7A). Place the outside of the waistband strip of fabric next to the inside of the back of the skirt, matching edges and allowing 2½″ to extend beyond the opening. Fold the waistband strip so that the other end comes back even with the opening. The fold should come exactly at the closed side seam. Fold the remaining free end of the waistband back plus ½″. This fold comes at center front. Pin the band all around the inside edge over the pleating, placing pins at right angles to the edge. Stitch the band on over the same rows of stitching which were used for the pleating. Now, double the band back, right sides of the fabric together. Stitch across each end of the waistband with ½″ seam allowance.

Turn the band to the right side and poke out the corners of the seam ends good and square with your point turner. Press a crease in the band (Fig. IX-7B). On the right side of the skirt, fold under the seam allowance of the banding against the pleats. Pin neatly all around with pins at right angles to the seam line. Stitch the band down on the right side, as close as possible to the edge. If you have a walking presser foot on your machine you can stitch right over the pins. Otherwise, you may wish (with this first skirt) to baste the band on before stitching. Try it on to see how well it fits.

Close the belt ends, and place pins on the upper and under thicknesses where the hooks and eyes will come. There is a sturdy large hook and eye meant for just this purpose (Fig. IX-8). There is one that may be sewed on and another that you may attach with pliers. Or, I like to attach two large Dot Snappers at the waistband, because then I never have to worry about having them come loose. Two are better than one in case you need to let out the band after eating a large dinner (Fig. IX-9).

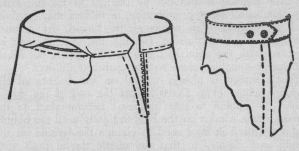

Fig. IX-9 Dot Snapper Closing

▶ Making a Dirndl Skirt

Some teachers of elementary sewing have abandoned the dirndl skirt as a first sewing project, because the shirring thread too often pops discouragingly halfway through the

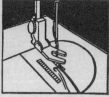

| Fig. IX-10 Winding Bobbin | Fig. IX-11 Regular Thread on Top | Fig. IX-12 Shirr-Stitching |

fitting. However, if you will use 100% nylon elastic thread for the shirring, there need be no such trouble. Nylon elastic thread shirrs at a ratio of 2 to 1. So, in planning for the amount of fabric necessary for a dirndl skirt made this way (again, using the 24″ waist measure) you need 48″ in the width of the skirt. There are now some lovely soft cottons and synthetics that come 48″ and 50″ wide, and all you would need is about a yard for today's short skirts. A dirndl should never be made of anything but a very soft, supple fabric. If you have to use a narrower fabric, you will need twice the length plus hem, or about 1½ yards. This you will have to seam together to get the width, and possibly you will have to cut away a left-over piece even after cutting off enough for the belt. After you press the seam flat it will be hidden in the fullness of the shirring, as will the fact that you haven't put a zipper in the placket.

Elastic shirring should not be thought of for full skirts only. Almost all shirring, gathering, or ruffling may be done most successfully with nylon elastic thread. Its greatest advantage is when pressing, because the shirring may be stretched with the point of the iron. This makes the fabric look much smoother close to the gathered fullness.

Elastic thread is always wound on the bobbin of the sewing machine (Fig. IX-10). Knot the end of the thread around the bobbin so that it doesn't become slack in the shirring. Then wind it on the bobbin tightly until the bobbin is almost full. You may need to change the tension on the bobbin case slightly so that the elastic thread pulls with considerable stretch.

Use regular sewing thread in the sewing machine needle (Fig. IX-11) in the same or contrasting color. Set the stitch gauge for a long stitch, 7 to 9 per inch. Test on a scrap of the fabric to be used. If the top thread loops, the top tension is too loose. With presser foot down, tighten the top tension enough to give the elastic thread stitching sufficient snap. It takes about 4 rows for the gathering to look tight enough (Fig. IX-12). A single row shirrs only slightly, and the more rows added the snugger the shirring looks. When beginning the second and subsequent rows, hold the previous row or rows stretched apart. Fasten the threads securely at the beginning and end of all rows with a few back-stitches. The rows may be as close together as one toe width of the presser foot, or spaced wider if desired. When you have finished your shirr-stitching, steam press with your iron at *nylon* or *rayon temperature* to improve the appearance of snugness. Sometimes, double nylon thread wound on the bobbin will give a look of even tighter shirring.

When you make a waistband on a dirndl skirt, it needs to be stiffened with an interfacing. Cut a piece of innerlining material the same size as the waistband piece, and stitch them together ¼″ from the edge all around. Then, you can treat them like one piece of fabric and apply the waistband just as you did with the pleated skirt.

▶ Hemming the Skirt

Now, dirndl skirt or unpressed pleated skirt, it's time to turn up the hem. These are both skirts that are straight around the bottom, and usually they can be turned up evenly without using a skirt marker if you are sure what length you wear. Check by measuring another skirt that is the length you like. First, stay-stitch ¼″ away from the bottom raw edge. Stay-stitching is just a straight row of stitches, 10 to 12 per inch, which prevents the threads of the fabric from fraying. With pinking shears, cut off the raw edge close to the row of stay-stitches.

Now, take out your hem pressing gauge and place it with the straight edge under the hem. We planned both of these skirts for a 2″ hem. So, turn the fabric over the hem gauge until it reaches the 2″ mark (or whatever amount of turn-up you desire). Press up the hem over this metal edge, always remembering to press in the direction of the fabric grain.

If your skirt is of a light weight wool you may wish to finish the hem with seam binding. Use 12 to 15 stitches per inch, and hold the seam binding firmly against the edge of the fabric, keeping the stitching on the stay-stitch line. If your skirt is a medium weight cotton or a blend of fibers you may not use seam binding, but will flat-stitch the edge instead. This means you fold the fabric back over the stay-stitched row, then stitch it down close to the turn. It could be that your fabric is firm enough (or of coarse, thick texture), so that you may leave the pinked edge raw, and sew the hem on the stay-stitch line.

Any of these hems must be neatly slip-stitched on the wrong side. A hand-done hem can be practically invisible when you learn to make tiny slip-stitches and bury them in the threads of the cloth. Or, you might learn to use your blind stitch hemmer (*see* Fig. VII-5K) or the automatic zig-zag hemming stitch on the sewing machine. The directions for doing these are in the instruction book which comes with your sewing machine or attachment. The results can be almost as unnoticeable as hand-hemming if you are working on a coarse-textured fabric, or one with a soft surface into which the stitches sink, or a "busy" print (a crowded design).

► *Blouse and Skirt Suggestions*

By now, you novice sewers are stitching straight, enjoying the results, and should be about ready to make a shaped skirt by a pattern. Or, as a change of pace, why not tackle a blouse? You might choose a simple blouse and fitted skirt pattern at the same time. Here, be sure to remember what I told you in Chapter 3 about figure types and sizing. All the things you will learn when making a blouse and skirt from a pattern will help you when you make your first dress.

My idea of a simple blouse pattern is one of those in which the sleeve is cut all in one with the blouse (Fig. IX-13). It looks like a "T" and is called a *kimono sleeve*. Save set-in sleeves for a dress. You see, I want everything you make to be something you will put on and wear. With a kimono blouse there is plenty to learn about in the facing of the neck and in fitting darts. This blouse pattern may come in several versions, with and without a collar. It may be one which closes in the back or in the front, part way down with a neck zipper or all the way, whichever you think will suit you best.

The many skirt patterns will give you more to decide about. There's the one with only two side seams (Fig. IX-14). Another has two side seams and a back seam ending in a pleat (Fig. IX-15). The four-gored skirt has seams in front and back and both sides (Fig. IX-16). These seams all in-

Fig. IX-13 Kimono Sleeve Blouse

fluence the fit of the skirt, as do the darts and tucks at the waistline. A tuck is like a pleat on the wrong side that is sewn down a little way and ends in released fullness. A dart is a tuck that ends in a point. Choose the skirt that flatters your figure.

The reason you use a pattern is to learn how to make a garment fit. Different styles do different things for your figure. If you have an ideal figure with a flat abdomen, and are a "long-stemmed American Beauty" in the leg department, the plain, no-gored slim skirt is fine. On the other hand, if your legs are less than ideal and on the chubby side, choose a skirt with more flare at the hemline or with a generous kick-pleat. If you are real broad through the pelvis and hips, get a four- or six- or eight-gored skirt to break up the wide area and give you some long vertical lines. Avoid wrap-around, double-faced or other complicated skirt patterns for now.

When you choose fabric for this blouse and skirt try something easy to sew that you may not have worked on before.

Fig. IX-14
Skirt with
Two Side
Seams

Fig. IX-15
Skirt with
Back Seam
and Pleat

But, remember, you may want to wear your blouse with various style skirts, either in a contrast color or a match-mate print. Or, make the blouse the same color and fabric as your new fitted skirt.

Turn, right now, to Chapter 3 and learn from the start exactly what you need to do on both your skirt and blouse pattern pieces to assure their perfect fit. Then, you are ready to lay the pattern on the fabric, cut it out and mark it according to Chapter 5.

▶ *Blouse with Neck Zipper in Back*

We'll use the collarless view for the first blouse lesson. Later on, if you feel you can go to the head of the class after

Fig. IX-16   Four-Gored Skirt

fitting your first neck curve, you might try making the collar and finishing the neck edge with bias seam binding.

Your choice of blouse style may have a neckline zipper part way down the back (Fig. IX-17). Then, both back and front pieces have been cut on the fold. Or, you may have selected a style that opens all the way down back or front with a lap closing. The open piece in this type, in simple patterns, has the facing cut in one with the blouse, and it is usually cut on the selvage. Of course, you have cut out everything grain-perfect, carefully marked the darts, gathers, or tucks which form the shaping over the bust or into the waistline. Wherever a center front or back is indicated, baste or chalk in the line on the wrong side of fabric.

There are sewing steps leading up to the assembly of anything you make, which are always the same. I cannot think of a time when they are not vital to the end results. Such a rule is that all neck edges and most off-grain edges are

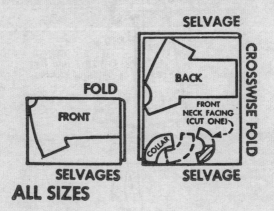

35" FABRIC

SELVAGE

CROSSWISE FOLD

BACK

FRONT
NECK FACING
(CUT ONE)

FOLD

FRONT

COLLAR

SELVAGES

SELVAGE

ALL SIZES

Fig. IX-17   Blouse Layout

stay-stitched inside the cut edge. This is the only way to keep off-grain fabric threads from stretching as you handle them in sewing preparation. At first thought it may seem like a lot of extra work. But, it saves so much time when you have to fit two such pieces together as, for instance, neckline and facing.

You practiced stay-stitching on a straight edge at the hem to learn to do it in an even line. Now you will begin off-grain stay-stitching, which always is done in a definite direction, *with* the grain threads (Fig. IX-18A). To determine which way the grain runs on an off-grain edge, tug the threads gently along the cut edge, pushing them backwards a little. See, they stay together in one direction, but stretch or pull out the other. The with-grain direction is from the shoulder down to sleeve edge on your raglan sleeve, ½" from the outside edge (Fig. IX-18B). Now, turn your work over and stay-stitch the other shoulder edge. If you are working on a blouse piece which has been cut on a fold, do not stay-stitch the neck curve from one shoulder to the other (Fig. IX-18C). Instead, begin at one shoulder edge and stitch to

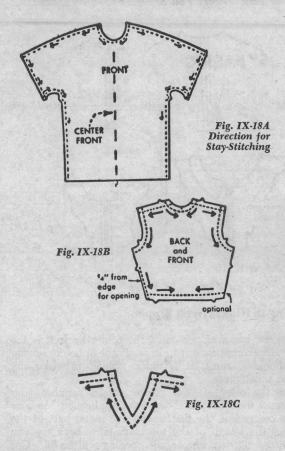

FRONT

CENTER
FRONT

*Fig. IX-18A
Direction for
Stay-Stitching*

Fig. IX-18B

BACK
and
FRONT

¼" from
edge
for opening

optional

Fig. IX-18C

the center mark; clip the threads and start over from the shoulder edge on the other side until you meet the first row at the center. Stay-stitch across bottom of the sleeve and around the underarm edge.

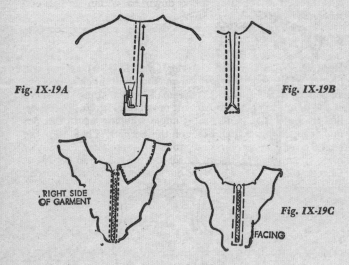

Fig. IX-19A

Fig. IX-19B

RIGHT SIDE
OF GARMENT

Fig. IX-19C

FACING

Applying Neck Zipper

▶ *Sewing in Blouse Neck Zipper*

If your blouse has a zipper down the center back, it is the easiest of zipper applications to learn. Put it in before sewing up the shoulder seams. It is much simpler to make any closure on a flat piece.

Be sure the color of your zipper exactly matches your fabric because the teeth will show in this application. Measure down the center line the distance of the metal part of the zipper plus the length of the top cloth tabs. Let's say you are applying a 6″ neck zipper, the opening will be 6¾″. Cut an extra small patch of fabric straight-of-goods, 1″ square. Pin it where the bottom metal part of the zipper will come on the center line.

Now, stay-stitch ¼″ away from the center line, straight down through the patch the necessary length (Fig. IX-19A). Now, you have to make a right angle turn. To do this, leave the needle down but take up the presser foot. Turn at right angles to the line of stitching you just did and put the presser foot down again. Stitch across for ½″ and turn again on the needle until the stitching can run parallel with the first line. Stitch this parallel row up to the neck edge. Then, cut through the center mark down to within ½″ of end stitching.

▶ *Mitering a Corner*

Here you learn to miter a corner (Fig. IX-19B) as you will need to know how to do it in making buttonholes, pockets, and many other details. Your small scissors must be sharp at the points so that you can cut on an angle from the center line to the corner of the right angle stitching up to but *not into* the stitches. Miter both of the corners. Then turn the edges in on the stitching all around the opening and pin or baste them close to the metal of the zipper (Fig. IX-19C). Change to the zipper foot on the sewing machine and stitch all around close to the metal teeth.

▶ *Blouse with Lap Closing*

Perhaps you have chosen the blouse style with the lap closing. With facing cut all in one (Fig. IX-20). You stay-

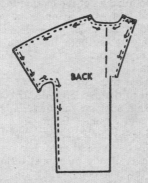

Fig. IX-20   Facing Cut in One With Piece

stitch around the shoulders, neck edge, sleeve edge and underarm, in the same order that was done on the other blouse style. But, here is where you decide what kind of closing you are going to use on your blouse.

If you choose decorative Dot snappers, say pearl-topped ones, they will look like buttons and you won't have to make buttonholes.

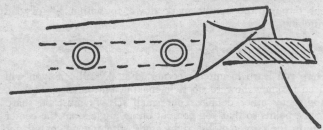

Fig. IX-21 Strip of Twill Tape Under Dot Snappers

► *Application of Dot Snappers*

Dot snappers must never be applied without at least three thicknesses of fabric. If there's no interfacing, use a strip of twill tape (Fig. IX-21) under the application area between facing and top fabric. The top half of the snapper will go on the right front or back edge, from ½″ to ¾″ in, depending upon where the center line comes, as the lap centers exactly on this line. Pin both halves of the closing together and decide how far apart you wish your snappers to be placed. If you think they should come closer to each other than buttons are marked, evenly redistribute the distances between the markings. Then mark both top and bottom halves of the closing, inside the facing.

A Dot snapper has two halves and four parts. The decorative top is applied to the overlap with its corresponding stud applied at the same spot on the underlap. You can buy a Dot snapper kit and hammer them on, or a dual purpose plier kit that will apply both snappers and belt eyelets. This practical tool will be pressed into service many times in your sewing. I have already mentioned using the plain ring Dot snappers at the belt band. They are excellent for children's snow suits, rompers and such, and numerous other places when you don't want to be eternally sewing on lost buttons. The pliers have soft rubber rings at each jaw so it'll be safe to apply pearl-topped snappers without crushing them. You will find the directions on the plier package very easy to follow.

► *Making Self-Covered Buttons*

Perhaps you'd rather close with buttons and buttonholes. This is the time, then, for you to learn to make stitched button-

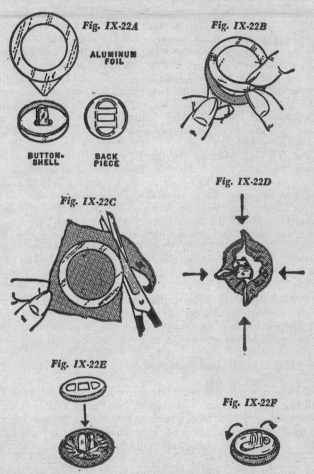

Fig. IX-22A

ALUMINUM
FOIL

Fig. IX-22B

BUTTON-
SHELL

BACK
PIECE

Fig. IX-22C

Fig. IX-22D

Fig. IX-22E

Fig. IX-22F

holes, with your buttonhole attachment, on this lapped closing. They must be made the right size to fit your buttons. So, you'd better decide first what kind of buttons you are going to use.

Why don't you make your own self-covered buttons from the scraps of your blouse fabric? The size 24 or 30 buttons are usually the best for a blouse closing. However, they come in other sizes up to the tremendous ones used for coats or decoratively in the centers of pillows. Make your buttons now so you may check the buttonhole measurements given on the pattern to make sure they are the right size.

You will find the easiest self-covered buttons to make are the ones which have aluminum foil ring patterns included in the package for each button (Fig. IX-22A). Peel off the paper backing from the foil pattern, taking care not to distort the ring (Fig. IX-22B). This exposes an adhesive on the underside of the ring which you stick down on the wrong side of your piece of fabric. Press it firmly to the cloth. Cut away the cloth around outside edge of the pattern (Fig. IX-22C). Center the curved metal front button shell over the cloth, inside the ring. Pinch the cloth evenly over edge of the shell. The aluminum ring helps to hold it easily against the metal (Fig. IX-22D). This foil keeps the edges from fraying as you manipulate and smooth the fold of fabric over the side of the shell. Center the flat metal back piece over the turned-in fabric so both tabs come through the slot (Fig. IX-22E). Press it down firmly so both parts come together to form the button, then bend each of the two tabs outward until they lie flat in their groove on the back shell (Fig. IX-22F).

This button will never come apart. If you see a shine of metal through the fabric, after you have placed the top over it, line the inside of circle with a piece of facial tissue or very thin cloth, before you begin to cover the button.

▶ *Making Stitched Buttonholes*

Machine-made or stitched buttonholes are done right through all thicknesses of outer, interfacing, and facing fabrics. Many times, on simple garments, such as this blouse, no interfacing is used where a machine-made buttonhole closure is preferred. The length of the buttonhole is usually the diameter of the buttons plus ⅛″. You may make a horizontal buttonhole or a vertical one, but follow the grain thread of the fabric either direction. The markings on the pattern indicate the best placement for your style.

Buttonholes of any kind, whether they are stitched or bound, are always made on the right side of your garment, and they are cut through it so that you must be absolutely accurate about their placement before you start. If you will make a baste-stitch ladder marking for the buttonholes before you make them, it is the easiest way to have them perfect

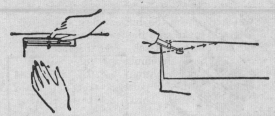

Fig. IX-23   *Fig. IX-24*

the first time. A baste-stitch is 7 to 9 stitches to the inch,
longer than stay-stitching, so that it is more easily removed
afterwards. Your tailorette, which chalks as it measures, is a
wonderful tool for checking the size and distance apart of
buttonhole tracing marks (Fig. IX-23). Baste-stitch from the
outside edge of the front through the center of the mark for
about 5″. Now, on the facing side of the work, connect all
the front ends of the buttonhole marks with your see-thru
ruler and chalk lightly. Do the same through the back end
of the marks. Baste-stitch through these parallel lines. Doesn't
that look like a ladder?

The direction book which comes with your sewing machine
will teach you how to make stitched buttonholes with your
particular type of machine or attachment. Stitched buttonholes are appropriate for any casual style garment or fabric.
Bound buttonholes are a sign of quality on dresses, suits, and
coats with interfacing.

▶ *Darts, Tucks, Gathers*

I know you are still working with unassembled blouse pieces!
However, haven't you learned a lot about closure construction on an uncomplicated flat piece of fabric? Your darts,
tucks, or gathering are still done on these unassembled pieces
to shape them to your body curves. On the wrong side of
the fabric, match the traced lines on either darts or tucks
and pin them exactly if you can't hold them perfectly.

If you are stitching a dart, be sure to do so from the
outside towards the point (Fig. IX-24). End off that point
sharply and lock with a back-stitch. If a dart is ended with
a wobbly, dull point it will show a "dimple" on the right
side which you simply will not be able to press out.

A tuck, too, must be stitched straight, exactly the length
marked, and ended with a back-stitch so that it will not
pull out in the wearing.

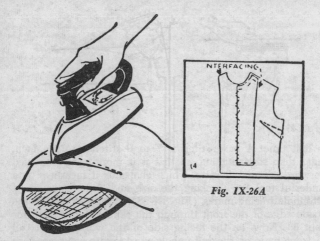

Fig. IX-26A

Fig. IX-25

Gathers are made by using a row of baste-stitches over the marking, which can be pulled up into the fullness later. Or, a couple of rows of elastic shirr-stitching makes very satisfactory gathers.

When you have these fitted marks stitched, they are turned flat against the fabric and towards the center and pressed over a pressing ham so they take on the curve of your body (Fig. IX-25). If there are darts at the elbow of the raglan sleeve, they are pressed towards the cuff edge.

If your pattern called for an interfacing piece to be cut out, you have doubtless prepared this already. If not, cut one for each side of closing, the size and shape of the facing turnback. Stitch in ¼" inside the marking for turnback on the facing, with the interfacing sandwiched inside (Fig. IX-26A). Pin together the neck edges of the facing and the blouse on the stay-stitch line. Press the outside fold flat.

▶ *Seams, Finishes, Facings on Blouse*

At last, you are ready to sew the blouse together at the shoulder line (Fig. IX-26B). Match the seams exactly at all notches and edges. Stitch with the grain from shoulder towards cuff with a ⅝" seam allowance. Press these seams over your sleeve roll also, because they must conform to the curve of your shoulder and arm.

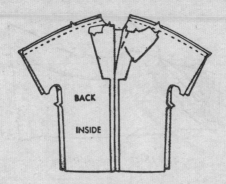

Fig. IX-26B   Attaching Blouse at Shoulder Seam

This is where you need to decide how to finish off your seams on the inside. It is easier to finish seam edges as you go, than to do all of them after your garment is complete. There are two practical finishes for you to learn on this simple first blouse, the pinked and stay-stitched seam, and the edge-stitched seam.

You now have a much larger flat piece and it is easier to finish the neck edge here than to wait until after the under-arm seams are closed. Follow your pattern instructions according to the style you selected for the final finishing details. But, here are a few things that have helped me in the construction of a perfect fitting neckline.

If the neckline interfacing has not been already cut, use the facing pattern to go by. Stay-stitch the edges ½" in and with the grain, just as you did for the facing and blouse. This time you will learn the kind of lap seam which is used mainly on stiff interfacing pieces to keep them flat between outer fabric (*see* Fig. X-13). Instead of placing the matched edges of your seams together, you lap one piece over the other so ⅜" extends beyond where seam comes on each piece. Sew through the center and cut away the raw edges of the interfacing to within ¼" of the seam.

Place this interfacing piece over the right side of the neck edge, all notches and edges matching exactly, and lap the seam of the interfacing over the shoulder seam of the blouse. Stay-stitch the neck and bottom edge of the facing pieces. Join the shoulder seams of the facing and press them flat. Finish off the bottom edge with a narrow edge-stitched hem. Lay this

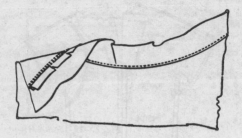

Fig. IX-27   Understitching

facing piece right side down, toward the right side of the blouse neck, with the facing between them. Place pins at right angles to the outside edge about 2″ apart and pin all these pieces together with notches, edges, and seams exactly matching. Stitch together with a ⅝″ seam allowance, carefully keeping a true neck curve.

I am going to give you a little advance information here because I wish that I had been taught to do it when I was a beginning sewer. It is the art of under-stitching (Fig. IX-27). If you finish the neck edge carefully this way, it will turn in and fit beautifully around a perfect curve. You are now looking at a raw edge that seems as though it will never look flat and pretty. First, trim away the interfacing raw edge as close as you can to the seam. Then, clip carefully with your pointed scissors toward the seam, about every 2″ around the edge of the neck curve. Turn the interfacing and facing back towards the wrong side of the blouse, against the clipped raw edges. Under-stitch inside the facing side of the seam all around as close as possible to the turn. You will have to stretch the fabric a little as you stitch to keep it flat under the presser foot. Trim away the raw edges of the seam underneath ¼″ from the seam. Turn the neck edge facing into the wrong side so the shoulder seams come together. Place the whole neck section, wrong side out, over your pressing ham and steam press the curve of the neckline so that it molds as it will on your own neck and shoulders. That row of under-stitching will be hidden inside the neck edge, and you will see that it helps to make the crease so sharp the facing will always stay inside without peeping out.

A simple pattern usually gives a sleeve hem cut in one with the sleeve. Finish the hem before sewing up the under-

Fig. IX-28 Stay Stitch Direction On Skirt

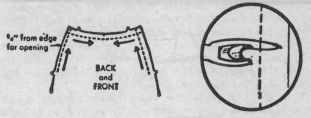

Fig. IX-29 Seam Ripper in Use

arm. Pink the raw fabric edge, turn under the stay-stitching to the wrong side and edge stitch. Press the hem crease over the hem pressing gauge at the required depth. Also, press up the hem depth on the bottom of the blouse. Stitch up your underarm seam with a ⅝" seam allowance. Stitch an extra piece of bias seam binding for about 4" around underarm curve to keep it from pulling out. Then, clip the seam about every 1" under this armpit area.

Consult your pattern instructions for finishing final neckline and facing edges, according to the style you choose. Finish the bottom hem with invisible hand hemming or a row or two of edge-stitching, depending upon whether your blouse is a dressy fabric or a casual cotton.

▶ *Fitted Skirt*

Since you have already made two skirts, this one should seem very simple and easy. The one new thing you will learn to do is to put in a hip-line zipper.

If you have not already cut out the skirt, do not forget to make any needed alterations on the pattern pieces before you cut. Cut on the grain, and accurately and plainly mark all darts, etc., including possible kick pleats.

No matter which style fitted skirt you have decided on making, you still have to pay attention to with-grain direction of raw edges, just as you did in the blouse. It is not necessary to stay-stitch the long edges, but stay-stitch across the waistline edge, ½" in (Fig. IX-28). Stay-stitch ⅝" in on both edges of the left hip seam opening as far as the single notch.

The with-grain direction for skirt seams is from the bottom to the top. So, stitch upwards from hem to waist with ⅝" seam allowance. Press each seam open as you go, pressing in the same with-grain direction. Be sure that you have accurately matched all notches, seam edges, and ends, which you may pin together if you wish, with pins running at right angles to the seam. However, here on these long seams might be a good place to practice your finger dexterity and try holding the edges together perfectly matched, pinning just once at hem and waistline.

If you go off, or get fullness where it doesn't belong, or end up with seams not coming out exactly together at the end as they must, there's always the seam ripper to make ripping easy (Fig. IX-29). When I rip with it, I stick the point under a stitch and cut every fourth or fifth stitch. Then, turn over the ripped area to the other side and pull away the long, loose threads which will pull out all the short threads at once.

As soon as all your skirt seams and darts or other details are stitched up and pressed, it's time to put in the zipper placket. This will be a concealed or lap seam closing, which differs from the one you put in the back of the blouse. Always get a special standard-length skirt zipper. Inside every package are complete instructions for the skirt placket application. These directions have been simplified to correspond with modern no-baste, no-pin sewing methods. However, I have an old fashioned way that I fall back on when the zipper application gives me trouble in a hard-to-handle fabric. After all, a zipper is a mechanical device going onto a piece of cloth, and besides it's a straight line going into a curve. So, it is not surprising that one sometimes runs into trouble here.

Baste-stitch the skirt placket closed on the regular ⅝" seam allowance (Fig. IX-30A). Press the seam flat over the seam roll. Because this width seam is sometimes too shallow to stand the strain of constant zipping and unzipping, it may be well to face the placket front edge. Cut a 1½"-width facing piece along the selvage of a piece of your skirt fabric, the length of the zipper tape. Flat-stitch this facing piece ⅛" inside the front placket seam edge (Fig. IX-30B). (I've also made the facing piece of a matching-color thinner fabric.) Turn the skirt to the wrong side and lay it in front of you on a flat surface. You're going to fit that hip curve to the straight tape of the zipper. Lay the zipper down, right side up. Fold the back half of the placket ⅛" inside the seam, and place this narrow fold from notch onto placket edge

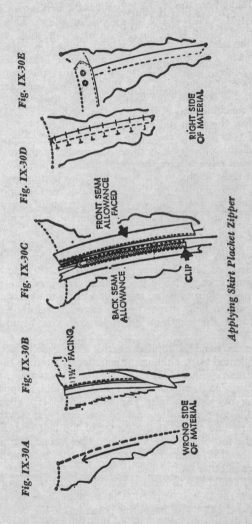

Fig. IX-30A   Fig. IX-30B   Fig. IX-30C   Fig. IX-30D   Fig. IX-30E

WRONG SIDE OF MATERIAL

1½'' FACING.

BACK SEAM ALLOWANCE.

FRONT SEAM ALLOWANCE FACED

CLIP

RIGHT SIDE OF MATERIAL

Applying Skirt Placket Zipper

close along the zipper chain. Pin down the turn of the fold above the notch at the closed end of zipper. Put another pin at the fold where the zipper is to meet the belt, about ¾" from the top of the skirt, at the tab end of the zipper. This shallow ⅛" fold of fabric between these two points must be eased along the zipper chain evenly and pinned in place. Then hand baste. Clip the back seam allowance below the metal of the zipper. When you are satisfied that the zipper tape and fabric fit together so that the curve has been accommodated to the straight tape, change to the zipper foot on your sewing machine and stitch over the basting (Fig. IX-30C) Press over the seam roll and remove basting.

Turn your skirt to the right side and fold the zipper back so the chain comes exactly under the center of the seam. The faced front edge is over the metal of the zipper. Now, place a pin at right angles to the seam over the bottom end of the zipper. Place another pin the same way over the zipper tab. Smoothing the seam line as you go, pin about every 1" in between (Fig. IX-30D). Evenly baste the fabric along the unsewed edge of the zipper tape, using a large cross-stitch basting across the bottom and top. (If this basting is done with matching thread, it won't show should some stitches not get pulled out later.) Remove the pins. Stitch exactly over the basting lines. Remove the basting. Top-press the placket with a press cloth over the fabric and using the pressing ham underneath to help shape the hip curve. Carefully rip open the hip seam the length of the zipper with your Seam Ripper (Fig. IX-30E).

The skirt band is applied on this skirt exactly as it was on the pleated skirt, although it is better to interline the band for stiffness (Fig. IX-31), so it doesn't crumple around your waist. As I said before, I like two Dot snappers for fastening my skirt bands. The belt should lap about 2¼" above the zipper closing. Attach two snappers so the top of the first one comes at the center of the belt end, directly above the top of the zipper closing. The second snapper top should be 1½" from the first. Apply the bottom half of snappers to other end of belt to match.

If you would like to conceal the top ring of the snapper, do so before the belt is applied. Cut a small piece of material 3" long and 1½" wide. Baste this patch inside the overlapping belt end. Apply two snappers so that the rings come on the patch side (Fig. IX-32A) and the sockets on the belt side (Fig. IX-32B). Snappers should be placed ⅜" from the end of

Fig. IX-31

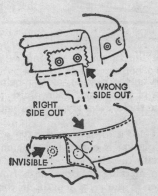

Fig. IX-32A

Fig. IX-32B

WRONG
SIDE OUT

RIGHT
SIDE OUT

INVISIBLE

Fig. IX-32C

the belt and 1½" apart. Fold the belt end and sew across, with the rings outside. When turned right side out the socket side of the snapper will be on the underside of the belt and the ring side of the snapper concealed (Fig. IX-32C). Apply belt to skirt so that the first snapper comes directly above the top of the zipper closing. After the belt is finished the studs of the snappers may be attached to match the concealed tops.

Now it is time to hem your fitted skirt. If your figure is very even and your pattern was adjusted exactly the right length, you can take up your hem without having to try it on and work with the skirt marker. If it is a pencil-thin, straight skirt, place the straight edge (Fig. IX-33) of the hem pressing gauge inside the hem and press it up the

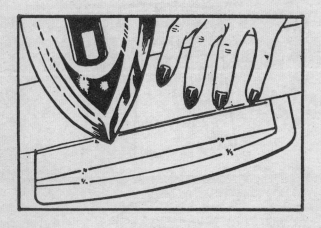

Fig. IX-33

amount indicated on the pattern, always being sure to press in with the grain of the fabric. Then, finish the edge of the hem in one of the three ways given when you hemmed your pleated skirt.

Neither a skirt nor a dress should have a hem measured until the zipper placket is completed. Put on the shoes you intend to wear with the garment, as well as the right girdle and bra. Do the marking in front of a full-length mirror. Adjust the marker to the right length. If you are not quite sure what length it should be, put on something that is the length you like to wear your skirts. Adjust the marker to that length from the floor up. It would not be fair for me arbitrarily to say, "Skirts are being worn 18" from the floor this season." This distance might not hit you at the same point that it hits someone else.

You may mark your own skirt without help when you use the squeeze-bulb type of chalk marker (Fig. IX-34A). Of course, if you have no self-confidence, have someone else mark your skirt with pins or chalk (Fig. IX-34B).

The chalk marks may then be pressed up over the hem pressing gauge and the edge trimmed even along the measure. Stay-stitching will complete the job ready for hemming.

In case the skirt hem is flared or circular, it must be well shaped with no little pleats on the underside of the hem.

Fig. IX-34A
Self-Marking Hem

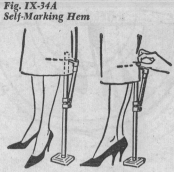

Fig. IX-34B
Help with Hem Marking

Here's where you learn to baste-stitch with ease. Long thread ends are left at beginning and end of each seam or gore. Let's assume it is a four-gored flared skirt. Baste-stitch (7 to 8 stitches per inch) ¼″ from the raw edge between gores, breaking threads and beginning anew at each seam.

If the skirt is completely circular with only two seams, it should be hung up for a day or two to stretch down as much as it's likely to. In this case the skirt length is taken first, then the hem depth is evened before the baste-stitching is done. Also, break the baste-stitching several times along the edge of each half.

Begin at a seam and turn up the hem depth over the curved edge of hem pressing gauge a single width of it (*see* Fig. VI-14). Find the half-way point of this gore and do the same thing; repeat at the end of the gore. Now place pins where the pressing has been done and wind one end of thread around the pin, to tack it. Ease fullness along the baste-stitching until it is all even along the entire gore and wind the other end around the pin. Finish pressing the hem depth over the gauge and adjust the fullness as you press in the grain direction. Now the skirt is ready for hemming.

► *Making a Separate Collar*

Before we leave the blouse-and-skirt project, let us make that separate collar. Your pattern instructions may show you how

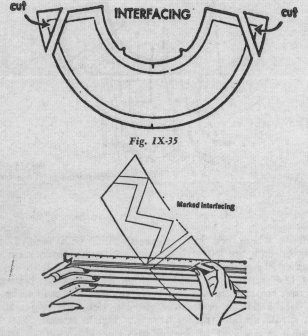

Fig. IX-35

Fig. IX-36

to sew it into the neckline before applying the neck facing. By all means do so, if you feel adventuresome enough. However, a round, collarless neckline does lend itself to jewelry changes, scarfs, etc., and you can make detachable collars one of these changes.

Let's say your collar is the Peter Pan variety. There is nothing that shrieks "home-made" like badly turned corners. So, learn to do them correctly from the start. Cut an interfacing by the under-collar pattern, but cut off the corners diagonally for about an inch (Fig. IX-35). Lay this interfacing on the wrong side of the under-collar and stay-stitch them together, ½" in from outside edge. With the see-thru ruler and tailor's chalk, draw off a few crossed lines (Fig. IX-36) at the center of the neck edge on the interfacing and stitch through them in a little design. This helps hold the two pieces of fabric together so the collar will roll better when

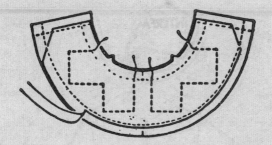

Fig. IX-37A

Fig. IX-37B

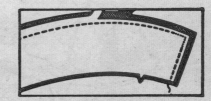

Fig. IX-39 Trimming and Beveling Seams

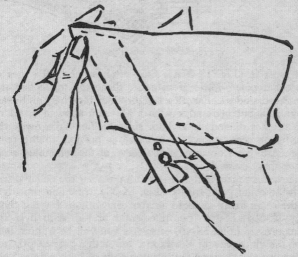

Fig. IX-38 Using Point Turner

Fig. IX-40   Point Presser

you wear it (Fig. IX-37A). Stay-stitch around all edges of the collar piece, ½″ in from edge. Place the top collar and interfaced under-collar pieces right sides together, and seam around all but neck edge with a ⅝″ seam allowance, taking two stitches diagonally at both collar points. Trim away the interfacing seam allowance as close as possible to the seam (Fig. IX-37B). Clip around the curve of the remaining seam edges about every 1″.

Turn the collar right side out and poke out the collar points with the collar point turner (Fig. IX-38), trimming the edges of the seam away as close as you can without fraying them (Fig. IX-39). Flatten out the center of the seam over the point presser (Fig. IX-40). Because you will be ironing here over the right side of the fabric, use a thin press cloth and press along the seam right into the ends of both points. Turn over and press the short side seams the same way into the ends of the points.

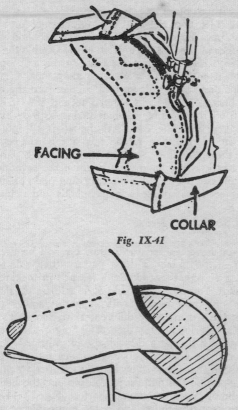

FACING

COLLAR

Fig. IX-41

Fig. IX-42 *Press Shaping Collar Over Ham*

With the under-collar side facing the presser foot of your machine (which is holding the seam), under-stitch along the seam (Fig. IX-41), working as far as you can into both corners. Under-stitch the short sides of the collar into the points as close as you can, too. Now, inside the seam trim away the excess seam allowance by "beveling" it (Fig. IX-42). This means that you trim one fabric edge a trifle narrower than the other.

Shape your collar over the pressing ham and pin it there as you would wear it on your neck. Then, press and manipulate the fabric until the collar lies nicely curved over the neck and shoulder area and flat on the edges. Bind the neck edges with a piece of your blouse fabric by using your see-thru ruler and tailor's chalk to measure and rule off a 1½" true bias the right length to fit the neckline. Stay-stitch both edges of the bias ¼" in from edge. Double the bias strip and press it folded. Apply one edge to the collar neckline and stitch it on flat with a ⅝" seam allowance. Clip the seam every inch and trim it down to ⅜". Then turn the other edge of the bias in on the stay-stitch line and sew it down neatly. Finish off the ends of this bias facing so they extend about ½" longer than the collar, to be snapped into the neckline of the blouse. You might sew a few silk-covered snaps inside the collar line. Sew the corresponding parts of the snaps onto the collar band. You might make several collars for your blouse; perhaps one a contrasting plaid or stripe, as a good project for learning to match plaids and stripes.

▶ Making Your First Dress

Everything you have learned to do thus far will be used in making a dress. So, select a dress pattern that will teach you something new that you have not learned in making the blouse and skirt. You might choose a style with set-in sleeves and a collar and front closing with separate facings (Fig. IX-43). Look for a completely different skirt, too. Let's line the skirt with innerlining this time. You might also decide to graduate to a little more difficult-to-sew fabric.

Lining pieces are cut by the same pattern pieces, except for the length on those that show hems, such as skirt pieces. In this case, you fold the pattern piece up along the hemline and cut the lining piece that much shorter (Fig. IX-44).

In order to keep the lining and outer fabric pieces absolutely grain-perfect, lay each section out on a large flat surface like your cutting board, with the corresponding lining piece on top of it. Then, pin them, notches and edges matched, and press once over lightly with a warm iron.

If you are making a slim skirt, stay-stitch the waistline with both fabrics together as though they were a single fabric. The darts and tucks are usually sewed in as though they were one fabric, unless the outer fabric is very thick. But, side seams must be sewn separately with the grain from bottom to top. Sew the lining seams first and press them and then do the same with the outer fabric seams. Only the section of the zipper placket from notch up is baste-stitched together as one.

Fig. IX-43 Basic Dress

Fig. IX-44 Innerlining Skirt

On the other hand, if you are making a flared skirt, all seams are sewn as though the outer fabric and innerlining were a single piece of fabric. When there is much flare in a gored skirt, it may be well to stay-stitch the innerlining and fabric pieces together ½" in around all edges before you seam up the gores. After all the skirt seams have been pressed in the same direction that they were stitched, put the skirt aside and begin on the blouse (or bodice section of the dress, as some patterns call it).

Here, you will learn two new things, (1) how to put on an applied facing to the collar and neckline, and (2) how to set in sleeves. We will not line the bodice this time, which may or may not be done when skirt is lined. Set-in sleeves are seldom lined.

► *Interfacing and Bound Buttonholes*

We must interface the front because you are going to make bound buttonholes on your dress. Don't shiver! The bound buttonhole maker will make it a pleasure for even a novice home sewer. Learn to use this simple tool and your bound buttonholes will add an expensive look to the most modest of frocks.

These buttonholes are easiest made on the flat piece before shoulder and underarm seams are sewn, just as you did with the machine-stitched buttonholes. I hope you have cut out all your facing and interfacing pieces at the same time that you did the rest of your cutting. Also, I hope you remembered that, if you had to shorten or lengthen your bodice, the facings and interfacings had to be altered and cut to the same length.

I can't guess exactly how to construct your particular style because I don't know what it is. So check with your pattern instruction sheet here. I am just using as my example a simple front closing with separately attached facings.

On the dress bodice, stay-stitch the same as you did on your blouse in the with-grain direction at the neckline. With set-in sleeves, you stay-stitch from the neck to armhole on the shoulder; from the shoulder to underarm around the armhole (*see* Fig. IX-18). If the front edge is somewhat off the grain, stay-stitch as close to the with-grain direction as you can. The underarm edges are not stay-stitched except below the placket notch on both sides of the left underarm. Stay-stitch around the edges of the facing piece and finish the inside edge of this piece with a flat-stitch turn.

Lay the interfacing to the wrong side of the bodice front. Lay the facing with the right side against the right side of this same piece, so that you will have facing, bodice front, and interfacing together, notches and edges matching. Seam these pieces together with a ⅝″ seam allowance at the front edge. Trim away the interfacing seam allowance as close as possible to the seam. Inside the facing edge, from the first buttonhole position down, under-stitch close to the seam all the way to the waistline. Trim away the excess seam allowance, beveling the edges. Press the facing inside the bodice over the interfacing with thin, neatly turned edges. If a bit of the interfacing peeps out beyond the facing, trim it away. Bound buttonholes are usually made through the interfacing, which supports and gives them body. With very thick fabric,

Fig. IX-45   Marking Buttonholes

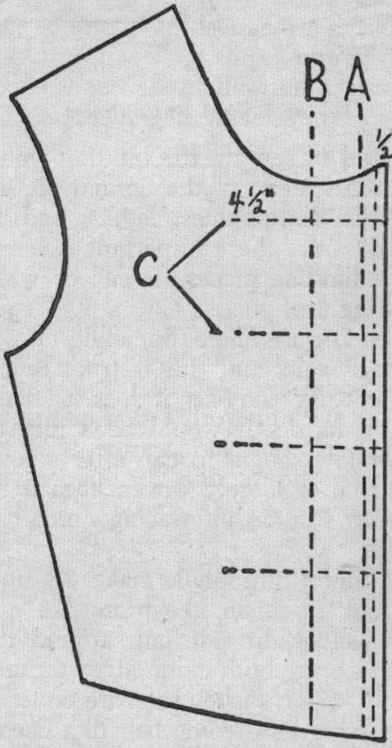

B A

4½"

C

½"

Fig. IX-46   Making Thread Ladder

a portion of the interfacing may be cut away and the welts brought through it.

Lift away the facing and make the buttonholes in the right front where the markings were transferred from the pattern (Fig. IX-45). With contrasting thread, baste-stitch the necessary ladder marking over these marks to bring them to the right side where work is done (Fig. IX-46).

If your fabric is cotton, satin, or other types that may permanently mar with stitch marking, make the ladder by hand with silk thread. If the cross threads of the fabric are

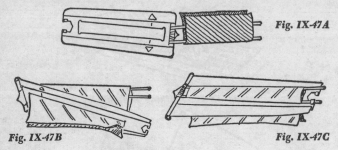

Fig. IX-47A

Fig. IX-47B   Fig. IX-47C

Making Bound Buttonholes

very wiry, you need to sew on the binding welts with about 20 stitches per inch instead of the normal 15. The best idea is to make practice buttonholes, ladder and all, on some fabric scraps to discover these important exceptions.

The buttonhole binding pieces are called "welts" and must be absolutely straight-of-goods. Cut a 2½" square of your dress fabric for each buttonhole. Someone may tell you that you can make bias welts and this is true. But, even if you are very good at cutting true bias, it does stretch more readily than straight-grain fabric. It would be a pity to have your first bound buttonholes begin to gap after a few buttonings. If your fabric is thin or loosely woven, firm it by pressing a same-size square of iron-on interfacing onto the wrong side of each welt piece.

Open up your bound buttonhole maker by unfastening the two wires that look so much like prongs of a hair barrett. Double a fabric welt, right side out, around the two wires (Fig. IX-47A) and bring both cloth edges through the center of the tool (Fig. IX-47B). Fasten the wire under the little side clips as though you were fastening hair in a barrett. Pull both fabric edges together evenly, and on the back there will be a ⅜" fold of it caught under the wires. Be sure it is absolutely straight-of-goods down the center, but it should not be pulled so tightly that the wire buckles in the center (Fig. IX-47C).

Lay the filled tool over the first baste-stitched buttonhole marking on the right side of your blouse piece. Slide the work under the raised presser foot on the sewing machine. Set your stitch gauge about 15 per inch for normal fabric. The two little arrows at the closed end of the bound buttonhole maker make an exact right angle with its center pointers. Correctly position the tool so that these indicators are over the center of the thread at the right angle marking on first

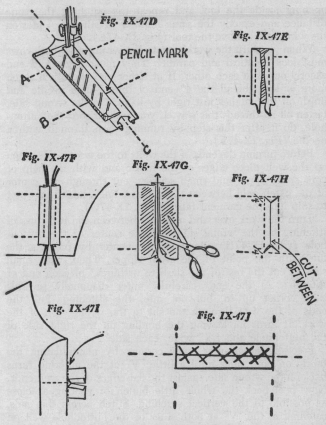

Fig. IX-47D

PENCIL MARK

A

B

C

Fig. IX-47E

Fig. IX-47F

Fig. IX-47G

Fig. IX-47H

CUT BETWEEN

Fig. IX-47I

Fig. IX-47J

Making Bound Buttonholes

buttonhole, with the pointer towards the faced edge of the work (Fig. IX-47D).

Beginning at the two crosswise arrows, bring the sewing machine needle through the fabric inside the opening of the tool. Then, lower the presser foot so it will ride along the slightly raised portion of the tool. Guiding the balance wheel of the machine with your right hand, and holding the bound buttonhole maker firmly in place with your left hand, stitch slowly from one vertical baste-stitched line to the other. Count the stitches as you go and cut threads off about 4″ long when you have finished. Now shift to the other side of the opening inside the tool and repeat the stitching the same distance and exactly the same number of stitches. Unfasten the wires and remove the tool (Fig. IX-47E).

When you turn the work over to the wrong side, both rows must look identical and parallel. They must begin and end exactly opposite each other. If at either end there is a stitch more or less, thread the 4″ end of thread in a needle and finish off the stitches just right by hand. On the wrong side, fasten off all threads this way. If you wish to cord the buttonhole, do it after this step by running yarn through with a needle (Fig. IX-47F).

Before turning the ends of the welts to the wrong side, open up the welt piece edges of the fabric and with the help of your seam ripper and small scissors, cut through the center of the patch *only* between the stitched lines, taking care not to snip into the garment fabric (Fig. IX-47G).

Turn the work over and, midway between the two rows of stitching on the wrong side, cut the center of the buttonhole (Fig. IX-47H). Begin at the center by piercing the line with the point of the seam ripper. Then, with small scissors cut the rest of the slash to within ¼″ of each end of stitching. At the ends carefully miter diagonally towards each corner up to, but not into, the stitching. Pull the ends of the welt through the slit to the wrong side of the work. It turns in, leaving the binding on the right side of the buttonhole about ⅛″ wide, each side.

Precisely square the outer corners by manipulating the fabric on both sides until a little "V" of the mitering turns back on the wrong side against the flat edges of the welt ends. Now peel back the whole little bunch of welting as close as possible to the vertical stitching. Stitch across the ends, catching in the "V" at both sides of the buttonhole welt on the wrong side (Fig. IX-47I).

Overcast the center of the welts together on the right sides (Fig. IX-47J). After all the buttonholes have been completed, rip out all the stitching of the baste-stitch ladder marking, then press over the buttonhole welts on the wrong side.

I had you begin by adding the facing to the front for more than one good reason. I want to tell you the neatest way I know to finish the facing side of buttonholes. The welts are probably larger than need be, so trim them down to within ½″ of the turn on each side. Fold the facing inside the bodice again, over the buttonhole welts. Pin each buttonhole in place where it comes against the facing, with the pins

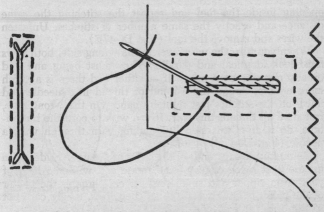

Fig. IX-48A

Finishing Buttonhole Facing

Fig. IX-48B

at right angles to the buttonhole opening at each end. Use your fine line tracing pencil and mark through the buttonhole slit onto the facing, a tiny bit longer than the outside opening. Unpin the facing, when all marks are drawn and stitch a small oblong around each one, using two stitches across both ends of the line. Slit the center of the stitched oblongs open very carefully (Fig. IX-48A). Turn in the edges of fabric around the stitching and hand hem them over the wrong side of the buttonhole (Fig. IX-48B).

► *Construction of Dress*

Now that the buttonholes are completed, we get on with the bodice construction. It is time to stitch up the bust darts or other fitted lines. This is done exactly as you did on your other blouse. Press the bust darts over the pressing ham so that you have fitted them over a curve. All darts are pressed towards the center (Fig. IX-49A), except underarm darts which turn towards the waistline. On the back bodice piece, stay-stitch the edges with-grain, finish darts and other details, and press. Matching edges and notches, seam the shoulders and underarms with ⅝" seam allowances, and press these seams flat over the pressing ham.

You are now ready to make your sleeves and set them in. Sleeves are so easy to put in and yet they are a bug-a-boo to many home sewers. Part of the difficulty comes in cutting. Perhaps the layout shows that you cut them from separate

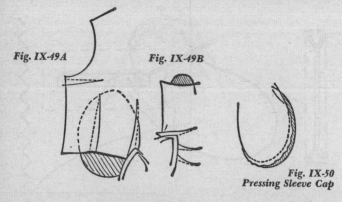

Fig. IX-49A   Fig. IX-49B

Fig. IX-50
Pressing Sleeve Cap

Correct Direction to Press Darts

areas of fabric instead of together. Then, you must be careful to cut left and right if your fabric has a wrong and right side. It is always best in this case to leave the first one you cut attached to the pattern piece so you can make sure to lay right sides of fabric together. Then, when you separate them from the pattern piece, chalk mark on the wrong side of the fabric "L" for the left and "R" for right. The pattern companies have a standard way of notching their sleeve and armhole patterns: the double notch is at the front and the single notch is at the back.

Stay-stitch ½" in around the cap edge of the sleeve from seam to seam (*see* Fig. IX-18). If there is an extra cuff, make and interface it as you did your collar. Or, if the sleeve is to be faced, apply facing and interfacing as you did with the front bodice facing, understitching the edge and all. If there are elbow darts, stitch them up and press them down toward the cuff edge. Snip a bit of a nick at the center top of the sleeve cap if it was not otherwise marked. At the sleeve cap, almost on the ⅝" seam allowance line, make a baste-stitch row from the single notch to the double notch. Sew up the sleeve underarm seam with a ⅝" seam allowance, matching notches and edges. Press this seam flat over the seam roll or sleeve board (Fig. IX-49B).

Measure the size of the bodice armhole from notch to notch. Place a pin at one of the sleeve notches and wind the first end of the baste-stitch thread around pin to fasten it. Stick the point of the pin into the first inch on your tape measure. Place a pin at the other notch of the sleeve cap and

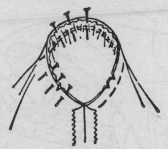

Fig. IX-51 Pinning Sleeve into Armhole

stick the point at the same distance on the tape measure as the area of the bodice armhole. Ease the fullness around the sleeve cap on the baste-stitch thread. Fasten the end of the baste-stitch thread by winding it on the second pin. Place the cap fullness over the wide end of the pressing ham, which is about the size of one's shoulder, and pin it down (Fig. IX-50). From the seam allowance edge in, steam the fullness slightly with your iron. This will help mold the sleeve cap to more easily fit the armhole.

Turn the blouse to the wrong side, and with the right side of the sleeve against the right side of the blouse match notches and begin pinning in the sleeve (Fig. IX-51). There are four main points to pin first. Begin at the underarm seams and pin them exactly together. Then, pin the top of the sleeve nick to the shoulder seam. Pin the double notches together, then the single notches together.

The sleeve curve is always a little larger than the armhole curve because there has to be ease in the sleeve to keep it from binding your armhole and shoulder as you move. This ease is what has to be allowed for when fitting these two curves to each other. Some people may allow a ¼" of ease into the underarm, but most of the ease is between the notches. The sleeve cap is mostly on the bias; that is, the grain goes in one direction on one side of the top of sleeve, the other direction on the other side. The top of the sleeve cap is on the straight-of-goods for an inch or less. It's simple enough to ease bias. So, adjust and pull up the thread between the pins at notches until the sleeve fits the armhole curve, as you place more pins at right angles to the sleeve seam edge every inch or so. You will be surprised how everything dovetails if you just don't get fidgety about it. If you still

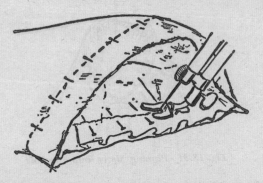

Fig. IX-52 Sewing Sleeve into Armhole

lack confidence in yourself on your first sleeve, baste it in. But, I never do, unless it is a delicate fabric.

Put the work under your sewing machine presser foot with the sleeve on top of garment facing you (Fig. IX-52). Begin stitching from the underarm seam, being sure to take up the whole ⅝" seam allowance as you sew. Stitch slowly and guide the ease under the presser foot with one finger so it won't form into tiny pleats. Continue stitching inside the baste-stitch line and remove the pins as you come to them, if you didn't baste. Patience does it!

Consult your pattern instructions for the finish on the particular style you have chosen. Use what you have learned about pointed corners and shaping curved collar edges. There's just one added helpful suggestion I may be able to give. Remember how we always trim away excess seam allowances? Just be sure they are no longer needed or that you'll never want to let out the line for any reason. Then, trim away the excess on crossing seams as you did on the collar points, or trim and bevel a seam where it allows flatter pressing, as after under-stitching.

You are ready to sew your waist and skirt together. The notches of both pieces should match at the waistline, as must all dart or tuck seams (Fig. IX-53). Be sure to pin the center fronts, center backs, and side seams exactly together, as well as darts and notches. Check the waist measurement to be sure it is like your own. If there is a little easing of the waistline into the skirt, make it come between the darts. Stitch the waistline seam with the usual ⅝" seam allowance. It is a good idea to place a strip of seam binding over the

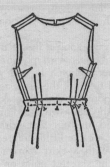

Fig. IX-53

waistline stitch, then stitch again over this binding (over the first stitch you made) to keep the garment from stretching at this vulnerable point.

Now, apply the dress placket zipper according to package instructions or see Fig. IX-30 or Fig. IX-54.

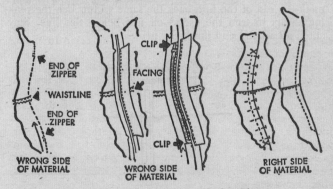

Fig. IX-54 Applying Dress Placket Zipper

Sew on your buttons or other closure. Button up, zip up placket, and fasten belt around your waist. (I hope it is a self-covered belt such as you will learn to make at the end of this chapter.) Put on the shoes which will be worn with this dress. I hope you have on your proper underpinning, too, such as bra, girdle, "falsies," and slip. Are you surprised that I came right out and said "falsies?" Why, indeed, shouldn't you improve a too flat bosom, even as you improve your natural skin tone with makeup, or your hair with a permanent or rinse?

I believe in having as good a figure in clothes as possible and, of course, this begins with posture. Stand up straight and tall, keeping your stomach in and your derrière tucked under. Then proceed to mark the hem, as explained earlier in this chapter in directions for making a skirt.

There are always the same ways of finishing a hem after it is marked, as you did on your first skirts. But, you use the hem pressing gauge here a little differently. Usually, when a hem is taken up with a skirt marker, the outer edge is somewhat uneven. The shortest point on this unevenness determines the width of the hem. So, bring the hem gauge up under the chalk marks, beginning at this point, and press the fabric back with the mark just a trifle on the wrong side of the turn. Here is where you will find your Tailorette most helpful (Fig. IX-55). If possible give a slim skirt a 2½" to 3" hem; a flared hem is best at 1" to 1½". Adjust the gauge where the hem turns up shortest, and this will be the width of turn for the rest of the hem. Gauging from fold to chalk, mark the rest of the turn-back the same width. Use the pinking shears to trim the excess off just below this line. Stay-stitch all around and finish the hem.

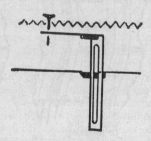

Fig. IX-55 Measuring Even Hem Turnback

▶ *Making Belt and Buckle*

Two types of self-covered belt kits are available. One is the kind of belt held together with eyelets and a prong, found on casual clothes (Fig. IX-56G). The other has a transparent ridgy plastic strip hidden under buckle and end, to keep them from slipping apart; this is best for most formal and dressy attire (Fig. IX-56L). You have a wonderful selection of belt widths, buckle shapes, and sizes in both types.

The belt is made the same regardless of its closing. Cut the stiff inner belting the length of your waist measurement, plus 4" or 5" for overlap. Example: Cut a 3" width of fabric to cover 1" belting, about 1" longer. Attach the zipper foot to sewing machine. Double the wider fabric over the belting, wrong side out (Fig. IX-56A). Hold the two fabric edges together evenly around it, and stitch with the zipper foot up against the edge of the covered stiffening. Stitch along the entire length and across one side of the pointed end (Fig. IX-56B). Pull the belting out of the fabric tube just made. Trim the seam to ¼" and turn the tube right side out with a bodkin or loop turner. Press. Now, attach the bodkin to the pointed end of the belting and pull it through the fabric covering (Fig. IX-56C). Neatly finish off the other side of the pointed corner by hand.

The unique buckle-covering pattern which is supplied with your belt kit to fit your choice of shape has two adhesive sides—one dark and the other light—hidden under a protective paper covering. This pattern is made from *Milar* which will stretch in any direction. Decide which side to use so as to least tinge the color of your outer fabric. Beginning at the slit, peel the paper away from this side of pattern (Fig. IX-56D). Lay this adhesive side of pattern down on the bias grain of the wrong side of the fabric. With your fingers, press and flatten the pattern securely to the fabric. Cut away excess fabric around the edges of the pattern. Pierce the inside center of the buckle covering with the point of scissors or a seam ripper, and cut exactly around the inside of the pattern and up the lines leading into corners (Fig. IX-56E). Do not cut beyond the end of these lines. Peel the paper from the adhesive on the other side of the pattern. Lay the fabric side down on a flat surface, and center the top half of the buckle over it carefully. Mold the lined fabric around the buckle (Fig. IX-56F). The fabric will stretch and mold smoothly around the buckle. If you manipulate it with a bit of patience you can coax out any little creases that may have formed. If they persist, pull the fabric and pattern away from the frame and remold at that place only. Push the under-frame firmly into the covered top.

To attach tongue and eyelets: If you got the belt kit which has to have eyelets attached, see the directions for adjusting your duo-purpose Dot snapper pliers and apply the eyelets

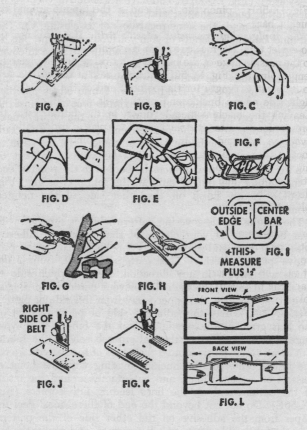

FIG. A   FIG. B   FIG. C

FIG. D   FIG. E   FIG. F

FIG. G   FIG. H

OUTSIDE EDGE   CENTER BAR

←THIS→ MEASURE PLUS ½"   FIG. I

RIGHT SIDE OF BELT

FIG. J   FIG. K

FRONT VIEW

BACK VIEW

FIG. L

Fig. IX-56A-L   Making Self-Covered Belt and Buckle

with them (Fig. IX-56G). Attach the first one 2″ from the pointed end of the belt, and the others as far apart as desired. Fold the end of the belt around the bar of the buckle with a 1½″ overlap and mark it. Cut slot, ⅛″ wide by ¾″ long, 1″ from the end at the center of the overlap. Slip the slotted belt end over the buckle bar and fasten it on the wrong side of the belt with a few overcast stitches. Place the bent end of the tongue, contained in the package, through the slot in the belting and around the bar. With mechanics' pliers

(Fig. IX-56H), pinch the bent end of the tongue around the buckle bar.

To apply ridgy concealed plastic strip: If you chose the no-eyelet type kit, measure from the center of the buckle bar to the outside edge of the buckle, cut a ridgy plastic piece this length plus ½" (Fig. IX-56I). Cut the rest of the plastic strip to 3" or 4" in length for the pointed end of the belt. On the right side of the buckle end of the belt, edge-stitch for 1". Leaving the machine needle down in the fabric, raise the presser foot. Center the short piece of plastic, ridgy side up, over the belt and touching the needle. Lower the presser foot and take two stitches through the plastic, by slowly turning the balance wheel by hand (Fig. IX-56J). Continue edge-stitching to within 4" of the pointed end. Leaving the needle down on the last stitch, raise the presser foot. Slip the longer plastic piece, ridgy side down, under the belt and close to the needle. Lower the presser foot, hand turn the balance wheel, and continue stitching, holding the plastic and belt together. Stitch around the point and up the other side. When coming to the second side of the short plastic strip at the buckle end, it may be necessary to repeat hand-controlled stitching. Attach the buckle to the straight end of the belt and tack it in place with a ½" plastic strip around the center of the bar. Kits with 2" or wider belting have two ½" plastic strips (Fig. IX-56K), one to be stitched each side as just described.

CHAPTER 10

Advanced Sewing and Tailoring

"To fit or style with trim, straight lines and finished handwork like that of a tailor's work on men's garments," is *Webster's Dictionary* definition of tailoring.

In a book written by a tailor, to teach tailoring to tailors, I found these fine rules on what to look for in good professional work:

1. Edges must be thin, even where you would expect seams to pile up thickly at their junctures.
2. All edges curve slightly inward on fronts, sleeve vents, pocket flaps, revers, collar corners.
3. A good coat has straight seams and edges all over, no puckers. All seams are pressed open flat in the inside.
4. Linings are always loosely put in so that they do not interfere with the drape when worn.
5. Buttons are sewn with a "neck" and not too tightly, avoiding strain at their bases. Buttonholes are handmade.
6. Hand sewing around collar and elsewhere is neat and inconspicuous.
7. The sleeves hang clean, with no diagonal twisting.
8. The collar sits close around the neck, but is neither tight nor loose.
9. The fronts and revers often have a narrow stitching along their edges.
10. A good garment is not necessarily a custom or tailormade garment, or one almost completely hand-sewn. Many have machine seams and are beautifully proportioned.

Just what makes a custom-tailored suit superior to one

ready-made? The answer is mainly better fit. A tailored suit may not be made of better fabric than a high grade commercial one, but if it is constructed by a good craftsman it should fit better. When doing your own home tailoring, then, it's your craftsmanship that counts.

You have already learned many of the things professionals require for good tailoring. You graduated from pleated straight skirt to blouse, to fitted skirt, to dress. You learned to stitch straight; to fit and alter patterns; to cut on grain and mark correctly; to make darts, tucks, and pleats; to press as you sew; to trim away excess fabric and finish collar edges; to set in sleeves; to under-stitch for sharply turned edges; to make buttons and bound buttonholes; to interface and innerline; to put in zippers. All of these things are repeated in advance sewing, only with even greater precision.

▶ Pressing for Good Tailoring

Pressing equipment is very important to tailoring. You need a sleeve board; press cloths (thin organdy-like cheese cloth, a treated drill cloth); a pounding block and point presser (sometimes called a *clapper*); a properly regulated steam-dry iron; tailor's pressing hams; ironing board.

Up until now I have not discussed steam irons. A good one is absolutely necessary to do good tailoring. I like the latest type with an extra steam spray. The following information is from an impartial report on the subject. There are two types of steam irons, the *flash* boiler type and the *kettle* type. Most of the brands on the market today are the first kind. It is somewhat the most convenient since the steam can be turned off and on at will without having to empty whenever you wish to change from steam to dry ironing.

This preferred flash boiler steam iron works on the principle that a drop of water on a very hot surface will dance about and turn into steam. It is marked with a specific temperature control with a very small range setting for steam. It stops steaming when the steam control is turned to "dry" and whenever the iron is placed on its heel plate.

The kettle steam iron contains a reservoir in which water is boiled, forming steam which passes through channels to the vent holes in the sole plate. It will generate steam at any temperature setting except, perhaps, the very lowest. It stops steaming only when it has been emptied of its water supply.

The latest steam irons can be set hot enough to iron linen or cool enough to iron acetates and other synthetics. An iron

Fig. X-1   Cleaning Steam Iron

which steams copiously is likely to be most satisfactory, but
it will require more frequent filling. None will steam much
longer than half an hour before refilling. The spray feature
is an additional measure of versatility. When spray is forced
out under pressure it should be finely atomized. The spray
can be aimed immediately ahead of the iron where it is
wanted, without pointlessly wetting any adjacent area.

The factors of convenience make ironing something you
approach with reluctance or enjoyment. The things to look
for are handle comfort, how it feels in your hand when you
lift it; ease of filling; placement of power cord—some swivel
either right or left or are plugged into either side for convenience of left-handed people. Thermostat locations should
be up front and easy to read whether iron is standing on its
heel or is in use. Heel rest must be stable—safest are those of
molded plastic. Watch for shock hazard and keep iron un-
plugged while filling. As far as corrosion resistance, aluminum
tank may be more susceptible to corrosion than brass or
stainless steel.

Most new irons allow the use of tap water. However, if
the water is hard it may build-up deposits, especially in the
area where water evaporates. Deposits may interfere with
the formation of steam, clog up and reduce the size of the
drip-holes, and ultimately plug up the steam vent holes in
the sole plate, or clog spray-holes of steam-spray irons. In
this event use a steam iron cleaner (Fig. X-1), to keep
your iron in good working condition. It comes in a plastic
bottle with enough for eight cleanings. It is non-toxic, odor-

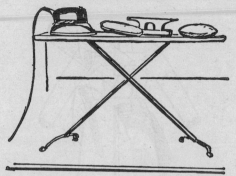

*Fig. X-2   Steam Iron, Seam Roll, Point Presser,
and Dressmaker's Pressing Ham*

less, and fireproof. Just pour the cleaner into iron's water receptacle and allow to remain for three minutes.

You can now buy three useful sizes in pressing hams (Fig. X-2) at the notion counter of a department store. The smallest sized pressing ham is called a seam roll. It is shaped more like a sausage than a ham and is useful for pressing long seams, elbow darts, and zipper plackets. The dressmaker's ham has a wide curve at one end just right for shrinking the cap on a set-in sleeve. You also use it to press darts to a body contour, which is part of good tailoring. The tailor's ham is truly a professional size that any tailor would use for shaping collars and revers on man-tailored suits and coats.

An important tailor's tool has always been a sharp-pointed, seam-width board for pressing seams flat and opening up the points and junctures. The clapper or pounding block was used to flatten steamed areas by spanking them with it. The clapper had shallow grooves in each side which were never quite big enough for a woman to grasp securely. So, now, these two tools have been combined into one, with the seam presser making a sturdy handle for the pounding block.

▶ Basic "Muslin" Pattern

Tailoring experts agree that fit is the thing. Also, they usually begin by making a "muslin" (Fig. X-3). This means they cut the whole pattern in a sturdy cotton fabric, and fit it to the figure exactly in every detail. Then, they use the "muslin" as the pattern by which they cut out the suit fabric. So, if you have not yet made yourself a basic "muslin" of your

Fig. X-3 Basic Muslin

figure, this is the time to do so. Every pattern you make up may first be altered according to this "muslin."

I asked a friend to play "guinea pig" for me at this point. We bought a size 38 half-size basic pattern for her 38-28-38 figure. She has what is often called the "pouter pigeon" figure; that is, full bust and slim hips. But she also has shoulders that droop. This makes her shoulders narrower than a 38 pattern; also one hip is a bit higher than the other. There is a sway-back tendency across the back of her skirt.

We cut a basic "muslin" from the pattern, tried it on her, then took the "muslin" off and made the following alterations in it: narrowed the shoulder, took out some excess across the bust, widened the back across the shoulder blades, and tapered the area across the back of the skirt so that it hung grain perfect. We then made up a two-toned basic dress to use to check all patterns by, whenever my friend decides to make anything. When she selected her simple suit pattern we were able to cut the fit into it from the beginning, as a good tailor should.

▶ Sewing with Difficult Fabrics

"Alertness" may be the key word in tailoring. Alertness to every detail is paramount for every home tailor to remember. Before we go into making this simple basic suit, let's talk

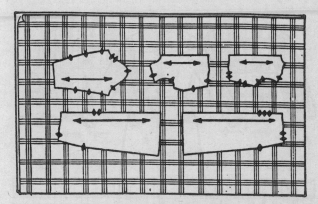

Fig. X-4 Cutting Even Plaid

about some more difficult-to-cut fabrics that have not been mentioned.

We all love plaids and stripes, but they can be tricky. There are even plaids and uneven plaids. An even plaid comes out the same on both sides of a single repeat (Fig. X-4). An uneven plaid is woven so that some lines and checks differ all the way across a repeat.

Choose a pattern of simple design with the fewest possible seams. Avoid circular yokes or many-gored skirts. Small plaids, easier to match, can be made up in a greater variety of styles. For average-sized plaids, purchase about ¼ of a yard extra fabric; purchase ½ yard extra for very large ones.

Carefully plan the position of the most noticeable lengthwise and crosswise plaid bars. The lengthwise bar usually looks best at center of the garment. Just below the shoulder is good for the crosswise bar. Before placing the pattern pieces on two thicknesses, pin the fabric layers together along the plaid lines in both directions so they match exactly and will not shift during cutting. If the plaid fabric has a right and wrong side, it is easier to determine matching points if the fabric is folded right side out for cutting. When marking you will have to reverse your tracing paper.

A plaid has to be considered from two directions, lengthwise and crosswise. Before beginning the layout, you should plan the matching throughout the entire garment. Study the pattern and decide all the areas where matching should be done: shoulder seams, center seams, armhole seams, skirt

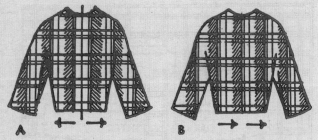

Fig. X-5 *How to Match Uneven Plaid*

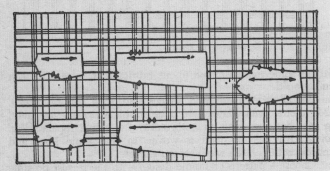

Fig. X-6 *Cutting Uneven Plaid*

seams. If you wish to be very exact, you can trace the design on the pattern tissue at matching points with a soft lead pencil.

Uneven plaids may be uneven crosswise, lengthwise, or in both directions (Fig. X-5). In all cases, it has to be cut all in one direction. Therefore the pattern pieces are all laid out facing the same way. If the uneven plaid is woven with no right or wrong side, it can, if very carefully planned, be balanced. Each piece has to be cut from a single thickness of fabric. Keep the pattern piece pinned to the fabric you have cut, and place both (pattern and fabric) on a matching area of fabric before cutting the second piece. When matching, your garment pieces are turned left and right. It is best to have a seam down the center back to even up this area. If an uneven plaid has a definite wrong and right side, the plaid cannot be balanced. In this event, the center front or back of garment may be laid on a fold. Only the horizontal lines can be

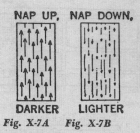

NAP UP. NAP DOWN.

DARKER   LIGHTER

Fig. X-7A   Fig. X-7B

matched identically. Vertical lines will continue around the figure in one direction.

Checks less than ¼″ square require little or no matching. Stripes and harlequin prints require matching at the seams and should be treated like plaids, by placing corresponding numbered notches on the same color stripe of fabric. Stripes are easier to handle than plaids because the design runs only in one direction, lengthwise or crosswise; thus they need be matched in only one direction. Stripes, too, come both even and uneven. There are no particular problems in matching even stripes. You just have to be sure to lay matching parts on the same stripe (Fig. X-6). But, uneven stripes also have to be cut with the tops of all pattern pieces laid the same way, and many of the other rules for cutting uneven plaids apply to uneven stripes. When working with uneven lengthwise stripes, and there is no seam at center of bodice or skirt, allow the stripes to follow right around the figure. When you cut the sleeves of such a pattern, watch out that the stripes move in the same direction as those on the bodice. If you wish to have the stripe design move in opposite directions from the center, you will have to plan with a seam in the center of the bodice and skirt.

Velvet, velveteen, and corduroy are pile fabrics with a surface produced by short, upright fibers woven into the fabric. Pile fabrics should be cut all in one direction with the pile running up (Fig. X-7A), except for panné velvet, which runs down (Fig. X-7B). This is a fabric to pin firmly to your cutting board because it has a tendency to squeeze away from itself when one layer is put over another, with the pile sides together. Also, the electric scissors will cut a pile

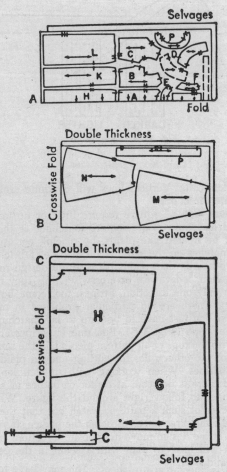

Fig. X-8 Cut Napped and Piled Fabric Pieces All One Way of Goods

fabric identically when doubled, whereas pile has a tendency to push against the blades of regular shears.

A nap fabric also has a fuzzy surface texture, anywhere from the flat flannel nap to a longer-haired fleece or camel's hair. It should be cut all one way with nap running down

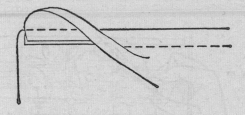

Fig. X-9   French Seam

(Fig. X-8). Napped and pile fabrics have a tendency to slip in stitching, so here is one time when basting is in order. If you use pins, put them fairly close together and stitch over them before removing, if possible. Use a longer machine stitch for best results.

It might be best to cut satins and other shiny fabrics all one way, too, so as to have no shading between different pieces.

I have always loved filmy chiffon and nylon organdy, which seem to be becoming to almost any figure or age. Chiffon skirts, especially, are often cut on several identical layers and should be cut together. One excellent method is to baste-stitch selvages and torn crosswise grains together. But, they may float away as you try to lay out pattern pieces on such fabric. I was never successful at cutting them grain-perfect until I had a cutting board. When I was able to pin those layers down on the straight marked lines, then they were really anchored and I could get the pattern pieces pinned grain-perfect to the fluffy material. If you interface chiffon bodice fronts, use nylon organdy or marquisette.

Be sure your sewing machine needle has a good point so it won't pull the fine threads of sheers. You may have to adjust tension and pressure and make stitches 16 to 18 per inch. Unless you have a zig-zag machine or attachment, you will stitch seams on the right side, trim them very narrow, then French-seam on the wrong side (Fig. X-9).

The armhole seams will have to be stitched twice, ½" apart, and trimmed. But, if you have a zig-zag machine you can make beautiful fine machine seams on the wrong side;

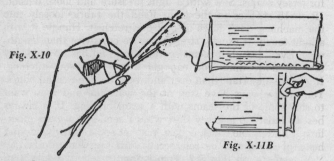

Fig. X-11A

Fig. X-10

Fig. X-11B

use the narrowest zig-zag stitch, and trim off the excess fabric right down to the stitching. Stay-stitch hem edges and hand roll (Fig. X-10).

▶ *Knitted and Stretch Fabrics*

Jersey or knitted fabric is made in a variety of fibers: wool, dacron, nylon, orlon, rayon, acetate, cotton, silk, and blends of several of these. The very newest type of jersey is double-knit and stretch-jersey. Sometimes these varieties come tubular like a seamless stocking, and sometimes cut with the edges fused. Knitted fabric never has a real woven selvage. If it is tubular, locate the rib which is the lengthwise grain and follow it with a basting. Then cut carefully on grain. Pressing in the lengthwise grain direction, steam out the other fold before cutting (Fig. X-11A). Place your see-thru ruler on a crosswise rib, and chalk a line to cut on for straight crosswise grain (Fig. X-11B).

At about the place where the center crosswise crease was pressed out, find a straight rib and run basting all through the length of the fabric to guide you for grain-perfect cutting. Jersey is a flattering and drapable fabric on any figure. Only be sure your pattern is not too tight-fitting. It must be cut so that it doesn't fit you like a bathing suit, but looks casual and clean-lined on your figure. So many people have come to me when I have given cutting board demonstrations in stores to ask about cutting jersey. It is so easy to cut when you can pin the fabric down both ways on those nice straight lines. Also, here is another fabric that I love to cut with electric scissors. Avoid stretching when pinning the pattern pieces into position.

Taslan-textured nylon sewing thread is resilient and strong for jersey seams. Sew with a light pressure and loose tension, 12 to 15 stitches to the inch. Feed the fabric loosely into the machine; don't force or pull or stretch it. Handle it with a light touch. It usually stretches more crosswise than lengthwise. Even though it seems so very firm and has no tendency to fray, don't think you can get away from stay-stitching. It is more important than ever and must be done on all edges. You must always have stay at the waistline and may want to stay some of the seams with a seam binding. It is always best to innerline a jersey skirt with a semi-soft woven innerlining. Buttonhole welts, collars, placket areas, waistband, and hems of slacks can be reinforced with press-on interfacing.

Woven stretch fabrics are no easier to sew at home than the jersey type. However, if you follow the rules you can sew on stretch fabrics without any fear. Most of the pattern companies have brought out special patterns for this new wonder fabric. At least be sure to use a proportioned pattern. If a pattern for slacks says they must have a stirrup, make them, otherwise they do not fit properly. The only caution is to be certain your pattern can be laid to have the stretch pulling in the desired direction. In blouses or shirts this would undoubtedly be horizontal to allow for stretch across the shoulders. Check the fabric before buying. Warp stretch will pull lengthwise, filling stretch will pull from selvage to selvage.

Although it is not always necessary to pre-shrink stretch fabric, it is a wise precaution. If steaming with an iron, do not use pressure, as you are not pressing, just shrinking. When laying fabric for cutting, do not pull but lay it smooth. It works beautifully on the cutting board, but lay it down and let it relax before pinning it. Use less pins than usual. Pieces cut from fabric under tension will not match those cut without tension. Use very sharp shears and here the electric scissors are wonderful.

In sewing smart apparel from stretch fabric, seams sewn in the stretch direction must be able to stretch or extend with the fabric. Seams which cannot extend with the fabric will not hold when the fabric is stretched. A fine needle, with 14 or 15 stitches per inch *minimum*, is advisable. Increasing the number per inch will add to seam stretchability. Also, you might stretch the fabric slightly while sewing, and you must take care not to skip or have uneven stitches. Increase the pressure on the presser foot if there is a slippage tendency.

But, too much pressure may cause the fabric to travel unevenly under the presser foot. You might make a test seam first on a scrap of the material. Taslan-textured nylon thread has more give than mercerized cotton thread.

When pressing, avoid high temperatures or excessive stretching. Use a synthetic setting on your iron temperature control. Fusible non-woven interfacing pressed on small areas such as plackets, waistband, and hem of slacks, adds stability. But, once the interfacing is fused, the stretchability is lost.

▶ *Foam Laminated Materials*

Foam laminates are another new type of fabric which is being used in linings of light weight warm sports clothes and rain coats. It is non-allergic, non-toxic, and will not retain odors. It stabilizes knit fabric, helping it retain its shape. It gives resiliency to fabrics to which it is bonded. It gives warmth without weight, yet it will not cause excessive perspiration, since it "breathes" and gives ventilated warmth. Unlike rubber, urethane foam does not stiffen or swell in dry cleaning solvents, and it is not affected by water or heat.

The foam is bonded to a variety of fabrics with an added adhesive, or by pressing the fabric to the foam when it is hot and tacky. The bonding method is usually governed by the fabric to which it is bonded.

Foam laminates are very easy to cut on the cutting board, but must be turned fabric sides together and foam side out. If laid the other way, foam sticks to foam. Use the very simplest patterns with no tricky seaming or seam detail.

In sewing seams, the foam may bind or stick under the presser foot. If your "walking" presser foot doesn't sew well, some machines have a roller foot attachment. Or you can use adhesive press-on sensitized tape on the foam side, to help it pass through the machine easier. Use a fine silk needle and loose stitch with Taslan thread. When I hemmed my coat at the bottom, I peeled away the foam at the turn line of the hem.

▶ *Meeting Cutting Situations*

Before we leave the subject of difficult fabrics, I'd like to tell you of a special problem I had recently that made one more point for the value of a pattern cutting board. The dress is a chiffon wool plaid, with the blouse of the dress cut in an all-in-one raglan sleeve style on the bias. The skirt is cut on the straight from an even plaid material. There is no front seam, so I basted a line down the center of the plaid and made this the fold. I had no trouble cutting the skirt and, by matching the notches on the same square in the side seams, I had a perfectly matching seam line.

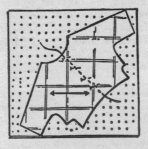

Fig. X-12

But, the blouse was a different story! I ran a basting line through the diagonal center of the 3″ squares, then pinned the pattern on the basting for bias grain (Fig. X-12). After the piece was cut, it was as crooked a bias plaid front as you ever saw. Fortunately, I had enough extra fabric to be able to cut another front. So, this time, I pinned the basted line down to a bias line of the cutting board. Then I pinned down the nearest selvage and crosswise grain. When I placed the pattern on the bias this time the fabric couldn't shift and it came out just perfect.

When there is as much thin bias fabric as there was in that whole front and two sleeves, don't wait a minute to stay-stitch all edges if you do not want them to stretch. Then came the problem of matching back shoulders down the center of the raglan. I used a special pressing technique to insure perfection. Pressing with the grain line, in the same direction as the stay-stitching, I turned under the ⅝″ seam allowance from the neck to the wrist on each sleeve. Then I placed the folded edge on a diagonal of the plaid, marking the neck and wrist positions, and drew a chalk line. The pattern piece was then placed with its seam line on the chalk line, neck and wrist edges turned correctly. Of course, all straight grain edges were well anchored to the cutting board before any pinning or cutting was done. Both backs had to be cut separately this way.

► Press as You Sew

Because correct pressing is so important to tailoring, here are a few basic rules to remember:

Pressing and ironing are different techniques. In pressing, the iron is lowered and raised over the same spot, not pushed along the material as in ironing.

Every stitched seam should be pressed before it is crossed with another seam.

Press curved seams over a curved surface such as a pressing ham.

Press seams in the same direction as that in which they were stitched. Skirt seams, for example, should be pressed from bottom to top.

Always press with the grain of the material. For instance, when pressing the surface of a four-piece bias-cut skirt, do not press straight up from bottom to top, but follow the grain which runs in a diagonal direction.

Darts are usually pressed toward the center front or back of a garment. In heavy materials they are slashed and pressed open.

Underarm darts are pressed down. Sleeve darts are pressed toward the wrist.

Wool should be pressed moist and usually on wrong side. Use a press cloth when pressing on the right side to avoid a shine.

Rayon is pressed either moist or almost dry, depending on the type of rayon. Test a scrap for temperature.

Cotton or linen should be dampened and pressed on the wrong side. It is necessary to use a press cloth with these two fabrics.

Sometimes it is very satisfactory to use a press cloth of the same fabric, if the material is napped or piled.

For completely professional finish, a garment must be pressed as you sew, and pressed on the outside after it is finished.

► Seams for Tailoring

Before we begin talking about the details of advanced sewing, let's take up the more complicated seams that are likely to

Fig. X-13A Single Top Stitched Seam

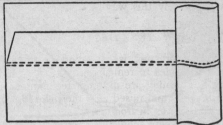

Fig. X-13B Double Top Stitched Seam

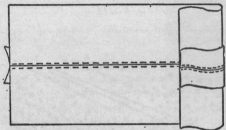

Fig. X-13C Flat Felled Seam

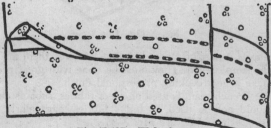

Fig. X-13D Welt Seam

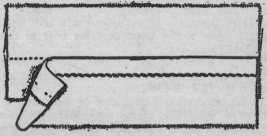

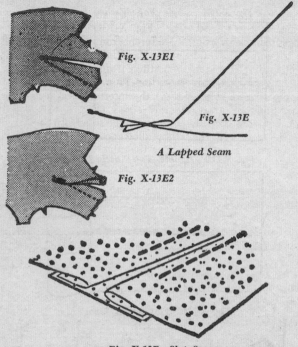

Fig. X-13E1

Fig. X-13E

A Lapped Seam

Fig. X-13E2

Fig. X-13F Slot Seam

appear as a part of tailored styling. Most of them are based on the simple seam. They must be done with great precision to make a good-looking professional finish.

The French seam is used on sheer fabrics, such as chiffons. It should not be used on bulky fabrics, particularly where curves are involved (*see* Fig. X-9).

The single top-stitched seam gives a neat, tailored effect where fabric might appear too bulky. After making the plain seam, turn both raw edges to one side and press. Then top-stitch close to the seam over the bulk of the fabric (Fig. X-13A).

There is a double top-stitched seam. In this case the seam is pressed open as usual and top-stitched close to both sides of the seam (Fig. X-13B).

The flat felled seam is often used on sport clothes. It may be done on either side of the work. Make the plain seam and press both edges to one side. Trim away under-seam to

¼". Turn the top seam under ⅛" to ¼" and pin or baste it, stitching close to turned edge (Fig. X-13C).

A welt seam is only slightly different from a flat-felled seam. After trimming the under-seam, lay the top seam over it without turning it under, then stitch it down. A second row of stitching is done near seam line (Fig. X-13D).

We lap-seamed (Fig. X-13E) the interfacing at a dart for flatness, trimming away the raw edges (Fig. X-13E1). But when a lap seam is to show on the right side, turn one edge under the width of the seam allowance, and press (Fig. X-13E2). Then it is lapped over the edge of the other seam up to the seam allowance. Stitch ¼" from the edge so the seam looks like a tuck.

The slot seam is very popular today as an elegant trim on tailored dresses (Fig. X-13F). Mark your seam allowances and press them back on the marked line. Cut a 1½" straight strip of self fabric, or contrast if desired, and mark a line at center. Lay the two turned edges so they meet at the center line on the strip and pin or baste in place. Topstitch ¼" away from center on both sides, or more than ¼" if you wish a wider effect.

▶ *Construction Details for Tailoring*

As I have emphasized over and over again, to make a garment properly, you must follow the pattern instruction sheet step-by-step to find out the best way to construct that particular style. But, you will argue that the new sewing methods I have given aren't on the sheet. Unfortunately, an instruction sheet of this kind couldn't possibly be made big enough to include a complete sewing technique every time. Even if it could, you probably would not follow anything that wordy. Your pattern instruction sheet can be considered like the blue print for a house. You can't get along without a blueprint and you consult it at every step of the building. But, you also consult outside sources of information for construction details and methods.

Now, let us first take a suit pattern instruction sheet, then a coat pattern instruction sheet, and fit into them some additional tailoring techniques as they are used. In this way you will learn how to coordinate your new knowledge with the blue print wherever it is needed.

▶ *Dressmaker Suit*

The suit style shown in illustration is the Chanel type, a very simple basic dressmaker suit, feminine but tailored (Fig. X-14).

Fig. X-14   Basic Suit

At the top of the diagram page we will use is the following useful reminder: Pattern pieces are numbered in the order they are used. To join seams, match each notch to a notch of corresponding number (1 to 1, 2 to 2, etc.). Shading denotes the right side of fabric. When fitting your first trial, check the following points: center and side seams should hang straight; front bodice and waistline darts should end slightly below fullest part of bust; check position of waist-line; note whether straight grain is at right angles at point

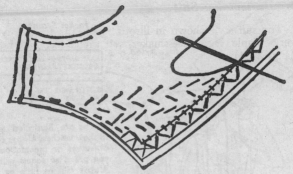

Fig. X-15 *Hand-Padding Stitches*

of bust, lengthwise from center shoulder to hem, crosswise from armhole to armhole. Stitch accurately on indicated seam lines. Trim and clip curved seam allowances so that seams will press flat.

After the pattern is altered according to changes in the basic "muslin" the fabric is cut out grain-perfect by following the pattern layout for your width of fabric. Both jacket and skirt of this suit will be innerlined throughout, sleeves and all. You need about 2½ yards of 45" innerlining. Get the woven innerlining specially made for the purpose to firm your outer fabric, and use a suit-weight hair canvas interfacing. Cut the innerlining by the same pattern pieces as the outer fabric, a hem depth shorter wherever there are hems. Lay the outer fabric pieces aside, and mark on the innerlining and interfacing pieces with the tracing paper and wheel all darts, tucks, center lines, slashes, buttonholes, etc.

According to the pattern instructions, you begin by laying the interfacing to the outer fabric at STEP 1. But, since we are going to innerline this whole suit, we will instead apply the interfacing to the front edges of the innerlining piece. At front, neck, shoulder, and armhole edges, as far as the interfacing extends, stitch on a ¾" seam allowance. Trim away the interfacing close to the seam. Now, find the corresponding outer fabric front pieces, and with the interfacing out, press the innerlining to the wrong sides, grain-perfect. Baste-stitch them together ½" from the outer edge and around the armhole and shoulder edges in with-grain direction.

The style indicates that there are three buttonholes to be made in the right front. It is so much easier to make them

Jacket Seams

Fig. X-16A

1 MAKE DARTS ON JACKET BACK 11 AND JACKET FRONT 12

2 STITCH SHOULDERS AND SIDES

Seams are illustrated unfinished to show notches. *Always clip seams at curves or indentations before you press, so seams will lie flat. Always clip as little as possible.*

PRESS SEAMS AND DARTS AS ILLUSTRATED

in the flat piece before the shoulders and underarms are joined to the back. So, with contrasting thread, make a baste-stitch ladder over the buttonhole markings and make bound buttonholes with the bound buttonhole maker.

In the days of meticulous tailoring, padding stitches were used on the roll line of the lapel at this point. But now, with our new tailoring methods, we home tailoresses have been getting along without padding stitches. However, since the finest men's tailors still use them to mold lapels, here's how and where (Fig. X-15). The roll line extends from the outside edge of the top buttonhole mark toward the neckline between the shoulder and center front. Roll the lapel over your hand with interfacing on top. Start your padding stitches about 1″ inside the roll line. Work the padding stitches up and down the lapel, being sure the right side stitches are invisible. Work inside the seam allowance line between the front and neck edges on both jacket front lapels.

Not all patterns indicate stay-stitching. This one does not, but it is always done first. Press and pin together the corresponding innerlining and outer fabric pieces, with the grain of each piece matching perfectly. Remember, this pattern has a straight skirt, and you only stay-stitch across the waistline edges and down the placket areas. You can finish this simple skirt in the same way as you made the one in Chapter 9.

Under section JACKET SEAMS on instruction sheet, follow

steps 1 and 2 (Fig. X-16A). After the shoulder edge has been closed on the ⅝" seam allowance, remove the basting across this portion, trim away the innerlining close to the seam, and press. Step 3 was done before the buttonholes were made. Refer to the new method of making an under-collar in Chapter 9 before following steps 4 through 7 (Fig. X-16B). Steps 8 through 16 on buttonholes were done with the bound buttonhole maker (Fig. X-16C). To begin the sleeves, follow steps 17 and 18. Before stitching up the sleeve seams, stay-stitch ½" from the edge of the cuff. With hem pressing gauge, press up the required sleeve hem width. Then follow steps 19 and 20 (Fig. X-16D).

Now for the section on JACKET COLLAR - FACING - HEMS, which is a new set of instructions. You have learned to first stay-stitch ½" from outside edges of all pieces like this before putting them together. Follow steps 1 and 2 here, but don't forget your careful pressing techniques and how to under-stitch at seam lines (Fig. X-17A). Before turning the corners of the front facings, rip out the baste-stitches which held the outer fabric and innerlining until the ⅝" seam was completed. Now, after you have trimmed and turned the seam, it will be knife-thin, as good tailored edges should be, without the bulk of any hair canvas to thicken them. After following step 3, stay-stitch ½" in from the bottom edge and pink with pinking shears. Press up the hem depth over the hem pressing gauge, and follow steps 4 through 7.

Braid is almost the trade mark of a Chanel suit. If some of the decorative wool, silk and leather braids are used, they may come already folded so you don't have to press a crease in them. In any event, follow steps 9 and 10 (Fig. X-17B). If there is a notch on a collar, run the braid around edge and miter it at the points. At the inside corner you fold it in reverse.

In section on LINING you begin with a new set of instructions again. Stay-stitch all off-grain edges of your lining pieces ½" from the edge, exactly as you did on outside pieces. Follow the lining instructions from step 1 through 3. Before stitching up the underarm seam at step 4 (Fig. X-18A) on the sleeve lining, stay-stitch the edge of the hem, then press up the hem depth over hem pressing gauge. Stitch the seam, press it open on a seam roll and press the hem edge at the seam line. At step 5, press up the lining hem depth over the hem pressing gauge and follow through to step 11 (Fig. X-18B). On step 12, pin up the hems of

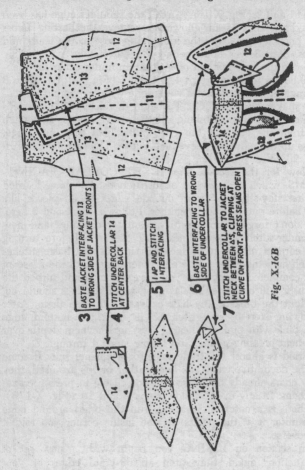

3 BASTE JACKET INTERFACING 13 TO WRONG SIDE OF JACKET FRONTS

4 STITCH UNDERCOLLAR 14 AT CENTER BACK

5 LAP AND STITCH INTERFACING

6 BASTE INTERFACING TO WRONG SIDE OF UNDERCOLLAR

7 STITCH UNDERCOLLAR TO JACKET NECK BETWEEN △5, CLIPPING AT CURVE ON FRONT, PRESS SEAMS OPEN

Fig. X-16B

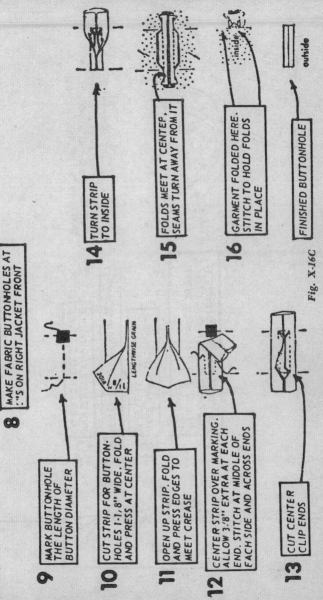

8 MAKE FABRIC BUTTONHOLES AT •"S ON RIGHT JACKET FRONT

9 MARK BUTTONHOLE THE LENGTH OF BUTTON DIAMETER

10 CUT STRIP FOR BUTTONHOLES 1-1.8" WIDE. FOLD AND PRESS AT CENTER

LENGTHWISE GRAIN

11 OPEN UP STRIP. FOLD AND PRESS EDGES TO MEET CREASE

12 CENTER STRIP OVER MARKING. ALLOW 3/8" EXTRA AT EACH END. STITCH AT MIDDLE OF EACH SIDE AND ACROSS ENDS

13 CUT CENTER CLIP ENDS

14 TURN STRIP TO INSIDE

15 FOLDS MEET AT CENTER. SEAMS TURN AWAY FROM IT

16 GARMENT FOLDED HERE. STITCH TO HOLD FOLDS IN PLACE

inside

outside

FINISHED BUTTONHOLE

Fig. X-16C

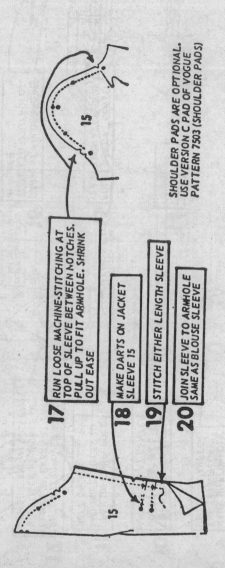

17 RUN LOOSE MACHINE-STITCHING AT TOP OF SLEEVE BETWEEN NOTCHES. PULL UP TO FIT ARMHOLE. SHRINK OUT EASE

18 MAKE DARTS ON JACKET SLEEVE 15

19 STITCH EITHER LENGTH SLEEVE

20 JOIN SLEEVE TO ARMHOLE SAME AS BLOUSE SLEEVE

SHOULDER PADS ARE OPTIONAL. USE VERSION C PAD OF VOGUE PATTERN 7503 (SHOULDER PADS)

Fig. X-16D

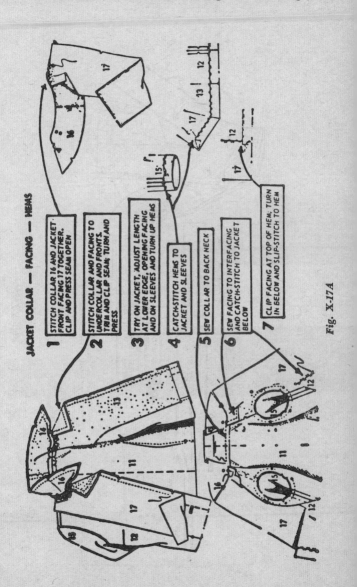

JACKET COLLAR — FACING — HEMS

1. STITCH COLLAR 16 AND JACKET FRONT FACING 17 TOGETHER. CLIP AND PRESS SEAM OPEN.

2. STITCH COLLAR AND FACING TO UNDERCOLLAR AND FRONTS. TRIM AND CLIP SEAM; TURN AND PRESS

3. TRY ON JACKET, ADJUST LENGTH AT LOWER EDGE, OPENING FACING AND ON SLEEVES AND TURN UP HEMS

4. CATCH-STITCH HEMS TO JACKET AND SLEEVES

5. SEW COLLAR TO BACK NECK

6. SEW FACING TO INTERFACING AND CATCH-STITCH TO JACKET BELOW

7. CLIP FACING AT TOP OF HEM; TURN IN BELOW AND SLIP-STITCH TO HEM

Fig. X-17A

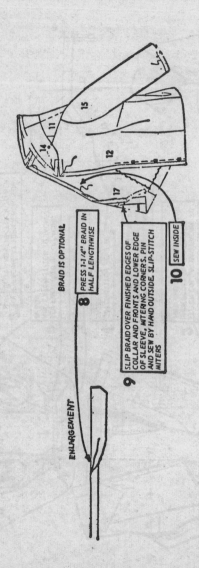

BRAID IS OPTIONAL

8 PRESS 1-1/4" BRAID IN HALF LENGTHWISE

9 SLIP BRAID OVER FINISHED EDGES OF COLLAR AND FRONTS AND LOWER EDGE OF SLEEVE, MITERING CORNERS. PIN AND SEW BY HAND OUTSIDE, SLIP-STITCH MITERS

10 SEW INSIDE

ENLARGEMENT

15
11
14
12
17

Fig. X-17B

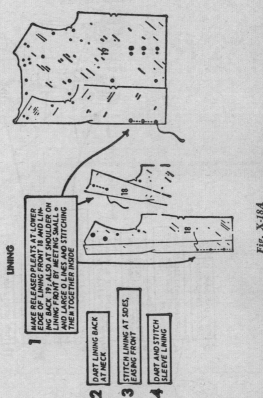

LINING

1 MAKE RELEASED PLEATS AT LOWER EDGE OF LINING FRONT 18 AND LINING BACK 19; ALSO AT SHOULDER ON LINING FRONT BY MEETING SMALL o AND LARGE O LINES AND STITCHING THEM TOGETHER INSIDE

2 DART LINING BACK AT NECK

3 STITCH LINING AT SIDES, EASING FRONT

4 DART AND STITCH SLEEVE LINING

Fig. X-18A

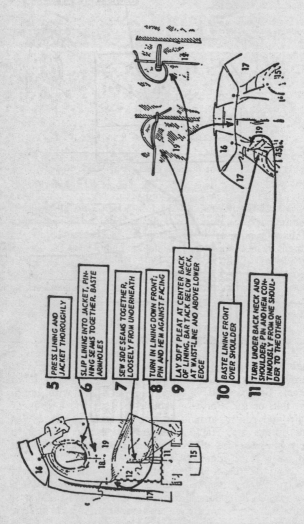

5 PRESS LINING AND JACKET THOROUGHLY

6 SLIP LINING INTO JACKET, PINNING SEAMS TOGETHER, BASTE ARMHOLES

7 SEW SIDE SEAMS TOGETHER, LOOSELY FROM UNDERNEATH

8 TURN IN LINING DOWN FRONT; PIN AND HEM AGAINST FACING

9 LAY SOFT PLEAT AT CENTER BACK OF LINING, BAR TACK BELOW NECK, AT WAISTLINE AND ABOVE LOWER EDGE

10 BASTE LINING FRONT OVER SHOULDER

11 TURN UNDER BACK NECK AND SHOULDER; PIN AND HEM CONTINUOSLY FROM ONE SHOULDER TO THE OTHER

Fig. X-18B

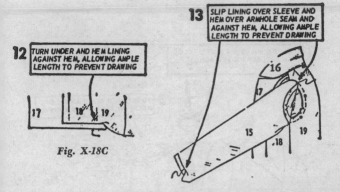

12 TURN UNDER AND HEM LINING AGAINST HEM, ALLOWING AMPLE LENGTH TO PREVENT DRAWING

13 SLIP LINING OVER SLEEVE AND HEM OVER ARMHOLE SEAM AND AGAINST HEM, ALLOWING AMPLE LENGTH TO PREVENT DRAWING

Fig. X-18C

the jacket and sleeves at the seams and at one or two places between. Try on the jacket to be sure the hem does not peep out from the sleeves or around the bottom edge. You can seam-bind the edge of jacket lining hem and blind stitch it separately if you wish. Bar-tack the hem at the side and center back seams or follow step 12. On step 13, if no adjustment is necessary at the sleeve hem, turn the sleeve wrong-side out (Fig. X-18C). Fold the lining back about ½" inside the pressed crease and blind hem at this point to the sleeve cuff. This allows a little "give" in movement, so the lining does not rip loose.

Section on FASTENING - TOP COLLAR: Before slashing the buttonhole facings at step 1, remember the much nicer finish you learned in Chapter 9. Also, on step 2 (Fig. X-19A), if you have used a fancy braid trimming, it is possible to make matching braid buttons with pieces of your braid that are left over (if the buttons are not larger than 1" in diameter). Self-covered buttons can be made with braid, leather, felt, or fur. For larger braid buttons use a gimp or ¼" braid and sew it around in a swirl from center out to turn of button top. Hand stitch it to a fabric backing to which you apply the aluminum foil pattern, and cut out around the pattern edges to make button.

You wouldn't use a velvet collar if you used the braid trim. Velvet collars are always added to another collar, seldom made a part of a collar because too frequently cleaning is necessary and velvet usually makes a garment look too wintry. So to add the elegance of a velvet collar, follow steps 3 and 4 (Fig. X-19B).

FASTENING — TOP COLLAR

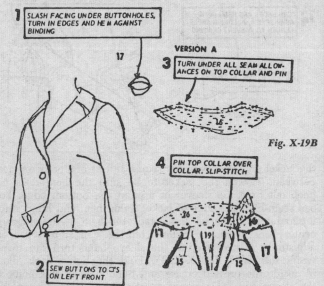

1 SLASH FACING UNDER BUTTONHOLES, TURN IN EDGES AND HEM AGAINST BINDING

17

VERSION A

3 TURN UNDER ALL SEAM ALLOWANCES ON TOP COLLAR AND PIN

16

Fig. X-19B

4 PIN TOP COLLAR OVER COLLAR. SLIP-STITCH

26

16

17   19   17

15   15

2 SEW BUTTONS TO □'S ON LEFT FRONT

Fig. X-19A

Perhaps you would like another version of a buttonhole to match the velvet collar. This is particularly smart on a black duvetyn, zibaline, or broadcloth. Why not try the decorative and easy to make triangular buttonhole? Remember, this decision should be made before you sew front and back pieces together so the buttonholes can be made in the flat. However, I have changed buttonholes in a finished suit easily enough. I ripped out the old buttonhole welts, pressed the slashes together and held them in place with transparent adhesive tape until new satin triangular wedges were made over them. These new triangular buttonholes (Fig. X-20) are made with a package that includes a plastic wedge pattern the right size, together with complete directions. Little touches like these are what turn an otherwise very plain style into a chic fashion that looks very expensive.

Before we leave the suit department, I should like to bring up a difficult detail, the gusset-type corner (Fig. X-21), that

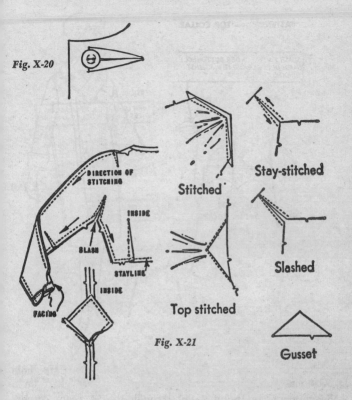

Fig. X-20

DIRECTION OF STITCHING

INSIDE

SLASH

STAYLINE

INSIDE

FACING

Stitched

Top stitched

Fig. X-21

Stay-stitched

Slashed

Gusset

one often finds in dressmaker suits and dresses. On the tissue pattern you find a slash mark. Here is a spot that should always be traced carefully, even though you may not trace all seam allowances. Mark the corner of the corresponding piece as well. In this detail of your sewing try to work on as flat a piece as possible to avoid too much fabric bulk in your way. On the wrong side, under the point to be slashed, press a small piece of *Fabri-mend*. Now stay-stitch very slightly inside the marked line, with shorter stitches on each side of the point and 3 stitches across it. Stay-stitch on the line of the other piece also. With the right sides together, match the raw edges of the slashed area and the piece that has to fit it. Slash up to (not into) the corner on the slash marking. Poke a pin up through the stay-stitched point on

Fig. X-22
Set-in Pocket

Fig. X-23
Simple Coat Style

the garment and bring it out through the ⅝″ seam corner line on the other piece. With garment side up, from the edge of the garment up to the point, stitch one thread beyond the stay-stitching, using small stitches for ½″ around each side of the point. Take a stitch or two straight across the point. To turn fabric neatly at the point, keep the needle down at the turn, raise the presser foot, turn and smooth the fabric with your fingers so it will lie flat behind the needle, then lower the presser foot. Try to keep the raw edges matched all the way.

If your pattern has pockets, the instructions are usually very detailed. When you make a slashed pocket, use the same kind of thread ladder and markings as you do when making bound buttonholes. When you make a patch pocket, remember you can make it a lot more uniform if you first stay-stitch, then press the seam allowance and hem edges over a hem pressing gauge. To shape the top of pockets your see-through scalloper might be helpful (Fig. X-22). Press on non-woven interfacing in the areas that must be slashed or to support welts and pocket flaps, to give you a crisp, tailored turn. Under-press the inside edge of a hidden pocket that goes into a seam so it will not have a tendency to stick out.

▶ Simple Coat

Now, let's make a coat and interpolate another pattern instruction sheet (Fig. X-23). This coat will be made of a bulky fleece and again we take liberties with the construction of the front because of two buttonholes. Wouldn't it be awful to put seams together and have to drag around all that heavy bulk for those two small openings? This pattern does not show any stay-stitching, either, but you have learned the rules in your basic sewing, so follow them forever and forever. Incidentally, you could cut out this heavy fleece coat, double thickness, with your electric scissors.

The pattern instructs us to interface the front edges, but if we did it on this bulky material exactly according to the instructions and used the right weight coat-type hair canvas interfacing, we simply could not get a good-looking, flat, tailored edge. So, after cutting out interfacing, something must be done to make the edges thinner as they turn on the seam. Cut a 1¼″ strip of unbleached muslin just like the front edge of the tissue pattern, on identical grain, as an interfacing edge (Fig. X-24A). Also, cut enough 3″ bias of muslin to cushion the coat hem (Fig. X-24B). Cut a similar 1¼″ muslin strip to outline the cuff edges, like cuff interfacing pieces (Fig. X-24C). When you have cut the interfacing for the under-collar, prepare 1⅛″ muslin edges for it (Fig. X-24D). Because heavy fabric sags through the shoulders, cut a piece of muslin from the back pattern and follow down about 5″ from the center back of the neck (Fig. X-24E). Now, stitch the muslin edge to the front of the interfacing, ⅞″ from the edge, and also at inside edge of muslin. Press and trim away the hair canvas to the ⅞″ line of stitching.

Stay-stitch the neck, shoulder, armhole and front edges of the coat front pieces. Stitch the darts. With this very bulky fabric, slash the dart to within 1″ of the end and press it open over the tailor's ham to make it look flatter. Place

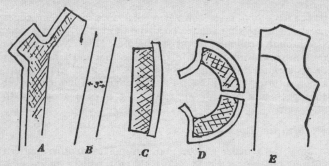

Fig. X-24   Softening Interfacing Edge

the interfacing to underside of the coat fronts, muslin strip facing coat. On both front edges stitch exactly on the ⅝" seam line.

The lapel and under-collar area of the coat is where a tailor might work padding stitches, as on our suit. However, many of our most expensive custom garments show a machine-stitched design on the under-collar. If you'll learn to stitch it neatly, as given here, you will really accomplish a modern tailoring technique.

According to the pattern instruction sheet, the buttonholes are only mentioned briefly in step 23. Also, the pocket (note enlargement detail on step 12) is more easily done before constructing the coat shell. Nevertheless, if you are going to make buttonholes and pocket now, it must be done only after you have assured yourself with a pre-fitting of the pattern that they are in exactly the right place as marked.

On the right front, the two buttonholes have been marked on the interfacing, and the pocket has been marked on the wrong side of the coat fabric. So, baste-stitch the contrasting color ladders over both the buttonhole and pocket areas. From the same instructions on that page, continue to work your bound buttonholes with the help of the bound buttonhole maker. In the case of a very heavy fleece fabric, you could make bias buttonhole welts. On the wrong side of these welts and on the pocket flap, press on adhesive type interfacing. Also use a bit of this press-on fabric on the under side of the pocket area. It will help keep the pocket from stretching. At the point of making buttonholes, just before turning the welts to the wrong side, cord each side by running through a needleful of tapestry yarn.

Under the section on COAT SEAMS (Figs. X-25A1 & 2),

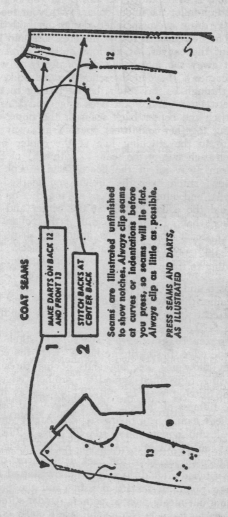

COAT SEAMS

1 MAKE DARTS ON BACK 12 AND FRONT 13

2 STITCH BACKS AT CENTER BACK

Seams are illustrated unfinished to show notches. Always clip seams at curves or indentations before you press, so seams will lie flat. Always clip as little as possible.

PRESS SEAMS AND DARTS, AS ILLUSTRATED

Fig. X-25A1

after you have constructed the pocket according to steps 10 through 18, go back to steps 1 through 4, up to where the under-collar is to be added. At this point you begin to learn how to stitch-tailor the under-collar. With your see-thru ruler and chalk, draw a crosshatched design on both interfacing pieces. The design must follow the crosswise and lengthwise threads of the canvas. At all four outside corners of each half, cut away the interfacing diagonally so it will be out of the corner ¼″ beyond the seam to avoid bulk. Following steps 5 through 7, stay-stitch the interfacing to the under-collar between ½″ and ⅝″ at neck edge and ¼″ from outer edge. Stitch the center back seam of the under-collar and interfacing together and press open. Trim away the interfacing up to the stitching line at the center back seam. Top-stitch each side of the seam to within ¼″ of the outside edge. Trim away all of the fleece seam except the lower edge. Now, stitch over the design you marked until the under-collar and interfacing pieces are together on grain both ways. Fold the collar in half at the center and pin down on a tailor's ham, forming the roll of the collar, and mold with your steam iron. Press on grain and shape the collar edges as they should fit the back of your neck. Trim away the interfacing to the ¼″ stay-stitching line and trim the wool to a point at the center back seam (Fig. X-25B). Follow steps 8 and 9 (Fig. X-25C).

Remember that steps 10 through 18 were done before the seams of coat were joined, to avoid bulk in handling (Figs. X-25D 1 & 2).

Skip to step 19. On sleeve piece 19, stay-stitch ¼″ around the outside edge. Baste-stitch a line ½″ from the edge within the seam allowance, keeping ends of the thread free for slight easing. Stay-stitch around the armhole edge of sleeve piece 18. Stitch pieces 18 and 19 together as in step 21. Ease the fullness of the cap of the sleeve and press over a dressmaker's ham. Then, follow step 22. Aren't you glad you didn't wait until now to follow step 23 (Fig. X-25E)?

Section on COLLAR - FACING - HEMS (Fig. X-26A): Stitch the collar facing at the back of the neck, only if you first stay-stitched around the edges. Follow steps 1 through 4, using your point presser for pressing and the point turner for digging out nicely pointed corners. Under-stitch between as many corners as you can on the inside collar edge. When you do outer pressing on the collar edge, use your pounding block to get as sharp edges as possible in this bulky wool.

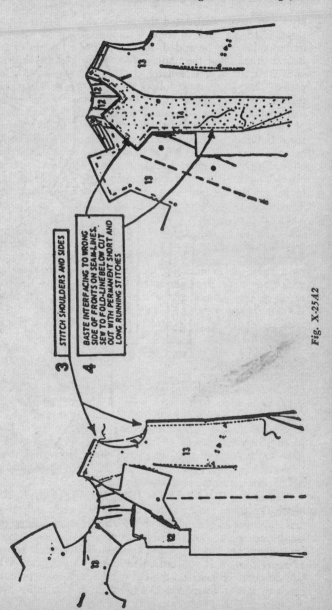

3 STITCH SHOULDERS AND SIDES

4 BASTE INTERFACING TO WRONG SIDE OF FRONTS ON SEAM-LINES. SEW TO FOLD-LINE BELOW CUT OUT WITH PERMANENT SHORT AND LONG RUNNING STITCHES

Fig. X-25A2

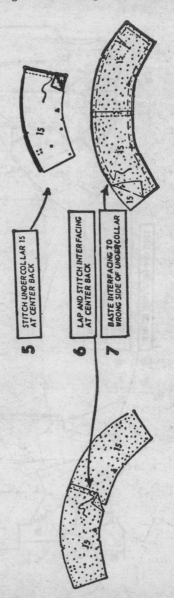

5 STITCH UNDERCOLLAR 15 AT CENTER BACK

6 LAP AND STITCH INTERFACING AT CENTER BACK

7 BASTE INTERFACING TO WRONG SIDE OF UNDERCOLLAR

Fig. X-25B

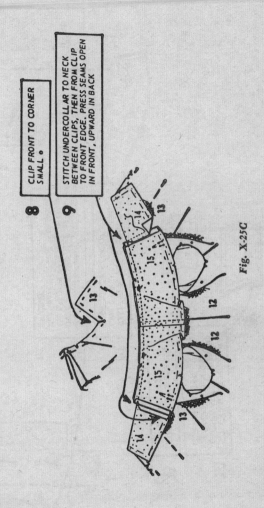

8   CLIP FRONT TO CORNER SMALL o

9   STITCH UNDERCOLLAR TO NECK BETWEEN CLIPS, THEN FROM CLIP TO FRONT EDGE. PRESS SEAMS OPEN IN FRONT, UPWARD IN BACK

Fig. X-25C

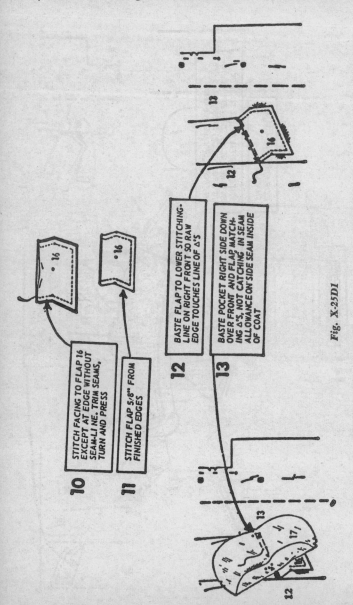

10 STITCH FACING TO FLAP 16 EXCEPT AT EDGE WITHOUT SEAM-LI NE. TRIM SEAMS, TURN AND PRESS

11 STITCH FLAP 5-8" FROM FINISHED EDGES

12 BASTE FLAP TO LOWER STITCHING-LINE ON RIGHT FRONT SO RAW EDGE TOUCHES LINE OF △'S

13 BASTE POCKET RIGHT SIDE DOWN OVER FRONT AND FLAP MATCH-ING △'S, NOT CATCHING IN SEAM ALLOWANCE ON SIDE SEAM INSIDE OF COAT

Fig. X-25DI

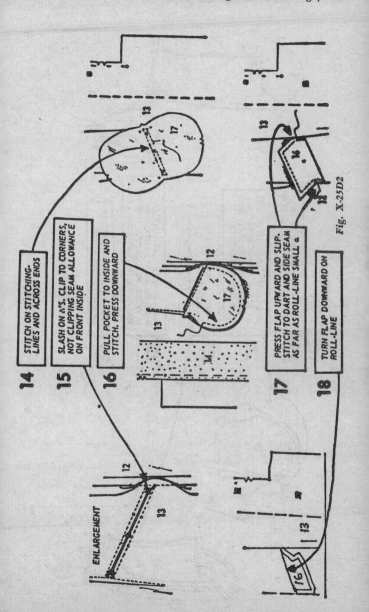

14 STITCH ON STITCHING-LINES AND ACROSS ENDS

15 SLASH ON Δ'S, CLIP TO CORNERS, NOT CLIPPING SEAM ALLOWANCE ON FRONT INSIDE

16 PULL POCKET TO INSIDE AND STITCH. PRESS DOWNWARD

17 PRESS FLAP UPWARD AND SLIP-STITCH TO DART AND SIDE SEAM AS FAR AS ROLL-LINE SMALL α

18 TURN FLAP DOWNWARD ON ROLL-LINE

ENLARGEMENT

Fig. X-25D2

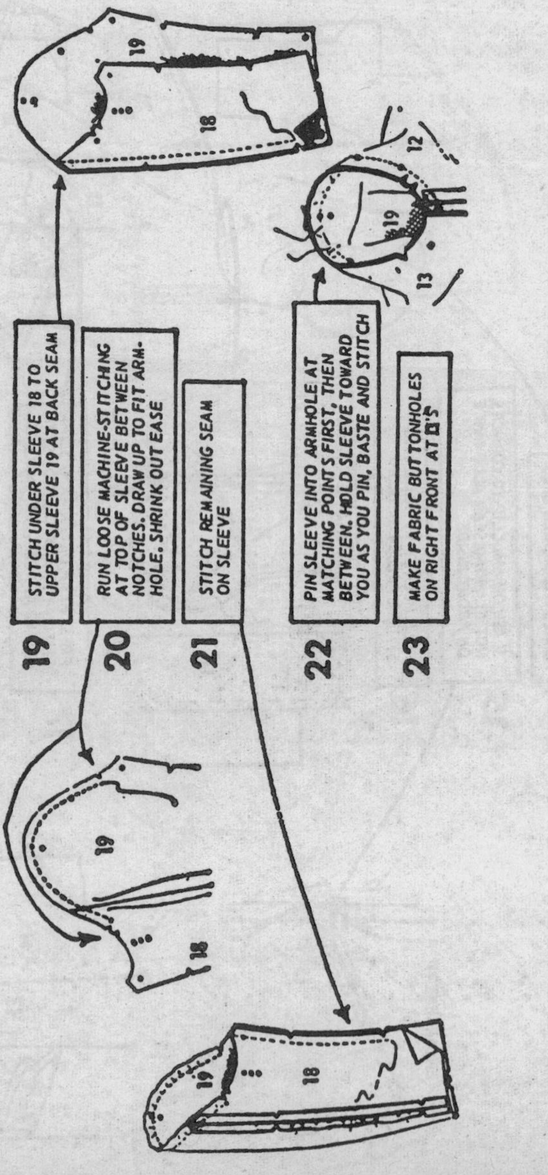

19 STITCH UNDER SLEEVE 18 TO UPPER SLEEVE 19 AT BACK SEAM

20 RUN LOOSE MACHINE-STITCHING AT TOP OF SLEEVE BETWEEN NOTCHES. DRAW UP TO FIT ARMHOLE. SHRINK OUT EASE

21 STITCH REMAINING SEAM ON SLEEVE

22 PIN SLEEVE INTO ARMHOLE AT MATCHING POINTS FIRST, THEN BETWEEN. HOLD SLEEVE TOWARD YOU AS YOU PIN, BASTE AND STITCH

23 MAKE FABRIC BUTTONHOLES ON RIGHT FRONT AT ☒'S

Fig. X-25E

COLLAR — FACING — HEMS

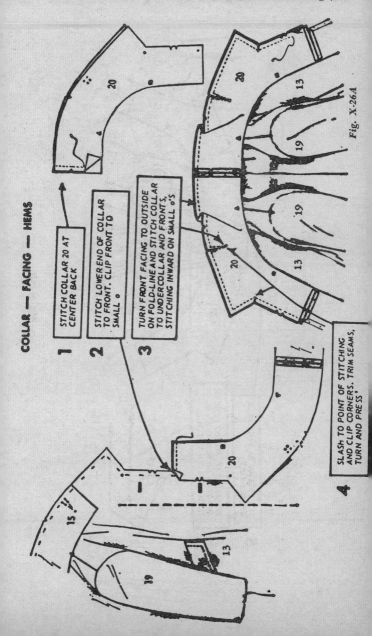

1 STITCH COLLAR 20 AT CENTER BACK

2 STITCH LOWER END OF COLLAR TO FRONT, CLIP FRONT TO SMALL o

3 TURN FRONT FACING TO OUTSIDE ON FOLD-LINE AND STITCH COLLAR TO UNDERCOLLAR AND FRONTS, STITCHING INWARD ON SMALL o'S

4 SLASH TO POINT OF STITCHING AND CLIP CORNERS. TRIM SEAMS, TURN AND PRESS

Fig. X-26A

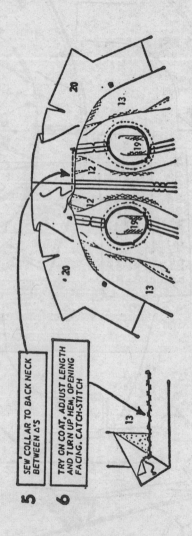

5 SEW COLLAR TO BACK NECK BETWEEN △'S

6 TRY ON COAT, ADJUST LENGTH AND TURN UP HEM, OPENING FACING. CATCH-STITCH

Fig. X-26B

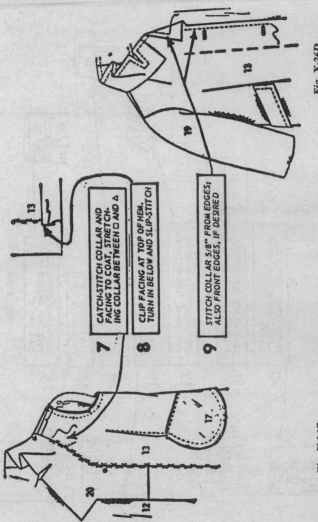

7 CATCH-STITCH COLLAR AND FACING TO COAT, STRETCH-ING COLLAR BETWEEN □ AND △

8 CLIP FACING AT TOP OF HEM. TURN IN BELOW AND SLIP-STITCH

9 STITCH COLLAR 5/8" FROM EDGES; ALSO FRONT EDGES, IF DESIRED

Fig. X-26C

Fig. X-26D

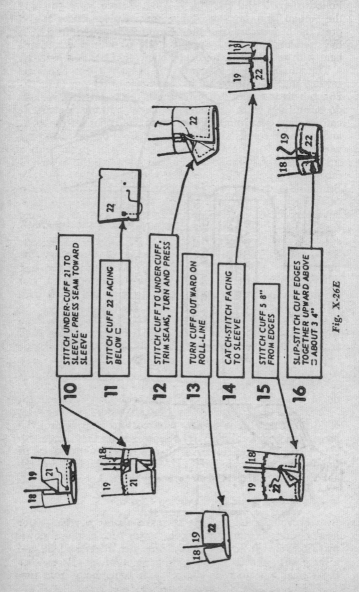

10 STITCH UNDER-CUFF 21 TO SLEEVE. PRESS SEAM TOWARD SLEEVE

11 STITCH CUFF 22 FACING BELOW □

12 STITCH CUFF TO UNDERCUFF. TRIM SEAMS, TURN AND PRESS

13 TURN CUFF OUTWARD ON ROLL-LINE

14 CATCH-STITCH FACING TO SLEEVE

15 STITCH CUFF 5 8" FROM EDGES

16 SLIP-STITCH CUFF EDGES TOGETHER UPWARD ABOVE □ ABOUT 3 4"

Fig. X-26E

Follow steps 5 and 6 (Fig. X-26B). Before catch-stitching the bottom hem, lay the 3" bias muslin piece under it and press the hem crease over the hem pressing gauge. In step 7, the stretching is aided by pressing and pounding over tailor's ham with the pounding block. Follow step 8 (Fig. X-26C).

The stitching that is mentioned in step 9 can either be sewing machine stitching or hand pickstitching (Fig. X-26D). This is a very expensive finish that a home sewer can do beautifully with a matching color of buttonhole twist. It can be done all around the edges of the collar on the coat, and around the cuffs and pockets flap. Hold the piece you are working on with right side towards you and begin with a small back stitch. Slide the needle between the layers of fabric and pick up another tiny stitch on the wrong side. Bring the needle to the right side again and take another small back-stitch. When you are working on the roll of a lapel, remember that the underside is the right side, so bring the needle all the way through the fabric and do the back stitch on the lapel side.

Continue with step 10, remembering to trim away the bulk on the seam before pressing. Now interface the cuff edge as you did the lapel. Follow steps 11 through 14, and in step 14, pickstitch the edge of the cuff and finish with step 16 (Fig. X-26E).

Section on LINING - BUTTONING (Fig. X-27A): Stay-stitch all off-grain edges of the lining pieces and follow all instructions from steps 1 through 13. Follow the instructions for finishing buttonhole facings given in Chapter 9 (Fig. X-27B). Self-covered buttons come in all the larger sizes that would be appropriate for this coat. Or, choose attractive metal, bone, or other type coat buttons to match or contrast.

It is sometimes a good thing to use weights at the hem of a suit or the front corners of a coat to help control the hang. You can buy them ready-covered, or they come un-covered so that you can cover them yourself with a piece of lining fabric. If you don't like the size, you can cut the almost butter-soft lead with ordinary shears.

▶ Advanced Sewing: Evening Clothes

By now you should be able to make almost anything your heart desires, including glamorous gowns such as those shown in (Fig. X-28). You will see in both styles there is a long and a short version of the same pattern, so you may select either the formal or informal length. With some help from me,

BUTTONING

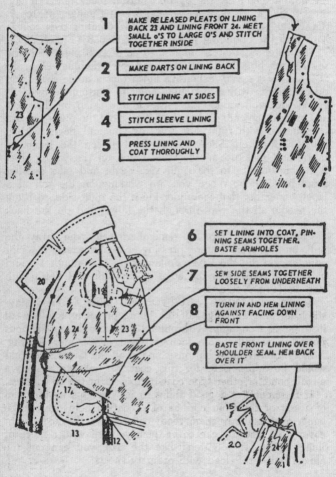

1 MAKE RELEASED PLEATS ON LINING BACK 23 AND LINING FRONT 24. MEET SMALL o'S TO LARGE O'S AND STITCH TOGETHER INSIDE

2 MAKE DARTS ON LINING BACK

3 STITCH LINING AT SIDES

4 STITCH SLEEVE LINING

5 PRESS LINING AND COAT THOROUGHLY

6 SET LINING INTO COAT, PINNING SEAMS TOGETHER. BASTE ARMHOLES

7 SEW SIDE SEAMS TOGETHER LOOSELY FROM UNDERNEATH

8 TURN IN AND HEM LINING AGAINST FACING DOWN FRONT

9 BASTE FRONT LINING OVER SHOULDER SEAM. HEM BACK OVER IT

Fig. X-27A

learning to use your new tools, lots more knowledge on how to follow and interpolate pattern instruction sheets, and much more practice, I hope you feel as I do that every new sewing project is an adventure. See (Fig. X-29) for complete instructions for constructing an evening dress.

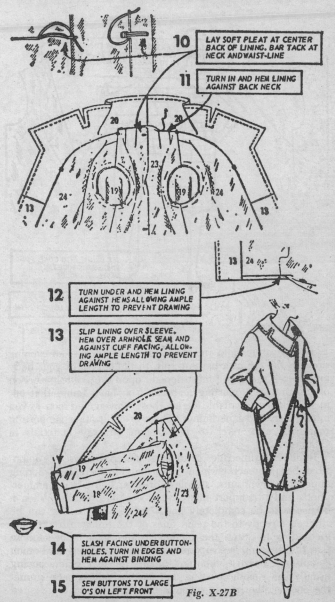

10 LAY SOFT PLEAT AT CENTER BACK OF LINING. BAR TACK AT NECK AND WAIST-LINE

11 TURN IN AND HEM LINING AGAINST BACK NECK

12 TURN UNDER AND HEM LINING AGAINST HEMS ALLOWING AMPLE LENGTH TO PREVENT DRAWING

13 SLIP LINING OVER SLEEVE. HEM OVER ARMHOLE SEAM AND AGAINST CUFF FACING, ALLOWING AMPLE LENGTH TO PREVENT DRAWING

14 SLASH FACING UNDER BUTTONHOLES. TURN IN EDGES AND HEM AGAINST BINDING

15 SEW BUTTONS TO LARGE O'S ON LEFT FRONT

Fig. X-27B

Fig. X-28

To intricately mold and shape anything, such as an evening dress or the top of a bathing suit, to the curves of your body and keep it there, you must depend upon the skillful selection of the proper supporting material. You have found that out in the choices available of all those woven and non-woven interfacings and innerlinings. There are still other supporting materials, also, refer to the section on stay materials in Chapter 2.

Rigid, inflexible rules as to what material to use are imposible, because each garment is an individual creation. Boning appears in swimsuits, strapless dresses, belts, and cummerbunds and to support many other costume details. When a bodice is to be completely lined, an encased boning can be stitched directly to the seam lines of the lining. An alternate method is to stitch the boning to the seam allowance so that the stitching is completely invisible. Encasing the boning is optional because the best quality of real featherboning usually has a cloth covering that may be pulled back around the ends of the boning when it has been cut to the desired

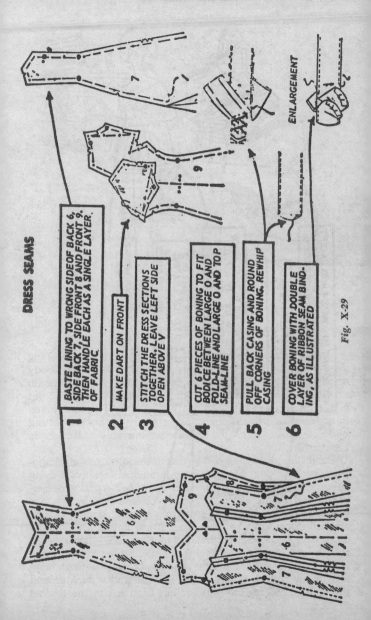

DRESS SEAMS

1 BASTE LINING TO WRONG SIDE OF BACK 6, SIDE BACK 7, SIDE FRONT 8 AND FRONT 9. THEN HANDLE EACH AS A SINGLE LAYER OF FABRIC.

2 MAKE DART ON FRONT

3 STITCH THE DRESS SECTIONS TOGETHER, LEAVE LEFT SIDE OPEN ABOVE V

4 CUT 6 PIECES OF BONING TO FIT BODICE BETWEEN LARGE O AND FOLD-LINE AND LARGE O AND TOP SEAM-LINE

5 PULL BACK CASING AND ROUND OFF CORNERS OF BONING. REWHIP CASING

6 COVER BONING WITH DOUBLE LAYER OF RIBBON SEAM BINDING, AS ILLUSTRATED

ENLARGEMENT

Fig. X-29

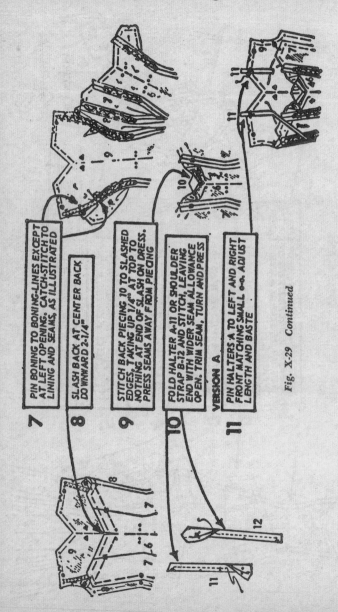

7 PIN BONING TO BONING-LINES EXCEPT AT LEFT OPENING. CATCH-STITCH TO LINING AND SEAMS, AS ILLUSTRATED

8 SLASH BACK AT CENTER BACK DOWNWARD 2-1/4"

9 STITCH BACK PIECING 10 TO SLASHED EDGES, TAKING UP 1/8" AT TOP TO NOTHING AT END OF SLASH ON DRESS. PRESS SEAMS AWAY FROM PIECING

10 FOLD HALTER A-11 OR SHOULDER STRAP B-12 AND STITCH, LEAVING END WITH WIDER SEAM ALLOWANCE OPEN. TRIM SEAM, TURN AND PRESS

VERSION A

11 PIN HALTERS A TO LEFT AND RIGHT FRONT MATCHING SMALL ↔ ADJUST LENGTH AND BASTE

Fig. X-29 *Continued*

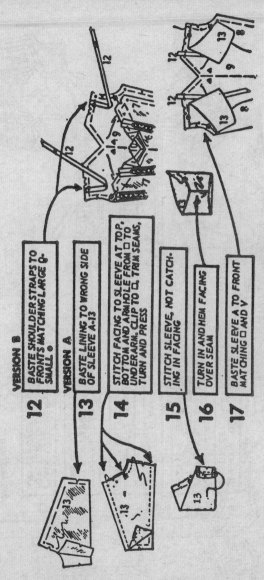

VERSION B

12 BASTE SHOULDER STRAPS TO FRONTS MATCHING LARGE O-SMALL o.

VERSION A

13 BASTE LINING TO WRONG SIDE OF SLEEVE A-13

14 STITCH FACING TO SLEEVE AT TOP, BOTTOM AND ARMHOLE FROM □ TO □. UNDERARM, CLIP TO □, TRIM SEAMS, TURN AND PRESS

15 STITCH SLEEVE, NOT CATCHING IN FACING

16 TURN IN AND HEM FACING OVER SEAM

17 BASTE SLEEVE A TO FRONT MATCHING □ AND V

Fig. X-29 Continued

BOW — SHOULDER STRAPS — HEMS

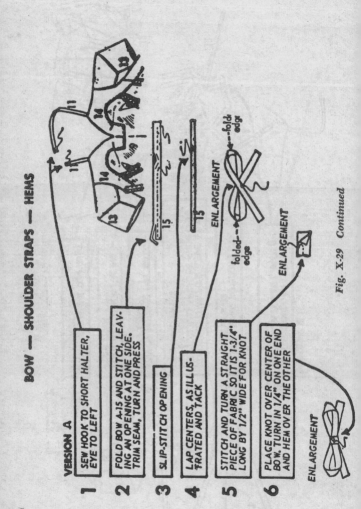

VERSION A

1 SEW HOOK TO SHORT HALTER, EYE TO LEFT

2 FOLD BOW A-15 AND STITCH, LEAVING AN OPENING AT ONE SIDE. TRIM SEAM, TURN AND PRESS.

3 SLIP-STITCH OPENING

4 LAP CENTERS, AS ILLUSTRATED AND TACK

5 STITCH AND TURN A STRAIGHT PIECE OF FABRIC SO IT IS 1-3/4" LONG BY 1/2" WIDE FOR KNOT

6 PLACE KNOT OVER CENTER OF BOW, TURN IN 1/4" ON ONE END AND HEM OVER THE OTHER

ENLARGEMENT

ENLARGEMENT

ENLARGEMENT

Fig. X-29 *Continued*

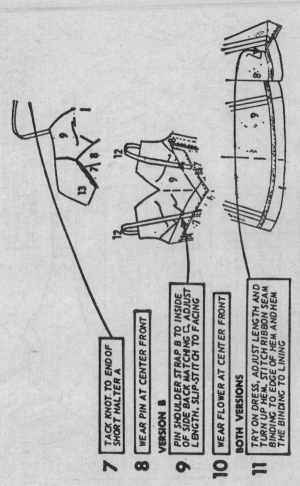

Fig. X-29 Continued

7 TACK KNOT TO END OF SHORT HALTER A

8 WEAR PIN AT CENTER FRONT

VERSION B

9 PIN SHOULDER STRAP B TO INSIDE OF SIDE BACK MATCHING C. ADJUST LENGTH. SLIP-STITCH TO FACING

10 WEAR FLOWER AT CENTER FRONT

BOTH VERSIONS

11 TRY ON DRESS, ADJUST LENGTH AND TURN UP HEM. STITCH RIBBON SEAM BINDING TO EDGE OF HEM AND HEM THE BINDING TO LINING

FACINGS — ZIPPER — INSIDE BELTING

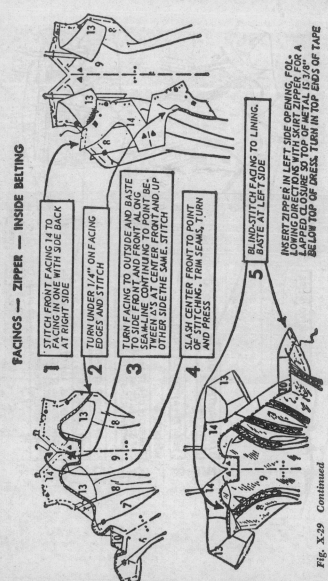

1 STITCH FRONT FACING 14 TO FACING IN ONE WITH SIDE BACK AT RIGHT SIDE

2 TURN UNDER 1/4" ON FACING EDGES AND STITCH

3 TURN FACING TO OUTSIDE AND BASTE TO SIDE FRONT AND FRONT ALONG SEAM-LINE CONTINUING TO POINT BETWEEN △'S AT CENTER FRONT AND UP OTHER SIDE THE SAME. STITCH

4 SLASH CENTER FRONT TO POINT OF STITCHING. TRIM SEAMS, TURN AND PRESS

5 BLIND-STITCH FACING TO LINING. BASTE AT LEFT SIDE

INSERT ZIPPER IN LEFT SIDE OPENING, FOLLOWING DIRECTIONS WITH SKIRT ZIPPER FOR A LAPPED CLOSURE SO TOP OF METAL IS 3/8" BELOW TOP OF DRESS. TURN IN TOP ENDS OF TAPE

Fig. X-29 *Continued*

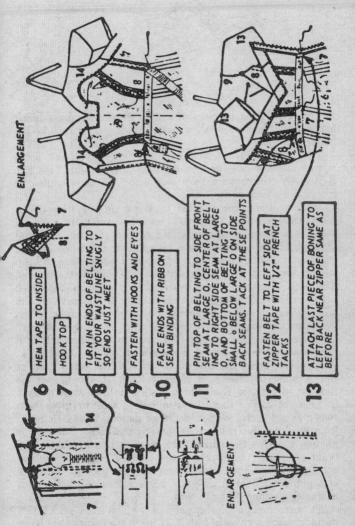

ENLARGEMENT

6 HEM TAPE TO INSIDE

7 HOOK TOP

8 TURN IN ENDS OF BELTING TO FIT YOUR WAISTLINE SNUGLY SO ENDS JUST MEET

9 FASTEN WITH HOOKS AND EYES

10 FACE ENDS WITH RIBBON SEAM BINDING

11 PIN TOP OF BELTING TO SIDE FRONT SEAM AT LARGE O, CENTER OF BELTING TO RIGHT SIDE SEAM AT LARGE O, AND BOTTOM OF BELTING TO SMALL o BELOW LARGE O ON SIDE BACK SEAMS, TACK AT THESE POINTS

12 FASTEN BELT TO LEFT SIDE AT ZIPPER TAPE WITH 1/2" FRENCH TACKS

13 ATTACH LAST PIECE OF BONING TO LEFT BACK NEAR ZIPPER SAME AS BEFORE

ENLARGEMENT

Fig. X-29 Continued

Fig. X-30

length. Twill tape or bias casings to match the dress fabric make a neat finish and their use enables you to remove the boning if desired.

The bodice may be completely boned throughout as in steps 4 through 7 of our evening dress sewing guide (*see* Fig. X-29). Or, the boning may stop short of the bustline to create a smooth midriff.

Some of the recommended uses for zig-zag wires (Fig. X-30) are in collars to give a smooth, permanent roll and stand, also in tabs and necklines to prevent drooping and sagging, as well as in the sides of cummerbund belts. Zig-zag wires may be shaped around the top of a decolletage to keep it from gapping. You never can do this with featherboning. The wire is usually sewn by hand to the seam allowance between the facing and the interfacing. Each curve of the wire, as well as the ends, should be fastened securely. When pressing a garment that contains the wire, special care should be exercised to pad that area so that imprints will not show on the outside of the garment.

Horsehair braid from ½" to 3" in width is often used at the hemline to create an elegant flare. It should not be thought of just for thin, filmy fabrics. I have seen it used in hems of heavy damask satin ball gowns to give them sweep as a graceful woman walks or dances. Horsehair braid is applied to the hemline to add extra body. Since it is pliable, it allows the garment to hang in billowy folds. The braid is usually placed along the creased edge of the hem and sewn into a thin fold. It may also be used at the edge of a petticoat. It most certainly holds ruffles and hems with character so they will not wilt.

The construction of the petticoat which goes under this evening gown is given in Fig. X-31 up to the point of applying the horse hair braid. Steps 8 and 9 give the details for doing this. Sometimes it has to be fulled a bit, and there is a little string at one edge so that you can pull it and gather to any desired extent.

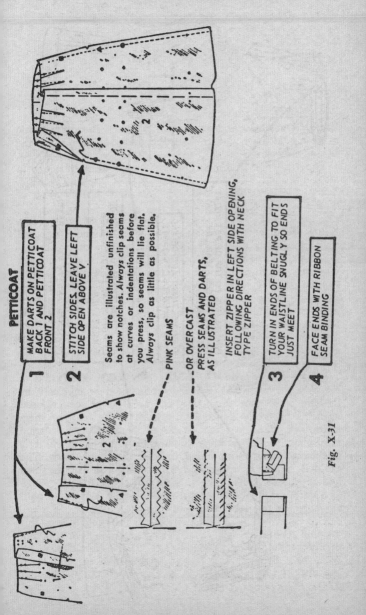

PETTICOAT

1 MAKE DARTS ON PETTICOAT BACK 1 AND PETTICOAT FRONT 2

2 STITCH SIDES, LEAVE LEFT SIDE OPEN ABOVE V.

Seams are illustrated unfinished to show notches. Always clip seams at curves or indentations before you press, so seams will lie flat. Always clip as little as possible.

PINK SEAMS

OR OVERCAST

PRESS SEAMS AND DARTS, AS ILLUSTRATED

INSERT ZIPPER IN LEFT SIDE OPENING, FOLLOWING DIRECTIONS WITH NECK TYPE ZIPPER

3 TURN IN ENDS OF BELTING TO FIT YOUR WAISTLINE SNUGLY SO ENDS JUST MEET

4 FACE ENDS WITH RIBBON SEAM BINDING

Fig. X-31

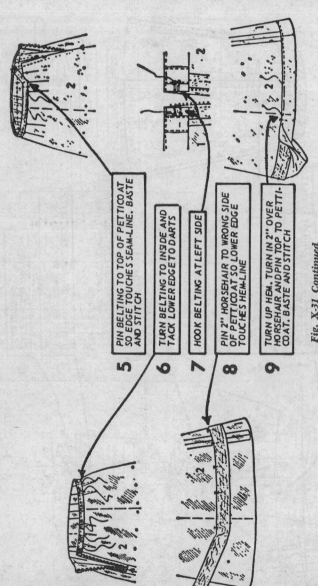

5 PIN BELTING TO TOP OF PETTICOAT SO EDGE TOUCHES SEAM-LINE. BASTE AND STITCH

6 TURN BELTING TO INSIDE AND TACK LOWER EDGE TO DARTS

7 HOOK BELTING AT LEFT SIDE

8 PIN 2" HORSEHAIR TO WRONG SIDE OF PETTICOAT SO LOWER EDGE TOUCHES HEM-LINE

9 TURN UP HEM. TURN IN 2" OVER HORSEHAIR AND PIN TOP TO PETTICOAT. BASTE AND STITCH

Fig. X-31 Continued

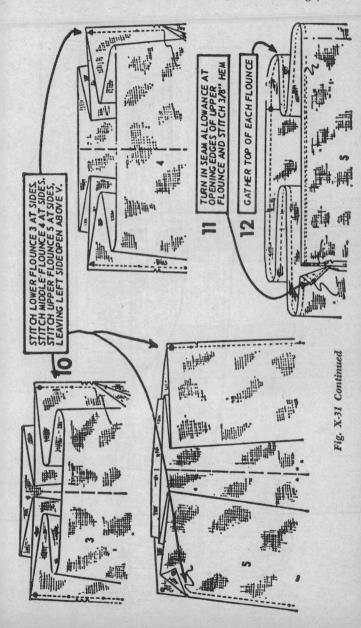

STITCH LOWER FLOUNCE 3 AT SIDES.
STITCH MIDDLE FLOUNCE 4 AT SIDES.
STITCH UPPER FLOUNCE 5 AT SIDES,
LEAVING LEFT SIDE OPEN ABOVE V.

10

11 TURN IN SEAM ALLOWANCE AT
OPENING EDGES OF UPPER
FLOUNCE AND STITCH 3/8" HEM

12 GATHER TOP OF EACH FLOUNCE

Fig. X-31 Continued

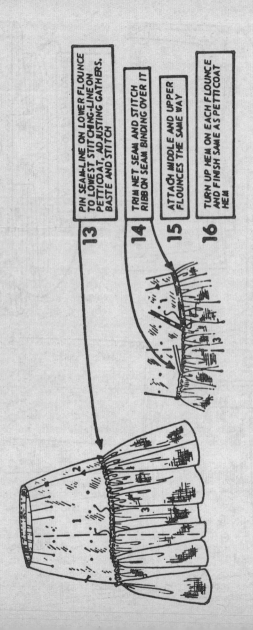

13. PIN SEAM-LINE ON LOWER FLOUNCE TO LOWEST STITCHING-LINE ON PETTICOAT, ADJUSTING GATHERS. BASTE AND STITCH

14. TRIM NET SEAM AND STITCH RIBBON SEAM BINDING OVER IT

15. ATTACH MIDDLE AND UPPER FLOUNCES THE SAME WAY

16. TURN UP HEM ON EACH FLOUNCE AND FINISH SAME AS PETTICOAT HEM

Fig. X-31 *Continued*

CHAPTER 11

Sewing Repair

Today's clever woman doesn't brag, "I can't sew on a button." Mending may seem a chore and a bore compared to hobby sewing. But, it is simple and can be quite a challenge to the imagination, even fun. It need not be terribly time-consuming if you just don't let it pile up. And, what a budget stretcher!

You sewing hobbyists should try to keep your mending sewing basket free of extra spools of thread and other items used for regular sewing. The basic articles needed for mending are given in Chapter 3, and they will fill your mending basket to the brim.

▶ Mending Accessories Needed

A few mending extras to remember are: keep small patching scraps separate from the larger pieces of something you have made, save hem shortening cut from ready-to-wear garments, hoard little pieces of net, lace, ribbon, denim, drilling, duck, muslin, and old sheets. They will come in useful for patching delicate details, papa's pockets and junior's constant rips and tears.

In notion departments you will find elbow and knee patches made of leather, new pocket linings, warm knitted cuffs, separate collars and cuffs for shirts, and iron-on mending materials, including some for invisible mending and for patching plastic.

There is a great variety of lingerie needs: shoulder straps, special bra hooks, garters, girdle elastic, etc. But, buy elastic items only as you need them because elastic loses its snap if kept too long. Always have a package of twill tape; it has numberless uses. Rayon hem tape and cotton bias fold tape are handy for binding frayed edges, but be sure to match it to garment color. Stay materials include featherbone, horsehair braid, and zig-zag wires to use as pepper-uppers for tired seams and corners. The 3″ zig-zag wires sewed into a décolleté neckline area and bent under keep lingerie straps from peeping.

Collecting buttons is a hobby all its own. For practical use, you need to accumulate "dress-up" buttons and "button-up" buttons. Save them from discarded clothing, and buy cards of staple underwear sizes (be sure they are washable and will not melt under an iron). Men's suit buttons come in colors to match the suit. If a button breaks, get a whole new set rather than sew on one of the wrong color. Keep buttons in a small box of their own, and string the sets together.

Sew-on snaps can be had all sizes on one card. Silk-covered snaps come in two sizes in basic colors. Fur hooks and eyes come in fur colors, covered with heavy silk thread, and there is a linked-together snap arrangement that keeps a fur piece from slipping off the shoulders.

There are also large flat hooks and eyes that are used above the zipper on trousers and skirt bands. These may be either sewed on or applied with pliers.

The duo-purpose Dot snapper kit which will apply both Dot snappers and eyelets is useful for making repairs. Also, there is another eyelet plier kit which attaches both eyelets and larger gromet-type eyelets.

Collect some dress and skirt placket zippers in basic colors. The "separable" zipper comes in both colored metal and heavy-duty plain gilt and nickel for coat-type garments. If the pull tab on a zipper gets lost, yet the teeth are perfect, there is a zipper repair kit for fixing regular size or heavy-duty zippers (Fig. XI-1).

There is a perfect all-in-one sock and glove darner which is dark on one side and white on the other. It's egg-shaped for the sock, and the handle fits into the finger of a glove.

Your skirt marker is also a useful sewing repair aid to help you cope with ever-sagging hems and ever-changing hemlines.

► *Before You Start to Mend*

Mending is a term for all sorts of fabric repair: replacing broken stitches, reinforcing worn spots, filling in holes, join-

Fig. XI-1 Repairing Zipper

ing tears, all those little jobs that prolong the life of worn but still-valuable fabric articles.

Don't face yourself with a whole mountain of work at once. Divide the darning from the patching, repairing, sewing machine jobs, make-over possibilities, and discards. Before you begin, make some firm resolutions:

1. Never put away another newly bought article before examining it for (a) knotty, broken, drawn or crooked stitching, and hanging or loose threads; (b) fraying too near the seam which might pull out; (c) hems too loosely sewn; (d) imperfect binding on any loose edges; (e) plackets, pockets and stretchy edges which need staying. Re-sew snaps, buttons, and hooks and eyes which were sewn on too loosely. Re-work faulty buttonholes. Next time check such details before purchasing.

2. Look over clothing or household linen after each trip to the washing machine, laundry, or dry cleaners for these same weaknesses. While ironing, watch for broken seams, thin spots, and frayed edges. Take the stitch in time before the button comes off or the pad comes loose, or the hole gets bigger. Don't put it off for another wearing when it becomes a larger task.

3. Teach the children some of the simpler mending chores. Even the littlest tot can be encouraged to tell you when stitches need taking.

Be comfortable while mending and sit in a well-lighted place. Arrange generous layout space within easy reach. Turn on the radio to a good program. Become such a proficient mender that your work basket can be picked up anywhere,

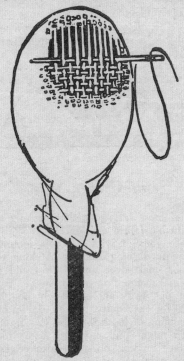

Fig. XI-2 *Darning Over Sock and Glove Darner*

anytime, even when friends drop in or during a cozy family conference.

What is the difference between darning and patching? Darning is mending with interlaced stitches. It may be done by hand or machine. Because it always shows, it should be used only when out of sight.

Patching is sewing an extra piece of cloth over a hole or worn place to strengthen it. It can be done so deftly as to defy detection. This is when you fool the eye by making it a decoration, which is in the mending fun department.

▶ Darning

Darning a sock: For nylon, rayon, or cotton socks, use 4-ply mercerized darning thread and a medium-sized darning needle. If you hand-knit the sock, use the same yarn to mend with. Cut off a 12″ length of yarn and split it 2-ply. If the wool sock is store-bought, match from wool sock yarn colors in your mending basket, and use a longer darning needle.

Thread your needle with not more than ½ yard at a time so as to save yourself a long snarl. If thread is not plyed, use two strands, doubled. Don't knot the end.

Slip your two-tone sock and glove darner (Fig. XI-2) into the sock until the hole comes over the bulge where the color contrasts with the sock. The function of the darner is to keep the threads from being drawn so tight as to pucker the edges of the darn. Be sure the hole is flat and stretched a bit against the hard surface. Grasp the rest of the sock at the handle so the hole stays taut, and put a rubber band around the handle.

If it is a little hole or a worn spot, begin darning without further ado. But, for a big hole, use the scissors and trim away the frayed edges. Take a small stitch, about ⅛″ away from the edge of the hole. Pull the thread through almost to its end. Take a back-stitch over the first stitch and pull it so it holds without a knot. Outline the hole with a series of running stitches. At one side, lay a thread across the hole in the same direction the sock is knitted. Take a stitch and turn back and lay another thread beside the first. Keep doing this until the hole is covered with parallel threads. Turn the work in a crosswise direction and with the point of the needle begin weaving, *over* and under, the threads you just laid. As you come to the end of the first woven row, take a stitch into the side of the hole and turn back. This time, go *under* and over, opposite to the first woven stitches. Continue this basket-weave effect until the hole is no more. End off your thread with the same back-stitch as you used to start. Pull the end to the wrong side and cut the thread off not too close to the work.

Mending a glove finger: While your darner is out, why not get busy on that ripped glove finger? About the only thing worth fixing on a glove is a broken seam. Is it a dress glove, with a machine-stitched seam on the inside? Put it with the pile of work to do when you open your sewing machine. If it is a casual glove with an outside hand-stitched seam, match the color of glove with buttonhole twist. There are three-sided hand and machine needles for sewing leather. Use a medium-fine needle that can be threaded with the

Fig. XI-3 Sewing Machine Darning

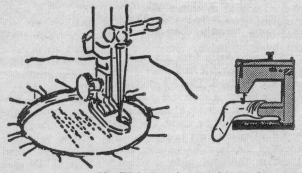

Fig. XI-4 Free-Arm Sewing Machine Darning

twist, and copy the stitch on the seam as closely as possible. Start with the back-stitch knot you learned when darning the sock, a little above where the rip begins. Hand-stitched gloves are usually done in a saddle stitch, a tiny, perfectly spaced running stitch. Occasionally, back-stitch or overhand stitches are used. Secure the end of the thread inside the seam with a back-stitch.

General hand darning notes: Though darning usually has to be more inconspicuously placed than patching, it is more practical for mending knitted fabrics. Hand-darn knitted underwear and outer wear by following the knit stitches as closely as possible. Fabric breaks in many ways. You may snag and pull threads. A tear may go with the grain of the material, or the threads may break in all directions. Hand darn a clean, straight tear on corduroy or velveteen on the wrong side, if there won't be strain. Weave the stitches back and forth across the tear for its full length. Then brush well on the right side to lift the pile. Sometimes a darn on the wrong side of tweedy wool may be almost completely disguised. Pull a lengthwise thread from a concealed section of the garment (perhaps from the seam or hem). Darn with it and see how good you are at copying the weave of the material!

Sewing machine darning: If you need to darn socks or anything else that has small tears or holes, you will find sewing machine darning quick and neat. Use regular mercerized thread and a medium needle. You might prefer to use an embroidery hoop, as shown in the illustration, to keep fabric smooth and taut (Fig. XI-3).

If you own a "free arm" machine, the sock which needs to be darned will fit over that arm (Fig. XI-4). Other machines provide special hoops to stretch a sock. Or use a small embroidery hoop to hold your work taut. Prepare the hole first by stay-stitching around it three times about ⅛" from the edge. If a hoop is used, grasp it with both hands and move it in time with the needle. Your machine instruction book gives you specific darning directions, but often the presser foot is removed. Then, stitch back and forth across the hole from one side to the other, in one direction, until hole is filled. Turn and stitch in the opposite direction across stitching just completed. It will look something like the basket-weave darn you learned to do by hand.

Darning sheets and other household articles: The shape and size of the tear or hole determines whether you darn or patch household articles. Iron-on mending should also be considered at this point. You will often find it the best solution for sheets. You may almost completely conceal a cigarette hole in a damask table cloth with a hand darn. Thread a fine needle with extra-fine thread and hand darn it cleverly, copying the weave. Or, experiment with the plastic mending film, which I'll explain later.

"Rounting" is an amusing mending term which I've discovered. It is the stitch used for sewing up a baseball. The two raw edges are brought together by the stitches being woven back and forth, from one edge to the other. A friend of mine tried it with success in a most unusual way. She accidently snipped a hole in the back of a dress she was cutting out. Her dress was almost completed when she found out about it. She was miserable until another look made her realize how near the color of her long hair the taupe of her dress was. So, she plucked out one of her longest hairs and threaded it in a very fine needle. Gently she wove together those cut edges on the wrong side with the baseball stitch. That hair was as sturdy as any thread and to her wild delight the result was a completely invisible darn! She finished making the dress and has been wearing it happily ever since. The darn never came apart and no one has ever known it was there.

▶ Patching

So many questions come up when you consider patching. What are the shape and condition of the area to be mended;

is it a slanting cut; a burn; a straight or three-cornered tear? Does it go with the fabric grain, or have the threads burst in all directions as with underarm strain? Does the fabric weave fray and have threads shifted, or is it sturdy, tightly woven, or jersey-like? Where is the tear and is it going to be strained constantly under the patch?

If you are working on clothing, table cloths, bed linen, or towels, can you trim the worn place imaginatively or make a fashion change over the bad spot? For instance, you might put a pocket over a moth hole; either a patch pocket to hide it or a slash pocket to make use of the hole. But, if it is a child's garment or a piece of household linen, can you place an appliqué over the spot to decorate the item?

Remember, a patch can be done so well as to be practically invisible. It is much better to patch than darn a large hole on anything but a sock. Make the patch of the same fabric, if possible. Cut a piece from the facing, hem, or under-collar or wherever it will not show. If you can't find a piece of the same fabric, match the color, weight and texture of the garment as nearly as possible. Trim away the ragged edges around the hole and square the opening exactly along the crosswise and lengthwise thread with your scissors. Miter diagonally at each corner (Fig. XI-5A). Turn the edges to the wrong side and press them down with your thumbnail or iron them toward each corner. Cut the patch about 1" larger than the hole. Place it under the hole, being sure you match the fabric grain of the patch and garment. If there is a design or special weave, see that each detail

Fig. XI-5A Cutting and Placing Patch

Fig. XI-5B Hand Sewing Patch

corresponds. This helps hide the mend. Turn the garment over, ever so carefully, to the wrong side. Hold the patch in position between your thumb and forefinger, or put a guide pin at each corner. Turn back to the right side and check the match of fabric grain.

To hand-stitch patch (Fig. XI-5B): If everything seems to be right, baste along the pressed crease. Use a fine needle and thread of the same color as the fabric. Take a tiny stitch at the corner of one turned-under edge, and hide the knot in the crease. Point the needle toward you and take another small stitch in the patch. Slide the point of the needle into the folded edge of the hole. The third stitch is taken in the patch, the fourth in the fold, and so on. This is called slip-stitching and is practically invisible.

Sewing machine patching: If you sew down the patch with the sewing machine, the stitches show more than fine hand-stitching. But, if you have an automatic zig-zag machine, here again is a way to point up a patch as an embellishment. On kiddies' clothes, for instance, why not make it an animal-shaped appliqué with a machine-embroidered edge?

Should you decide on straight machine stitching, the spool color can match one thread of a tweed or two-tone fabric, and the bobbin thread another, and so be made inconspicuous. Use a medium stitch and sew along the basted line on all four edges of the hole. With the stitching completed, trim off the edges of the patch. Clip off the patch corners to remove bulkiness, and press.

Press-on patching: A most practical and time-saving method is when you use the available press-on materials. There is a clear plastic which allows you to use self-fabric with it. Or, a variety of fabrics have a bonding agent impregnated on the wrong side.

Fabri-mend is a new clear plastic material which makes possible a press-on mend with your own fabric. Set your iron for dry ironing at the temperature for the type of fabric being used. It is better to press over the patch twice than to scorch it. Remember to allow no part of the iron to contact the shiny side of Fabri-mend. There are three ways to repair with this clear plastic mending agent: (1) Apply it with a self-patch to hold edges together on the underside of a tear. (2) Apply it *under* a large damaged area. (3) Make it an *outside* patch.

Fig. XI-6A

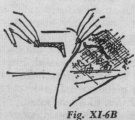

Fig. XI-6B

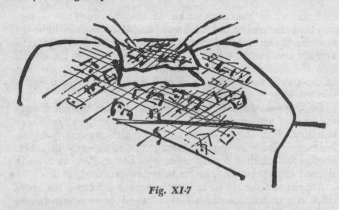

Fig. XI-7

To apply heat-seal patch to a tear: First, cut a patch piece of the same material ¾" larger than the torn area. Cut a Fabri-mend patch the same size as the fabric patch. Place the fabric patch *right* side up on ironing board, and place the Fabri-mend patch (shiny side down) over it. Iron over the paper side of the plastic a few seconds, being careful it remains centered exactly over the fabric (Fig. XI-6A). Let it cool and peel off the paper backing to expose the other adhesive side. Trim the patch to ½" larger than the area all around, and your heatseal patch is ready to bond to the garment. Turn the garment to the right side and place it over the ironing board. Slip the prepared patch under tear (shiny side up) against the fabric (Fig. XI-6B). Use a light press-cloth, such as transparent permanent-finished organdy, over the mend area and rotate the iron there for 10 seconds. Allow the fabric to cool and check the edges of the bond. If it is not completely sealed, iron over it again. Different fabrics may require more time to bond completely.

To apply heat-seal patch to a large damaged area: Prepare the edges of a large hole by trimming away frayed threads. Make up a heat-seal patch as you did before. Then, make a fabric patch only, same size as the hole, by laying the hole over a piece of fabric, drawing around inside it and cutting out the piece. Turn the garment right side out and place it over the ironing board. Place the heat-seal patch (shiny side up) under the large hole and center it there. Fit the identical size patch (wrong side over shiny side of heat-seal patch) so it fits the hole exactly (Fig. XI-7). Using a thin press cloth over the mend, press until completely bonded.

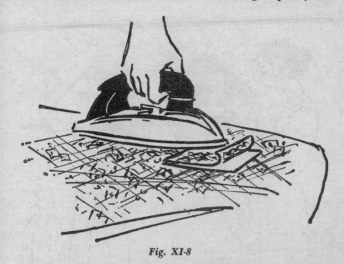

Fig. XI-8

To make an outside patch: This time the fabric and Fabrimend are prepared for the heat-seal patch so the plastic is bonded to the *wrong* side of the patch piece (Fig. XI-8). Place the garment right side up on the ironing board. But place the patch *over* the hole with the plastic side down. Put a piece of wax paper underneath to keep any plastic that may be exposed through the hole from sticking to the ironing board cover. Iron as before under a thin press cloth until completely bonded. Peel the wax paper away from the under side.

Using ready-prepared press-on patches: The ready-prepared press-on patches come in a variety of fabrics and sizes. These too can be used under a tear or over a hole. Take, for example, a pair of blue jeans. They often get whopping big holes that are hard to mend because the fabric is heavy and you can break a couple of needles before you finish stitching patches on them. You can get press-on patches that are made of the same blue denim as the jeans. Cut the patch about ½″ larger all around than the hole. Lay the hole area on the garment over the ironing or sleeve board, whichever side out you wish the patch to be placed. Put a piece of wax paper under the hole, to keep the underside of the patch from sticking if it faces the ironing board cover. Set the iron temperature for cotton (hot) and use it dry, no steam. Place the patch (coated side down over the hole, and cover with a press cloth if on

Fig. XI-9 Patching Plastics   *Fig. XI-10 Leather Patches*

the right side of the fabric. Press down hard for 30 seconds.
Allow the fabric to cool before touching. Then, peel off the
wax paper from the under side.

Here, too, you might cut your patch in a decorative shape.
There are many patterns to use in the embroidery section of
the pattern books. The newest is a stencil appliqué which
leaves a design on plain fabric in many lovely colors. A more
complicated two- or three-piece appliqué is cut from several
colors of fabric and assembled into a complete design.

Patching plastic articles: This is a perfectly clear plastic
tissue called *Plasti-mend* (Fig. XI-9), which may be finger-

Fig. XI-11 Sewing On Buttons

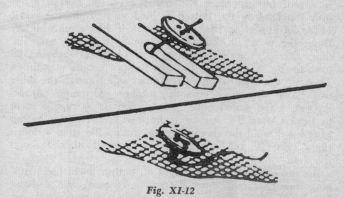

Fig. XI-12

pressed over damaged areas on vinyl plastic articles such as table cloths, raincoats, curtains, and covers. It must be applied to a clean, dry surface. Cut the Plasti-mend patch slightly larger than area to be mended (½″ all around.) Peel away the paper backing from the patch and place it in position. Smooth down with fingers. If the area is subject to heavy wear, a second patch can be applied on the reverse side for additional strength.

Leather patches (Fig. XI-10): Leather patches are a style feature on many Ivy League type sports jackets. Some thrifty mothers put them on new jackets of this type even before they are worn. However, you can add them to cover threadbare elbows and knees and call them smart. They come in a variety of leather colors and must be sewn on by hand. The best thread to use is either buttonhole twist or ready-waxed button thread.

▶ *Sewing On Buttons*

Often, tiny flat buttons are used as reinforcement, and are sewn on the wrong side under larger buttons; as long as they are neutral in color they don't have to match. Thread a fairly coarse needle with a double strand, not too long, and knot the thread. Take out your filled beeswax holder and pull the thread through the slotted opening several times, to strengthen it and keep it from tangling. Start by drawing your knotted thread from the top side of the garment, where the button belongs, to the underside and through the small button. If it is a coat button, place the big slot of the button gauge over the knot so the button is held away from the fabric (Fig. XI-11). Use the smaller slot if it's a suit button. Bring the point of the needle through the next hole and down through the opposite hole in the button. Go back and forth in this way through the two buttons about eight times. Then, do the same thing on the other side through the other two holes. Curiously enough, stitches are made parallel through a four-holed button, not crisscross as people seem to think. After the sewing is finished, remove the button gauge and wind the thread tightly around the stem a dozen times (Fig. XI-12). Finish with a knotted stitch through the stem.

Sewing on shank buttons: Not all buttons have holes running through them. Many decorative buttons have a shank attached to the back. Whether you add a thread shank too depends upon the height of the shank and the amount of strain the button may receive.

Sewing on buttons by machine: Shank buttons always have to be sewn on by hand. However, if you have a zig-zag machine, this is one of your rewards for investing in it. All utility buttons with holes running through them, such as coat, suit, or underwear buttons, have one thing in common, regardless of size. The holes are always the same distance apart. So, these buttons can be sewed on with a sewing machine. Consult the direction book with your machine to learn the proper procedure, because some machines have a special presser foot for the purpose. But, with a little practice, you'll find it simple enough to do.

▶ Applying Hooks and Eyes and Snaps

What about that blouse with the eye hanging by one loop at the neck and the skirt that had the hook crushed in cleaning? Replace both of these fasteners with completely new ones. If it is a white blouse, small white *silk-covered snaps* would look so dainty on it. Use a sturdy, flat hook and eye (such as is standard equipment on tops of men's trousers) for the skirt, so it withstands the pressure on its next trip to the cleaners.

Mechanically-applied hook and eye: Trouser hooks and eyes sometimes have to be replaced, too. But, usually they are stapled on. You can now put them on with mechanics'

Fig. XI-13 *Mechanically Applied Hook and Eye*

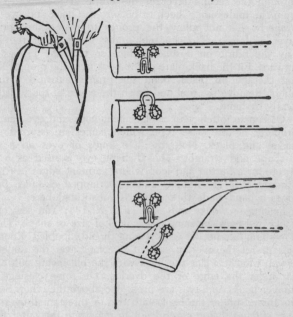

Fig. XI-14 *Sewing On Wire Hooks and Eyes*

pliers, so they will outlast the garment (Fig. XI-13). Get the kind that has a little tool included in the package to hold hook and eye open when you have to press down the jaws of the pliers. Each piece of the fastener has two parts, the working section and a metal plate which secures it to the fabric without thread.

Rip open the end of the waistband so that back plate of the hook section may be hidden behind a layer of fabric on the upper belt. The eye is to be placed to meet it on the under belt. The back plate of the eye is concealed within the layers of the waistband. Mark the exact position. To attach the eye, push the prongs of the eye through the marked area of the fabric from the right to wrong side. Place the flat side of the tool under the eye and lay the garment down on a solid surface, with prongs facing upward. Center the back plate of the eye over the prongs. Bend the prongs over the back plate with the pliers. Remove the tool from under the eye. To attach hook, push the prongs of the hook through the second layer of the fabric at the marked area from the underside. Check to be sure the hook and eye align properly. Do not allow the prongs to pierce the covering layer of fabric. Slip the tool under the turn of the hook. Lay the fabric on a solid surface so that the prongs face upward. Fit the back plate of the hook over the prongs. Keeping the tool in place, bend the prongs outward with the pliers. Remove the tool and finish the edges of the waistband neatly by hand.

Of course, often your replacement hook and eye can only properly be the wire type which comes in assorted sizes, nickel and black. Note the two kinds of eyes on a card, U-shape and straight. The U-shape eye is used as a substitute for a button and loop where garment edges just meet. Straight eyes are hidden under overlapped closings. Sometimes a hand-made thread eye is substituted here.

Sewing on hooks and eyes (Fig. XI-14): You sew on all hooks and eyes the same, regardless of size or shape. Thread a medium-fine needle with sewing thread, doubled. Knot and wax it. Fit the overlap so that it comes over the underside as you want it. Place the hook with the bill facing out, about ⅛" under the edge of the overlap. On some closings two smaller hooks and eyes are used, one above the other. Secure the thread under the hook with two or three small over-and-over stitches, being careful not to penetrate the outer thickness of fabric to prevent its showing on the right side. Keep overcasting around the first loop of the hook. Skip to the second loop and fill it with stitches the same way. Skip to the bill of the hook and pass the thread under the curve, stitching around it several times to hold it flat against the garment. Fasten the thread with a few back-stitches. If you have to sew on more than one hook at a time, do not cut off the thread, but take a few running stitches to where the next one goes and repeat the performance. Finish off the thread with several back-stitches and conceal the end between the layers of the fabric.

When you sew on the straight eye, place it on the underlap of the garment so as to just meet the end of the hook's bill. The curve of the eye faces the outer edge of the closing. Sew it on with overcasting stitches through both loops the same way you did the U-shaped eye.

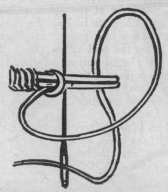

Fig. XI-15   Thread Eye

On custom clothing you may have seen a thread used instead of a straight eye (Fig. XI-15). This is the most invisible. The thread eye is made with buttonhole twist in a buttonhole stitch. There is an art to making a neat thread eye which you can easily master with a little practice. It may also be used as a button loop at a neckline. Fasten a double thread at the underside of the material. Draw it through to the right side and take a stitch the desired length of the eye. Leave a little slack and go back with another stitch at beginning, giving you four strands of buttonhole twist. Work around these in buttonhole stitch as follows: Make a loop of thread around the eye with needle coming out under it. Pass the doubled thread around the point of the needle from right to left and draw it up tight so a twist forms into a tiny knot. Make another loop beside the first and form a knot over it. Continue with stitches coming close together along the eye without lapping over each other. Fasten on the underside when eye is properly filled.

There are special large twist-covered fur hooks and eyes as well as a linked arrangement to keep neckpieces from slipping off. They come in the usual fur shades. They take a lot of punishment, especially on heavy coats. Use doubled buttonhole twist or carpet thread. The U-shaped eye is often placed flat on the fur a distance in from edge, and should be sewed

Fig. XI-16 Fur Hooks   *Fig. XI-17 Snap Fasteners*

through two thicknesses of pelt very thoroughly if you don't want it to tear a hole in the fur. The hook is usually concealed under the edge of the top half of the closing, sometimes between lining and fur, but more often at the facing edge between two thicknesses of fur (Fig. XI-16). Be sure the stitches go through both thicknesses many times.

When the proper size hook and eye is used, this taped closing will probably withstand more strain than sew-on snaps. However, snaps can often be made less conspicuous, particularly the dainty silk-covered snaps.

Sewing on snaps (Fig. XI-17): Silk-covered snaps come in two sizes and several basic colors, one size and color to a card. Nickel and black metal snaps now come with all sizes of one color on one card. When they are separated to be sewn on, begin with the ball-half first. Sew it in position, ball side up, on the underside of the overlap. Sew through all four holes with the same over-and-over stitches you used when sewing on hooks and eyes. Now, rub your tailor's chalk over the ball of the snap and press it into the underlap where the socket half of the snap is to be placed. In this way, you mark the spot exactly. Sew on the socket section over the mark just as you did the top.

Mechanically-applied snaps (Fig. XI-18): Probably you have many times blessed the ready-made-clothes manufacturers who use permanent fasteners on crotches of children's

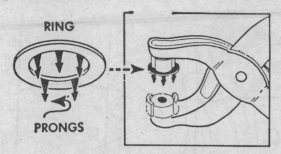

Fig. XI-18   Dot Snapper Pliers

play clothes, down legging sides, and on men's shorts. You, too, can apply them or replace them in one of two ways. If you are handy with a hammer, you will like the Dot snapper kit consisting of three little tools to help hammer them on. Or, if you're all thumbs with a hammer, the Dot snapper pliers kit suits your purpose.

Pliers Kits: There are four types of pliers kits, two of which apply Dot snappers. I've mentioned the duo-purpose one which applies both belt-sized metal eyelets and Dot snappers with a simple adjustment of a screw in one jaw. There is also one which applies snappers only. It has nylon jaws that do not cut into fabric. The third pliers kit is for applying belt-sized metal eyelets only. The fourth pliers kit is also duo-purpose to accommodate two sizes of metal eyelets—belt-sized and grommet-sized for shower curtains, bags, and many other household articles.

When you decide which kind of applying tools best meets your needs, you will find specific instructions for using them included with the package.

Mostly, they are used for utility closings on underwear or wherever they don't show. There are some with decorative tops that are attractive on sport clothes. These come packaged with their own little applicator tool, or may be applied with the duo-purpose pliers kit with the rubber-encased jaws.

If buttonless clothing is always popping up in your mending work basket, why not replace the buttons with the mechanically-applied snappers? They are laundry-proof and go through the wringer without damage.

If there are two or less thicknesses of light weight fabric, reinforcement is needed. Cotton twill tape is ideal for this purpose, laid between the two outer thicknesses.

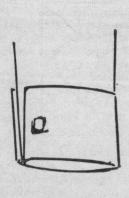

Fig. XI-19A   Fig. XI-19B

► **Replacement Mending**

Now for the repair jobs which require a trifle more skill,
but which don't turn up quite so often. Here you can get
out your sewing machine.

Turning shirt collars: Pick out from the pile of sewing machine mending that shirt with the badly frayed collar. You'd
be surprised at the number of women who would rather
make a dust rag of it than give a man's shirt a new lease
on life.

First, rip the collar completely off the neck band. Don't use
scissors because there is danger of cutting the fabric with
those exceedingly fine stitches. Your seam ripper, shaped like
a little pointing finger, is about the only thing that does this
ripping right. The blade of the ripper is in the curve. Slip
the point under the small stitches down to the blade and
cut quickly. Cut every fourth or fifth stitch across the row
in the same way. Turn your work over and pick up the loose
thread end on the other side. Pull, and in a jiffy all the
stitches come out.

Separate the collar from its band and turn it inside out.
After it's turned, poke the points out precisely with your
collar point turner. Press out the collar exactly on the creased
line where it was turned before.

Fit the newly turned collar between the collar band shafts
exactly the same depth as before, pin in place and baste.
Adjust to small machine stitch. Use the same color thread

as that with which it was stitched originally, and stitch the collar and band together along the same stitch lines.

Don't give up in despair if, after you have ripped and turned the collar, it seems too far gone. As long as the shirt is still good, particularly if it is white, you can purchase white replacement collars and cuffs.

Turning French cuffs: French cuffs are the ones that fold back and fasten with cuff links. (Fig. XI-19A). Turn them just as you do shirt collars, if the frayed edge is at the crease. If only the edges of the cuff fray out, rip seam all around. Turn it in just the ¼" seam line smaller and restitch.

Turning straight cuffs: Usually the edges fray first on the straight, buttoned cuffs (Fig. XI-19B). So, turn in and re-stitch the edges as you did with the French cuffs. If the edges again wear threadbare, rip off the cuff at the wrist and turn it upside down. You are going to say you can't do that without having to change the buttonholes. However, if you reverse the cuffs, put the cuff from the right sleeve on the left sleeve and vise versa, only the buttons have to be reversed.

Turning trouser cuffs: If you examine trouser cuffs after every trip to the cleaners, you'll keep up with the rough treatment they are given. Cuff edges may be repaired several times before trousers are noticeably shortened. Cut and rip loose the thread tacks at the side of the cuff. Rip open the hem. The wear usually shows up first along the last of the three sharp press creases. You cut the cuff off at this crease line, being careful to cut very evenly. If the wear goes up inside the hem, you may need to trim off a little more to get a straight edge. Seam the cut-off piece back to the pants leg, with not more than an ⅛" seam. Press the seam toward the facing. Fold the cuff and press again so the seam you have just made comes inside the crease line. Turn down the cuff and hem by hand or machine. Sharpen the new crease line with another pressing.

To half-patch or replace men's pockets: If only the lower part of the pocket is worn, cut it off and use it for a pattern for two new pieces. Figure in the seam allowance on the edge of the new piece where it is sewn to old pocket. New fabric should be a sturdy drilling. If the whole pocket looks about to give up, purchase new pocket linings and replace the old entirely.

Hems—up, down, and extended: How often have you admired a smart woman in a stunning costume, until you looked at the hem? It was uneven, too wide, too long, or too short, or perhaps it was coming out! Let this never happen to you.

There is an old rule of proportion, which was followed before hems began to rise. For street clothes, stand erect in heels and let someone measure your full height. Reduce the amount to inches and divide by four, then subtract 4". For example: 5' 4" equals 64". Divide by four and you get 16". This is just about right with current fashion. But, if you subtract 4", you get 12", which is long enough for the most conservative older women. A real full skirt looks prettier on the short side than a straight skirt which usually rides up when you sit down. For full-length evening gowns, finish the front hem 1" from the floor, even if the style leaves the back longer or trailing.

Consider the fabric and style of the garment before deciding upon the depth of a hem. Unless used for decorative purposes, hems should be inconspicuous. You can turn up a deeper hem on a straight-line garment than when the style is circular. In fact, a chiffon hem is often made very deep when it hangs straight. Circular hems should be made shallow enough to preserve the curve. Of course, children's clothes are given deeper hems for later lengthening. Here is a professional fitter's guide to hem-depth proportions:

	Straight	Semicircular	Circular
Coats	3"	2"	1½"
Dresses	2"	1½"	1"
Children's Garments	4"	3"	2"
Skirts	2"	1½"	1"
Jackets	1½"	1"	1"

Shortening hems: Whether you shorten or lengthen a hem, you have to take out the old hem, remove the seam binding or stitching and press out the crease. Put on the shoes you normally wear with the garment. If you are shortening a coat, button it completely. If it's a suit skirt, put on the blouse and jacket with it and button the jacket. The steps in turning a hem are marking with the skirt marker, pressing in the new crease over the hem pressing gauge, marking the new hem depth with the tailorette, pinning or basting, finishing the edge, and stitching in the hem by hand or machine.

Hand heming: Whether you finish by hand or machine depends on the weight and surface weave of your fabric, and the type of garment you are working on. You wouldn't dream of machine hemming a lovely party frock, now would you?

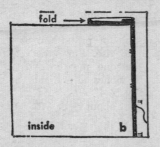

Fig. XI-20

The best way to hand hem is to use the most invisible stitches possible. The slip-stitch method is probably least noticeable. Of course, when you line a garment, the problem of tell-tale stitches is solved because your work comes on the lining, not through the outer fabric.

Sew a slip-stitch hem with carefully matched thread and fine needle. Hide the beginning knot under the hem edge and take the tiniest stitches under a mere thread of fabric on the surface. Insert the point of the needle in the fold of the hem and slip it inside the fold ⅛" to ¼" (depending upon fabric weight). Then, the needle is pulled out and inserted back of the thread and another tiny stitch taken in the fabric. This stitch is used not only for hems but for hand-stitching linings into coats and in other instances where practically invisible stitching is desired.

Inconspicuous machine-stitched hem: If you do not have a special attachment for blind-stitch hemming for your machine, you can try the following method. Thread your machine to match the color of the fabric. A slightly darker shade thread shows up less than a lighter one if you can't find a perfect match.

Put your garment down on the machine, wrong side out (Fig. XI-20). Then, turn the width of the hem under so the edge of the seam tape sticks out just the tiniest fraction of an inch. Run your machine *very slowly* by guiding the balance wheel with your right hand. Stitch along the absolute edge of the seam tape for 1" to get used to the precariousness of the operation. Shift the fabric a hair's breadth to puncture it with one stitch, get back on the tape for four or five more stitches, take another stitch in the fabric. Keep this up from tape to fabric every six stitches until you have finished the hem.

Lengthening hems: Mothers of growing children know too well the race with the hem lines. One of the worst problems in letting down a hem is erasing the crease. Here is a solution which very often works with woolens, and sometimes with other fabrics if the garment is perfectly clean.

Stretch and fasten securely a piece of nylon, such as the top of an old stocking, over the cap of a pepper shaker, after the shaker has been filled with hot water. Place the garment (right side out) on the ironing board so the crease line is flat. Rub the nylon-covered shaker over the crease until the water comes through, then steam iron over the area. The friction of rubbing seems to flatten out the crease and raise the nap of the fabric. If the crease simply will not come out, decorate it. A nice way to do this would be to cover with rick-rack or braid. In the following chapter on make-over there are several novel ideas on this theme.

▶ Household Mending

So far, I've covered clothing repair only. Of course, lots of mending and patching is done on household articles, too. Small holes and rips on sheets can be machine darned, or patched with iron-on fabrics. When sheet tears get so long that toes catch in them and make them longer, tear the sheet completely in two through the tear. Flat seam the outside edges together and then trim away frayed edges and hem for a new outside edge. This makes them only a seam-width smaller so they'll still tuck under the mattress, or they can be used on a smaller bed.

Hems on table cloths get frayed or tear apart at the hem-stitching. They get cigarette burns or become permanently stained. Try facing the hem with a contrast color or a lace edge. Appliqué or embroidered design over the holes and stains might solve the problem.

Curtains get faded or wind-whipped. Tint them anew with a commercial dye, or salvage the good parts and make into gay café curtains for another window or a change of decor. If you move, and the old curtains don't fit the new windows, lengthen them with a scalloped, faced hem which you can create with the help of your see-thru scallop measure.

Sometimes tufted buttons come off pillows and such, or a mattress seam pops open, or a leather chair gives, or you have to cover the garden shrubs with burlap to keep out frost. Here's where the home repair needle kit comes in handy with its special curved mattress needles, sail needle, packing needle, toy and yarn needle, glover's needle for sewing leather and heavy materials.

CHAPTER 12

Alterations and Make-Overs

After consulting my dictionary, I confirmed my impression that alteration and make-over are not the same thing; this is what I found:

"Alteration—to make different without changing into something else," and, "Make-over—to construct something once more afresh, or from beginning to end."

I had almost come to the point of thinking women were not interested in learning about alterations or make-overs, until a television show (on a nation-wide hookup) had a ten-minute segment on how to make over a man's suit into a woman's suit. The deluge of requests for a booklet on the subject, from the TV viewers, convinced skeptics that this is something you do quite frequently.

► Restyling a Garment

This takes almost more imagination than any other kind of sewing. Make-new should be the motive, rather than a dreary make-do attitude. If you've just learned new sewing skills here is an ideal way to practice and perfect them without taking chances on expensive mistakes with new fabrics. The average man's suit offers exceptional opportunities for making-over because of its excellent color, texture, and quality. And this is the time to observe the best tailoring as you rip away. It makes you want to take notes for future reference. However, first let's talk about some simple alterations that you should learn to do before you begin pulling something apart to completely remake.

Here is a short list of alteration ideas that came to me while looking through a single copy of a recent fashion publication:

1. Fit and shorten an old dress and add new buttons and belt. From left-over fabric cut from the hem, self-cover the buttons and make a new belt. Or, cover contrasting buttons in grosgrain, velvet, or satin ribbon; floral printed or bold striped French ribbon makes wonderful buttons and belts on summer cottons. Satin or velvet scraps would make ideal buttons or new triangle buttonholes on an old wool suit or dress.

2. Seams bursting because garment too tight? Let out the front of a dress with a contrasting buttoned band all the way down center front, or a bit to one side.

3. Plot a new sleeveless style. Rip out old sleeves that have begun giving way under the arm, and take off the collar. Lower the neckline and face it and armholes with a contrasting fabric. If it's a casual style suit, remove sleeves, then knit new sleeves and collar and sew them into armholes and re-styled neckline that have been faced with bias tape.

4. Recut the sleeves of an afternoon dress, add a lace yoke and make new sleeves in lace. Rejuvenate an old dress with contrasting color sleeves and yoke. Try eyelet embroidery shoulder ruffles or puff sleeves in an old summer cotton, add a matching apron-like peplum. Camouflage an undesirable shoulder or front treatment with braid, yarn, ribbon or bias piqué, satin or velvet cording.

5. If there's a stain, or a moth or cigarette hole in the wrong place, cover with rhinestones, sequins, self-covered buttons, ready-cut press-on appliqués, braid, or ribbon bows. Then add more of the same here and there on the garment to form a dotted effect or a design. Cover a larger tear or hole with a pocket, plastron, panel, fichu, or scarf.

6. If you are heir-apparent, there are many novel ways of making what you have into maternity clothes. You can put a ready-made stretch panel into any skirt; they are available in several colors where you buy other mending and sewing supplies. Then, convert a blouse into a butcher-boy (smock) style with an eyelet embroidery strip down the front, edged in lace or rickrack. Add a pretty paneled front to a plain dress by softly shirring the waistline area with elastic thread, or add a completely new roomy front.

7. For the overweight person, cut up a too tight shirtmaker dress into a redingote by slicing it open down the front and facing both sides with a contrasting color. Then, make a new sheath dress to go under it, in same fabric as facing. For a too tight basic black dress, let out the hip with a diagonal drape over one side which, when done in contrasting stripe or print, subtracts inches.

8. When a full circular skirt is old style, unbecoming, and too long, recut it into a slim four-gored skirt. Sometimes a blouse and skirt team do an encore in a bright new alliance with something else from your cast-off pile that mixes or matches.

You, too, can study advertisements and fashions this way, and get many other ideas for altering without having to make-over.

▶ Altering Ready-Made Clothes

An excellent booklet, *Fitting Dresses (Bulletin #1964),* is available if you write to the U. S. Department of Agriculture, Washington 25, D. C. It tells what to avoid when making a dress or buying ready-mades.

The typical alterations necessary on ready-made dresses, to watch for, are:

1. Shoulder seams are too far to the front or back, or too long.
2. Back neck line is too wide and stands away from the neck.
3. Crosswise fold appears at back of neck or over shoulder blades.
4. Neckline too high in front.
5. Armhole too tight.
6. Sleeve cap twists.
7. Sleeve too long or too short.
8. Sleeve uncomfortable because elbow fullness is misplaced.
9. Bustline too tight.
10. Waistline fullness poorly placed.
11. Waistline too tight, too loose, or stretched.
12. Waist too long in back or front.

13. Crosswise folds appear in back of skirt near waistline.
14. Skirt too loose or too tight at hips.
15. Side seam crooked or puckered.
16. Ends of pleated section pull.
17. Hem uneven or too long or short.

You should never buy a ready-made dress without trying it on, while wearing the undergarments or foundation garments with which it will be worn. If a part of your figure is particularly hard to fit whether hips, bust, or shoulders buy clothes that fit there. Often, it's not easy, practical, or even possible to alter a ready-made.

Fussy designs, complicated details and many insets may make fitting difficult or well-nigh impossible.

Examine all seams to see if there is enough cloth to allow for letting out. A narrow sleeve cap or back cannot be enlarged by letting out seams, unless there are wide allowances because narrow seams soon tear out. Think about the kind of fabric of which the garment has been made because, in some fabrics, previous stitching lines show when seams are let out. Many misfits cannot be remedied.

▶ Altering After Weight Loss or Gain

It seems easier to take in a garment when you reduce, then to let it out when you gain. Whether taking in or letting out, before any actual fitting, study yourself carefully from all sides in a full-length mirror to determine what needs changing. Check to see if the lengthwise threads of fabric drop straight at the center front and back, and if crosswise threads are parallel to floor across bust and hips. Tie a string around your waist to see whether the waistline has changed with your weight.

To fit a dress after weight loss: Rip out the hem and press out the crease. Turn the garment wrong side out and put it on. (A side seam zipper will be on the right instead of the left.) The only time when a garment is fitted right side out (which entails a lot more work and expert, accurate attention) is if there is a great difference between two shoulders or hips. Then, you must fit the sides that vary over the body differences where the fabric comes. You may not have to remove a zipper placket completely, just try working from the zipper down on that seam. With a wrist pin cushion

Fig. XII-1A   **Fig. XII-1B**

on your wrist, so you don't have to stretch for pins, start by fitting blouse first (Fig. XII-1A).

Since properly placed shoulder seams act as an anchor to the rest of the dress, begin with the shoulder fitting and decide whether you look best with a bit of padding. Here you can make your own or buy what are called "shoulder shapes," either set-in or raglan style. These are not highly padded like old-fashioned shoulder pads, but mold to the contour of the shoulder to help you out if yours are too narrow or sloping.

Now, check the neckline which helps to hold the shoulder seams in place. The bust, back, and sleeves are fitted next, in that order.

Take up or let out any adjustments that make the waistline come at the right level all around. If there are more than two side seams on skirt, distribute the amount to be altered, a little in all seams.

Take the garment off and baste carefully where the pins were placed. Then, turn it wrong side out and try it on again. If there is no further adjustment, stitch over the basted lines. Now, use your seam ripper to carefully rip out the old seams and press them all flat on the new lines. Pink away excesses of fabric beyond a normal ⅝″ seam. When all alterations are completed, make a new hem (Fig. XII-1B).

To let out after gaining weight: This usually means a lot of ripping. However, don't rip until you know exactly where it will help. Are there enough seams and seam allowances to give you the extra fabric you need? Will old stitching lines show? Experiment with a small ripped section and your nylon-covered pepper shaker to see whether the stitch marks and creases will press out. If your waistline girth has not changed, but the hips are too tight, rip down from the area where needed and widen all the way through the hem. Otherwise, your skirt will cup. All you may need to do across the bust is move the buttons, or let out the underarm seams. If the facing is in one piece with the fronts, examine the buttonhole on the facing side. You may be able to carefully sew up the slit and make a new one and thus give the front edge ½″ more room. Or, try one of my alteration suggestions by changing the style.

► Style Changes by Alteration and Make-Over

I'm going to tell you some of the things I have done with my own clothes to make them look better and last longer. Not much additional equipment is needed for alteration and makeover. After all, it is a thrift measure, so plot how to keep from spending any more extra money than you can help. You've already accumulated your staples in your mending and sewing supplies. If new zippers, seam binding, and thread are necessary, buy them to match in color and texture after you've decided on all your changes. When you need patterns for new details, they can almost never be with a raglan sleeve. A two-piece set-in sleeve may come out of old cut-up material better than a one-piece sleeve. Skirts will have to be simple, straight, and probably gored. Steer clear of styles with big collars or double-breasted effects. Match the style and size of pattern pieces as nearly as possible to the amount of fabric useable in the old garment. Almost always, it's more practical to get new lining and interfacing. Good professional interfacing is an economy because nothing crisps old fabrics like this kind of supporting material. A remnant may or may not be a bargain if you are combining any new fabric with old. If the remnant shows more yardage than you need for your project, can you use what's left over for an added accessory? If not, buy only what yardage you need from

Fig. XII-2   Relining A Suit

regular stock. By all means, do not try to economize with cheap new fabric that is completely inappropriate in combination with the old.

How to reline a suit (Fig. XII-2): I wear a lot of suits. However, I usually choose them in practical colors and styles, even when I make them myself. Yet, how tempting are those luscious fashions with gay matching blouse and lining! So, I have often taken out my yen for these by pulling out the lining in an old drab jacket and re-lining with the brightest fabric I could find. It costs the price of a new blouse pattern and about 5 yards of pretty new fabric.

Rip out the old lining and take it completely apart, darts, tucks, gathers and all. Note as you go how it had been constructed and sewn into the jacket, if it was a good ready-made suit. Put on the jacket and skirt to see whether they need any refitting. If you've discarded old shoulder pads, must the sleeve caps be raised? Would shortening help make it look more in fashion just now? Would it look smarter with rounded instead of square corners at the two bottom fronts of the jacket? How about a change of buttons, or adding the new three-cornered buttonholes faced with the new lining fabric?

Lay out your new fabric and pin it down grain-perfect on the accurate markings of your cutting board. It may be best to lay out the paper pattern and first cut out your new blouse. The ripped-up pieces of the old lining must be pressed carefully, and will be your pattern for the new lining.

If your jacket opens down the center front, choose the best of the two front lining pieces for the front pattern and cut front lining double. Also, if the sleeves were set in, you only need use one sleeve lining. If the jacket has an asymmetric front closing, the lining pieces are cut single thickness, and you must be sure to have them face left and right as they should. Note whether the back lining was seamed down the center back or cut in one. It may have a let-out pleat at the center back for ease. Examine the fabric of the old lining pieces until you know what's the straight-grain thread, crosswise and lengthwise. Pull thread to be sure. Lay your see-thru ruler along this grain and chalk the line exactly through its full length, both ways, on every piece you will be using for the pattern. Be sure your marking comes on the wrong side as then you are not so likely to confuse the left and right.

Fit the pieces into the new fabric, double or single, as economically as possible, placing the chalked old pieces on new fabric, grain-line for grain-line, and pin completely flat. After all the pieces have been cut out, mark the darts, tucks, or gathers as they appeared on original with your tracing wheel and paper, on the wrong side of the new fabric. Before stitching the new lining pieces together, stay-stitch ¼" inside all the off-grain edges of the neck, shoulders, armhole, or front to preserve the shape and keep them from stretching. Sew the seams and press them flat as you did when making the blouse. Sew the sleeves into the armholes as though it were the outside jacket shell. Now put on the new blouse and skirt. Slip into the jacket lining and try on the jacket over it. Then, you will know how well it fits and how deep the hems have been allowed at the bottom of the sleeve and jacket. Press these hem depths up over your hem pressing gauge, after you take off the lining.

Did you notice how the lining was sewed into the suit originally? Turn the jacket wrong side out, sleeves, facings, and all. First baste the sleeve seams together, beginning at the underarm and matching the wrong sides of the seams which face towards each other. Baste loosely along one side of the corresponding raw edges, three quarters of the way towards the wrist, and fasten the thread. Do the other sleeve lining the same way. Then, turn both sleeves right side out so the lining is inside the jacket. Now, baste the wrong sides of all other body seams together the same way, beginning at one underarm seam. After the lining has thus been fitted into the body, lay the outside edge of the lining over the inside edge of the facing, turning the raw edge under about ⅜". Pin it all around carefully, adjusting any fullness between the seams and pleating the inverted fullness at the center back, if any. Invisibly slip-stitch the lining over the facing. Slip-stitch the sleeve linings to the wrist facings. Hem the bottom lining last of all. Do not slip-stitch it to bottom hem. Bartack it loosely on all seams.

Re-lining a coat: This follows the same general rules as re-lining a suit. Today there are very expensive combinations of dress-matched-to-coat linings. But these are not practical for the budget-minded unless you are smart enough to perform this kind of change on an old coat. Match the old coat with a new floral print or smart dotted bengaline, decide on a simple dress pattern, and allow 2½ to 3 yards more for lining than the fabric yardage specifications call for. A coat is somewhat heavier to manipulate than a suit, when putting in the new lining. If you try to spread it out on a table to fit the lining, it slithers away from you maddeningly. Better fit it wrong side out on your dress form. Or, if you do not have a form, you could do a measuring job by hanging the coat on a sturdy hanger on a strong hook (on the back of a door, or perhaps even on your shower rod).

Making a suit from an old coat: If the fabric of the coat is sufficiently light weight, you can make a suit of it. This is not as difficult as it sounds. Simply remove the coat lining and possible innerlining. Try the coat on and decide the length you want the jacket. The coat might be long and have a good deep hem. So, a skirt can easily be made from the coat skirt, even if you need to face the hem. Most coats are fairly loosely fitted so that you would probably have to settle for a boxy, loose-fitting jacket. See whether you wish to remove the cuffs or change the sleeve lengths. Possibly you will like it better without a collar. If the coat is a wrap-around without buttons, perhaps you will wish to add a buttoned closing for the suit jacket. Your bound buttonhole maker makes new buttonholes a simple process. You can probably crop the length to hip or midriff length and have enough left over for a simple skirt. If the coat has a seam down the center back, you may need to make a four-gored skirt.

► Make Over Old Styles into New

If a suit is several seasons old and outdated, you can re-style it by chopping inches off and making a shortie jacket style or a bolero. Shorten the sleeves to bracelet- or elbow-length. Remove the collar and change the shape of the neckline. Use small pieces of fabric to add new details, such as patch pockets or amusing triangular buttonholes.

A couple of years ago I made a "sack" dress and was then slim enough to wear it. The next season, it was not only a dismal outdated style but I had taken on some poundage. But, this year it is one of the smartest things I own. Because of the original style, the back was plenty wide. I needed the changes around my thighs. So, I tied a string around my waist and cut the dress apart 1″ below the string all around. This allows a little blousing at my naturally high waistline plus a ½″ seam. I darted the skirt back about 3″ each side of the center, where darts normally go, and slightly gathered the blouse back so it would fit. The front skirt and blouse were both given release pleats over the pelvic area. A new waistline seam was made and a dress zipper added at the left side. Because I still needed more room in the dress I used the see-thru ruler and tailor's chalk and drew a straight line from the neck to the hem about 2″ left of the center front. Then, I machine-stitched a double line ½″ apart, each side of chalk line, and slashed through the center all the way. When I make a dress, I always save fabric pieces until it is worn out or given away, so I had enough scraps to make a 4″ insert band, facings, neckline trim, buttonholes, and buttons. One yard is enough if you have to buy new material in same color or contrast. The insert band is made double, 4″ wide, the full length of the front opening, pieced at the waistline. Face the fronts back 2″. I cut the dress neck into a low, wide "boat" shape, faced it with a bias of the fabric and added a 2″ bias fold for trimming. With the aid

Fig. XII-3   Fig. XII-4

of my bound buttonhole maker, new buttonholes were placed strategically down both sides of the opening (Fig. XII-3). The insert was then buttoned-in with good-sized self-covered buttons.

Here's a suggestion for making an old shirtmaker dress look new (Fig. XII-4). Begin by tinting it a new shade with a commercial dye. If the skirt has stitched-down pleats and the stitch marks can be removed, rip them out and turn them into new unpressed box pleats with the help of pleated stiffening at the waistline. Take off the collar and lower the neckline by turning it in at the depth you want. Baste along the turn, cut on the basted line, and face with bias. Close with a giant-sized self-button and large buttonhole. Rip out the sleeves and bias-bind the armholes, then shorten or otherwise adjust the hem. Add a stiff, wide belt made from the sleeves.

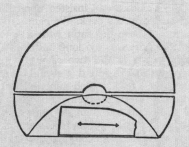

Fig. XII-5A Straight Skirt Cut From Circular

Fig. XII-5B

Not long ago a friend came wailing that she had been invited to a banquet and hadn't a thing to wear! I knew her closet was full of clothes and insisted upon pulling out some of the things buried in the back. We came upon an imported French creation of beautiful satin with a flattering decolleté neckline. But the skirt was too long and full. Like most completely circular skirts it had two seams, with one of them straight of goods. So, we found a straight skirt pattern with only two seams and folded each generous half-circle so that the pattern pieces fitted into them (Fig. XII-5A). In a single evening, we made this new slim skirt and had enough fabric left for a bias-fold cummerbund. My friend went to her banquet and never had more compliments than on her beautiful gown which no one had seen for five years (Fig. XII-5B).

Did you ever get a permanent stain or cigarette hole right on the front of a dress when it was almost new? Put a lovely contrasting plastron over it. (Fig. XII-6); make several of them to switch-change. The one I made, after spilling nail polish, was full-length. It is a straight strip of fabric, just shoulder-width wide and the length of the dress plus a 3″ hem. Cinch it in at the waistline with a double contour belt which you can make by half-hitching two single self-covered contour belts at the back. Weight the bottom corners of the plastron with lead weights, to keep it from flapping awkwardly as you walk. Make a 1″-wide hem around all edges except at its hem, or make it two-faced in two colors to switch around. Button it on at shoulder and hip line with large self-buttons and contrasting buttonholes. The last step is to make the hem, after you try on the completed make-over.

This front plastron idea could be adopted by expectant mothers who need to extend their maternity wardrobe. The dress beneath may be adapted with a stretch panel. It is applied at the waistline of the skirt section. When working with the stretch panel, use a loose machine-thread tension. Gently stretch the fabric when sewing. This stretch panel comes in nylon stretch-jersey of a size large enough to convert regular clothes into maternity clothes, and with matching draw tape (Fig. XII-7). Test the panel for the direction of maximum stretch, which should be sewn on the horizontal (Fig. XII-7A). Use a maternity pattern to shape the piece, allowing 1½″ at the top of casing and ⅝″ seam around other sides (Fig. XII-7B). On the right side mark the position for one eyelet slot 1¾″ down from the center top and ½″ deep. Face the eyelet area by basting 1¼″ square of fabric

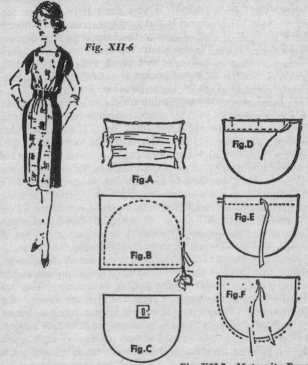

Fig. XII-6

Fig.A

Fig.B

Fig.C

Fig.D

Fig.E

Fig.F

Fig. XII-7   Maternity Panel

(like muslin) on the wrong side. Stitch the eyelet with the machine buttonhole attachment (Fig. XII-7C). Cut the center of the eyelet open and trim away the excess facing material. To form the casing make a ⅜" hem (Fig. XII-7D). Cut the draw-tape in half and insert the tape through each side of the casing and out at the eyelet (Fig. XII-7E). Stitch through all thicknesses at both sides of the casing. Make the necessary opening in the garment by cutting it with the help of the pattern and insert the maternity panel by top-stitching all around the panel edges (Fig. XII-7F).

▶ *Pockets to Camouflage Holes*

If there is a tear or hole you can make it an excuse for a fashion change on your garment. Is it in a place that you can disguise with a pocket? If you don't have enough material to make the pocket like the garment, choose a contrasting fabric. A half yard is plenty to make a pocket or two, plus a matching belt, tie, or collar. Make it just a plain patch pocket, a fancy decorative pocket or, if you are real good, try a slot pocket. The patch pocket is easiest to make. However, first darn the hole as flat as possible. Then, mark where pocket is going with a basting line for the top edge. To make your pocket, cut out two flat pieces, same way of the goods, any shape you wish. With the right sides of the fabric together, sew them up on three sides. Trim the seams to ⅛" and turn to the right side, shape, and press, using a point turner for good clean corners and edges. Turn in the edges of the fourth side and slip-stitch them together. If you like, add a saddle-stitch by hand or machine. Place the pocket over the darned area, and blind-stitch or machine-stitch it down.

A decorative pocket may be made scalloped with the help of your see-thru scalloper or by arrangement of points and decorative buttons. The material for the pocket must be prepared with a stay-stitch marking for width and position. Use press-on interlining on the wrong side to reinforce the pocket. Draw the design of the pocket on the stay. The top of the design should come ¼" below the center line of the marking. Start stitching at the center of the top line, using a short stitch. Take exactly the same number of stitches across each end and pivot the material on the needle at each corner. Overlap the stitches when you come back to the starting point. Press. Cut through the three thicknesses of the material to ¼" of the ends. Then miter the corners. Trim carefully around the scallops, leaving a ⅛" seam. Press. Turn the pocket to the wrong side and shape the scallops or points perfectly with your point turned. Press the seams away from the opening at the top and ends, and press the design so the edges or points are sharp. Turn up the lower portion of the pocket section to form a welt and cover the opening. Pin and baste. Press down the back section of the pocket and pin the sections together. Turn back the garment and stay stitch across the ends of the pockets and stitch the pocket section together. Press.

▶ *Lengthening Hem with Contrasting Material*

When hems creep up and you don't know how to save the growing-up girl's dress that seemed only to have been bought

Fig. XII-8 Lengthening Growing Child's Dress

yesterday, you might borrow an idea from the mother of a teenager, whom I know. She let down the hem all the way and added 4″ so that her style-conscious miss was simply sensational in the eyes of her set (Fig. XII-8). The dress was an all-over dark green paisley print. She bought ½ yard of plain orange to match one of the bright colors in the print. After measuring the full width of the hem, she made a double 4″ band to go around it. She used her see-thru scalloper and made scallops on the hem faced in orange. At the center of each curve she machine-stitched small buttonholes. Then, she covered enough small paisley buttons (of dress fabric) to attach the band to the bottom of the scallops. She had some orange fabric left over for a buttoned-on plastron front on the bodice. The whole dress turned out even cuter than when it was new.

▶ Men's Clothes Made Over for Women and Children

The perennial make-over source is dad's suit which may become many things. The thin or worn parts are usually found at the cuffs and in the knees, seat, and pockets of the trousers. However, a suit needn't be shabby to become a discard. Perhaps it no longer fits. Or, it may have a damage in one area that would necessitate a too expensive professional re-weaving-job. Sometimes you might prefer using the wrong side of the fabric for making your new piece of clothing. Men's wear fabrics can usually be used either side and the other side may look fresher and newer. Take a common-sense view, if the suit you are planning to remake is too badly worn it may not be worth the effort. The color may have faded in spots, or the worn places may come up too often to allow pattern manipulation on the right grain. Only good fabric is ever worth re-using. Make over an old suit only if you know you're going to have something to be proud of. Does it need to be cleaned before you rip? If it's not too soiled you might wait until after ripping and have all the pieces cleaned and pressed well at the ripped edges. If you have it cleaned before ripping warn the tailor *not* to press the creases into the trousers and sleeves.

A large variety of clothing can be made from a man's suit if you keep in mind fullness as the one limitation. If mother is making over the suit for herself, dad has to be several sizes larger than she is. Also, wide or flared skirts are out, as are raglan shoulders. Here's a list of possible items: You can easily make a suit, a jumper or tailored dress, a short jacket or jerkin, shorts, slacks or a skirt, a hat, a bag and several other things for yourself. For the children, you can manage a coat or ski suit, a skirt or shorts, trousers or overalls, a vest, a jacket and a hat. If you use a size 38 man's suit, which is average, you should be able to make any of the following combinations: Slacks and a short jacket; a jerkin, skirt and hat; a suit-dress and small clutch bag; a child's coat and hat; a suit with a vest for a boy; a skirt or overalls, jacket and hat; a pair of ski pants and a cap. That's quite a yield, wouldn't you say?

Probably you'd better consider the kind of men's wear fabric most appropriate for various types of garments before you decide what you will make. For instance, a light weight flannel would be just the thing for a coat for a little girl, while a sturdy tweed would make a boy feel most masculine.

First, several worthwhile tips before you start. *Do not* pull the seams apart when ripping because you run the risk of tearing your fabric and losing valuable inches. Use your *seam ripper* to rip the fine stitches. Be careful to pick off all ripped threads when finished. If you think you have plenty of fabric, you can cut close along the seam line with your scissors and throw away the old seam. This assures you of having no-stitch-marks where they might show. Trousers are always ripped apart completely.

If you're planning to make a tailored suit jacket for yourself, much the same style as the man's jacket you are remaking, if you are very ingenious, you might be able to lay your pattern so as to save some of the collar and lapel tailoring. In this event, remember that a man's jacket buttons just the opposite to a woman's. So, perhaps a bolero pattern might hold the collar line and yet allow cutting away at button line. The thing is, carefully select your pattern as much as possible like the style of the suit. If you intend using fabric on its reverse side, rip the jacket apart entirely.

Depending entirely upon the style of suit you've ripped apart, you usually have about nine large pieces and several small ones (one back section, two front sections, two lapel facings and four trouser sections). If you did wait till now to have fabric cleaned, pin the related sections together and send to cleaner with instructions to take special care to flatten seams.

Some men's suits are fully lined, but sometimes they are only half lined. By the time you get the suit for make-over, the lining is rather the worse for wear. Also, lining fabrics in men's suits are very masculine and drab of color. Unless the suit is being converted into something for a young boy, you'll want a more feminine lining fabric and color. Perhaps you have an old dress of gay color or print which you can convert into the lining. Or have fun with patchwork and make up a lining of many colors.

Before you shop for any new lining or interfacing, look over the old pieces. When you ripped it apart, did you notice the tailor's padding stitches you had to remove? This is one of the fine tailoring details you should remember for your own future tailoring skills. It was done to hold the interfacing in place at just the right roll line on the collar and lapel. When you buy new interfacing try to get the same general quality you found in the old garment.

Your cutting board is as important to you when recutting used fabrics as though you had new fabric with selvages. I am not sure it isn't even more so. Figuring out the layout for make-over pieces takes longer than with new fabric, because you have no layout guide to work from (Fig. XII-9). Examine each piece for lengthwise and crosswise grain threads. Then, with your tailor's chalk and see-thru ruler, draw a straight line on the wrong side through both grains, at right angles to each other. Pin the pieces down on the marked off lines of the cutting board, on these chalked grain markings. Note the sections having buttonholes and darts that must be avoided in the layout. Also, try to circumvent the most worn areas.

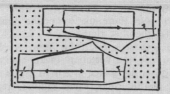

Fig. XII-9 Laying Out Skirt On Trouser Pieces

When you start to lay out your pattern, begin with the biggest piece. In the case of a child's coat, for instance, I found the largest was the front, especially if it was double-breasted. So, I discovered the trouser sections were just right. That meant laying the two back trouser sections grain on grain, right sides inside, so both fronts could be cut at once. The back pattern piece came next and it was laid on the trouser fronts. The sleeves came out of the best part of the coat sleeves, and the worn area around the elbow was avoided.

▶ Make-Overs from Men's Shirts

When a man's shirt reaches its retirement age, because of some worn spots or the size no longer fits, it may be cut down for the younger male members of the family by removing cuffs, shortening the sleeves and then replacing cuffs. Possibly by taking in the seams a bit, the old shirt will make a good fit for the smaller boys. Any worn spots should, of course, be properly darned or reinforced.

There are some wonderful, easy tricks that you can use to convert the man's old shirts into articles of apparel for yourself. You'd probably get many more wearings out of a fine piece of broadcloth than your young boy. Why not make yourself a tailored blouse to go with that new skirt or jumper?

To make a pleasant blouse: The requirements are one old white shirt and 11 yards of gaily embroidered trimming tape. Remove the shirt collar and sew enough bands of tape around the neck to completely cover the neckband. Remove the cuffs and do the same on sleeves. Also, edge each side of the button tab with rows and rows of tape. Of course, the front buttons all wrong for a woman. To change the button line use your eyelet pliers over places where the buttons and button-holes were. Attach eyelets to blend with color of tape, and use studs through them. The button side will come over the buttonhole side if you sew up the buttonholes before attaching the eyelet.

To make a beach coat: If the old shirt is a bold check or plaid, or a gaudy Hawaiian print, make a beach coat from it. Get 4½ yards of cotton fringe and a couple of packages of pearl Dot snappers. The snapper package tells you how to apply snappers to the front with the attached tool. Or you can put them on with a duo-purpose Dot snapper pliers kit. Remove the collar and cuffs from the shirt. Sew a border of cotton fringe around the top and bottom of the neckband. To get a more finished look, open the neckband seam both top and bottom, insert the fringe, and sew it into the seam line. Sew a border of fringe around the edge of the sleeve, carrying it up to the end of the sleeve opening. If you would like a puffed sleeve look, about 3″ from the fringed edge make several rows of shirr-stitching with nylon elastic thread. To have a belted back effect, you can make ½″ pleats across the entire back of the shirt at the waistline by using a strip of pleated stiffening underneath.

To make a night-shortie: I have a note here that says "Teenagers love night-shorties," but don't we all in the summertime? Turn a man's old night shirt into a female glamour version of same. All you need is about 4½ yards of assorted widths of eyelet-embroidered ruffling and some nylon elastic thread. Remove the collar and cuffs, and puff the sleeves with several rows of nylon elastic shirt-stitching. Then, extend the edge with a ruffle of 2″ eyelet embroidery. In the same way, edge each side of the bottom tab with ½″ ruffling. Sew two rows of 1½″ eyeletting together and apply it to the edge of the neckband. Add a border of 3½″ ruffling around the bottom of the shirt to give it more length if desired.

►Miscellaneous Make-Overs

Since I began this chapter I've found so many good ideas for altering and make-over that I could almost fill another book! For instance, a baby's layette of nightgown, sacque, bootees and carrying blanket may be made from a soft, oft-washed old summer blanket. A baby's christening dress, petticoat and bib may be made from great-grandfather's ruffled evening shirt. A summer play dress and a mother and daughter look-alike bathing suit duo may be made from an old bedspread. New blouses may be made from old shirts, a lady's handsome topcoat from a man's coat.

A helpful booklet which you may obtain by writing to the U. S. Department of Agriculture, Washington 25, D. C., is *Make-Overs from Leather, Fur and Felt (Miscellaneous Publication #614.* This shows a variety of things that can be made over from these materials; it runs the gamut from boys' weskits to mittens, and other accessories for family use or to make as gifts.

CHAPTER 13

Sewing for the Home

Every woman has a divine spark and a talent to create beautiful things for her home, and the home sewer has the advantage of being able to make many things with her needle to enhance the interior decorating theme and to be able to do so within the budget she can afford.

Dressing your home, like dressing yourself, can be done on a strictly personal basis through your choice of color, texture, fiber, fabric, and design. By mastering the techniques of elementary sewing and the simple stitches of needlepoint, crewel embroidery, appliqué, smocking, patchwork, and sewing machine embroidery, you put your own signature on your achievement. Today it is just as smart to individualize our homes with crafts our feminine ancestors used as it ever was.

Even when turning to patterns to sew for your home, your own interpretation of how to use them brings out your individuality. While leafing through the current pattern catalogues, I have found the following: (1) bedroom ensembles, some very simple to make, others more complicated with all-over smocking; (2) some very attractive curtain and drapery ideas; (3) pillows and bolsters of all sizes and shapes; many of them smocked, quilted, crewel-embroidered, flower- and fruit-shaped, with tuft button in center, and some very simple ones; (4) slip-cover patterns for almost all simple, straight-line furniture shapes; (5) lovely patchwork quilts, patchwork designs and appliqués for curtain borders, pillows and whole room schemes; (6) crib cover designs and other decorating items for baby's and child's room; (7) utility covers for various appliances, such as mixers and toasters, also bird cage covers; (8) simple and fancy embroidery stitches and appliqué designs for towels, place mat sets, and pillow and sheet edges; (9) various initial designs for monograms to personalize household linens.

In just one chapter of this book I cannot possibly cover all the avenues of self expression possible in sewing for the home. You alone know your own needs and capabilities. Over a period of time I have collected many good ideas from home magazines, and have obtained many home-decorating booklets (which are available at upholstery fabric departments in good shops) which give information on how to use fabrics and fixtures; there are excellent sources to stimulate your own ideas. The sewing departments offer a large variety of paper patterns for articles to be made for the home, and in each case the instruction sheet, giving step-by-step directions, is included with the pattern in the same way as for sewing clothes.

Sewing for the home should be as easy as, if not easier than, sewing for one's self or family, because a window or chair stands still when you go to measure it and you do not need to accommodate that measuring apparatus to pulsing curves or bulging flesh. There are, in fact, homemakers who think nothing of whipping up some curtains who have never dared to attempt the intricacies of making a dress.

▶ *Tools and Accessories to Sew Home Decorations*

A good sewing job depends, in large measure, on the tools which are used, in addition to your sewing skill. The following lists the aids which you can buy to make your sewing easier and to enable you to produce a more professional finish to your work:

Roll-up yardstick, which bends to measure around curves, corners, sills or other jutting places

Tape measure

Cutting board

See-thru ruler and tailor's chalk and chalk holder, for marking before cutting into fabric

See-thru scalloper for marking curves

Heavy-duty sewing thread, or synthetic thread for synthetic fabrics

Beeswax, to add strength to thread and make it easier to sew with

Sewing machine needles and hand needles, various sizes for different fabric thicknesses

Mattress needles (curved), and other special needles in the home repair kit

Two-way Dot snapper pliers kit and the large and small eyelet pliers kit, for sturdy fastenings

Self-covered buttons for tufting, or the large ones for pillow centers

Fig. XIII-1A   Rubber Cushion Protectors

1" wide ready-pleated stiffening, also special 4" stiffening for curtain and drapery pleats, ruffle pleats, and pinch pleats

Nylon elastic thread for shirr-stitching

Dress belting for stiffening

Lead weights to use at bottoms of curtains and draperies

Steam iron, ironing board, and press mit, so you may press as you sew

Hem pressing gauge, for pressing hems on curtains and upholstery covers

Point turner, for shaping square corners

Wrist pin cushion

Seam ripper

Bodkin, for turning narrow pieces inside out

Tweezer, to pick out ripped stitches

Little foam rubber cushions (Fig. XIII-1A) to affix on back of wood furniture to keep walls from getting marked. Also to apply on back of pictures to hold them straight and on back of doors to prevent banging

Felt pieces with adhesive backing, to apply to bottoms of lamps, book ends and bases of small dishes to prevent sliding and scratching on polished table surfaces

Knobby twist pins (Fig. XIII-1B), to anchor fabric firmly to cushioned surfaces to prevent slip-covers, etc., from slipping

Fig. XIII-1B Knobby Twist Pins in Cushioned Surfaces

Sewing machine attachments such as the hemmer, ruffler, quilter, binder, hemstitcher, and corder

Staple gun, for attaching fabric to wooden surfaces

Rug back adhesive (Fig. XIII-1C), to prevent scatter rugs from slipping

► Types and Fabrics for Curtains and Draperies

When you start to sew for your home, you will find the simplest thing to make is curtains. They may be as plain or fancy as your decorating plan determines, and as your pocketbook permits.

These are the types of curtains you could make: café, shirred glass, traverse, sash, criss-cross, ruffled tie-back, French door.

Window draperies come in these classifications: traverse (1-way draw and 2-way draw), slanting traverse, swinging door draw, cascade, and swag. Draperies often are made with these special treatments: swinging rod, dimensional curved, and arched.

In addition to curtains and draperies, windows are often dressed-up with: Austrian blinds, Roman shades, fabric shutters, as well as the conventional roller shades and the popular Venetian blinds.

There are as many types of curtain and drapery fixtures as there are types of windows. You and I are most familiar with the simple extension rods for sash curtains that we've been buying at the dime store to put up in a hurry. However, we should aim to make our sewing for the home as professional-looking as our dress fashion sewing. This largely

Fig. XIII-1C Adhesive Rug Backing

depends upon our choice of proper rods and fixtures for the purpose and type of window.

Windows come in these types: double hung, inswinging and outswinging casement, ranch or strip, awning, jalousie, picture, dormer, bay, bow, slanting, double, corner, French door, swinging glass door, Dutch door, and arched.

When your windows or doors are standard sizes you can usually find a display of good rods and fixtures in the drapery fabric department of any good department store or upholstery shop. However, if your windows are out-sized, smaller or larger than standard, it is worth the investment to have your rods and fixtures cut to order and installed by a professional. I know you may think that if you move you'll never be able to use them again. Actually, an investment in good fixtures is a lifetime thing because you can usually use most of the parts again except the lengths of rod and cords, if the new windows or doors are larger. If the spaces are shorter or smaller in a new place, the old rods and cords could be cut down.

I've discussed fibers, fabrics and finishes at length in Chapter 4. The best curtain, drapery, slip-cover and upholstery fabric can rarely be found in a dress piece goods department. Department stores and fabric shops, alike, usually have separate drapery fabric departments. My safe buying rules apply here on bargains versus brand name, only more so, because even the smallest yardage requirement means a greater investment.

Most important to a drapery fabric's serviceability are: dimensional stability, shrinkage, breaking strength, tear strength, elasticity, resilience, moisture absorption, abrasion resistance, color-fastness, resistance to moths, mildew and fire, whether or not the fabric is allergenic. All kinds of fabrics in all kinds of blends of fibers are used in modern drapery fabrics: cottons, silks, wools, linen, metallics, glass and man-made. Possibly the man-made fibers have made the greatest strides in producing economical and, at the same time, durable home decoration fabrics. Figure XIII-2 shows a very fine chart on these from *Be Your Own Decorator* by Betty Pepis. You have to be the judge of just which qualities you need to consider in your particular case.

There is only one of these man-made, fireproof fabrics that I will discuss here. *Fiber glass*, because it is the one so many people hesitate to sew on. Yet, it is one of the best in so many ways and most economical. This drapery material is made of the only fiber that cannot be combined with other fibers. In measuring for curtains of fiber glass, let them clear the ceiling and floor by at least an inch. You never need to allow for shrinkage, so be sure your measurements are absolutely accurate.

Glass-fibered fabrics are never used in everyday apparel, so we home sewers have little experience in sewing it. You may have been told that it is dangerous to work with because of the fabric dust. However, it has been proved, in factories where it is made and sewn, that there has never been any permanent ill effect to workers. When you are cutting and sewing it, the frayed edges may give off lint. Wear a long-sleeved smock, buttoned to the wrist. Wash your hands and arms frequently in cold water and sprinkle baby powder on yourself generously. Be sure to use the best permanently-sized crinoline sewed into the headings, because you'll be washing this material often.

Particularly because it's so slithery in long lengths, pin this fabric down to your cutting board carefully before you cut it, and electric scissors will do the cutting beautifully with the least amount of fabric dust.

Be sure that feed plate and presser foot on sewing machine are in perfect condition. Keep your machine and plate perfectly clean while you work. Use a fine needle and change to a new one whenever it seems to snag or pucker the

MAN-MADE MATERIALS FOR CURTAINS AND DRAPERIES

As with carpeting, man-made materials are beginning to dominate the window covering picture. Ease of maintenance of many of the newest ones and color fast qualities make them particularly adaptable to the large glass areas of today's homes.

FIBER	BRAND NAME	MAINTENANCE
ACETATE AND SOLUTION-DYED ACETATE	ACELE ARNEL CELAIRE CELAPERM CELANESE ACETATE CHROMSPUN COLORSPUN ESTRON FIBER 25	DRY-CLEANING, SOME ARE HAND WASHABLE.
ACRYLIC AND MODACRYLIC	DYNEL ORLON VEREL	IRON AT LOW TEMPERATURE, HAND-WASHABLE OR DRY-CLEANING.
GLASS FIBERS	FIBERGLAS FIBER GLASS	EXCELLENT EASE-OF-CARE, WASHABLE, NO-IRON, QUICK-DRY.
NYLON	CHEMSTRAND NYLON DU PONT NYLON	FOLLOW MANUFACTURER'S DIRECTIONS.
POLYESTER	DACRON KODEL	OFTEN MACHINE WASHABLE, SOMETIMES MUST BE HAND WASHED, LITTLE OR NO IRONING.
RAYON AND SOLUTION-DYED RAYON	AVISCO RAYON AVLIN AVRIL AVRON COLORAY COLORSPUN CORVAL II BEMBERG ENKA RAYON FLAIKONA FORTISAN JETSPUN ONDELETTE TOPEL	FOLLOW MANUFACTURER'S DIRECTIONS.
SARAN	ROVANNA SARANSPUN	EXCELLENT EASE-OF-CARE. HAND WASH OR DRY CLEAN.

Fig. XIII-2

COLOR-FASTNESS	GENERAL CHARACTERISTICS
AVERAGE.	SOFT LUSTROUS FEEL, GOOD DRAPING, GOOD RESISTANCE TO CREASING, MILDEW, HEAT AND WRINKLING.
FAIR, TEND TO DARKEN IN SUN.	SOFT FEEL, EXCELLENT DRAPING.
FAIR TO GOOD.	DURABLE, ALTHOUGH TENDS TO BREAK WITH EXCESSIVE FOLDING OR HANDLING. FIREPROOF, RESISTS SUN, HEAT, MOTHS, MILDEW, WRINKLING.
GOOD.	WRINKLE-RESISTANT, CREASE-HOLDING —FIBER MELTS BEFORE BURNING.
EXCELLENT, STRENGTH DECREASES AFTER LONG EXPOSURE TO SUN.	CAN BE PERMANENTLY PLEATED, DURABLE, WRINKLE-RESISTANT.
EXCELLENT IN SOLUTION-DYED, AVERAGE FOR OTHER TYPES.	SOFT FEEL AND GOOD DRAPING ABILITY. BURNS RELATIVELY FAST. ALTHOUGH GOOD HEAT RESISTANCE, FAIR TO GOOD BREAK-RESISTANCE, FAIR TO GOOD DURABILITY, WRINKLE RESISTANCE, DEPENDING UPON MAKE, POOR CREASE RETENTION.
EXCELLENT.	SOFT-FEEL, GOOD DRAPING ABILITY. NON-FLAMMABLE, GOOD CREASE RETENTION, GOOD RESISTANCE.

Fig. XIII-2

fabric. Use three-cord mercerized thread or nylon, 8 stitches to the inch, with an easy tension. Pile the bulk of the material on a table nearby so the weight of it will not drag down while you work.

Fiber glass draperies will stay beautiful and new-looking for a long time if washed frequently. Because soil does not penetrate the fiber itself, removal of dirt is simple. No ironing is required. It's best to wash by hand in moderately warm water (100° to 120° F.) if possible, and squeeze out the best part of the water, but do not wring. Draperies may be hung back at windows because they dry very quickly. Or, hang over a pole until almost dry and complete the drying hung at the windows. The only automatic washer that should ever be used is a front-loading one, at reverse low speed, with a high-water level. Wash no more than a two-minute wash cycle with two one-minute rinses at the same temperature and speed. Agitation which causes abrasion is death on fiber glass. Glass-fibered fabrics are made into light weights for transparent curtains, as well as plain and printed heavier draperies.

► *Kind of Window Treatment*

What's the difference between curtains, draperies, blinds or shades? A curtain is defined as a "hanging screen," put up to hide or obscure the view but let in the light, so it is most frequently of transparent or translucent fabric.

Blinds or shades are pulled up or down, closed or opened, to shut out or let in light at will. They can be anything from wooden shutters to metal Venetians, or bamboo matchstick, or the new fabric blinds now so popular to make at home.

Draperies are added to a window treatment to decorate and dress it up. They may be opened or drawn to regulate light and air. They are usually thought of as window treatment, but in modern homes they may be used as decorative treatment of blank walls without windows. Consequently, transparent fabrics are seldom used for draperies. Draperies are also used as room dividers.

► *Making a Roller Shade*

Sometimes only curtains or only draperies are used at a window. Most often, curtains and draperies are combined for a full window treatment. But, when blinds or shades are needed for light control, they are thought of first. Since a shade requires no shaping or fullness, let's begin learning to make hems on a shade. The fabric should be firmly woven and opaque. A very pretty effect with plain, sheer curtains is to make your shades of a printed chintz.

You can use the old rollers and sticks—which stiffen the hem from former shades that were hung at your window, or buy rollers and sticks and they can be cut to correct size. The roller shade is completed the width of the wooden part of roller plus the two metal ends, but not as long as the spring projections. Add enough for 1" hems on each side. Take accurate measurements, with a yard stick, from the roller to the window sill. The casing hem at the bottom of the shade has to be large enough for the stick to fit into, which will probably be 1½" or 2" wide. So, add that amount to the length, plus ½" seam allowance. The top edge of the fabric will be stapled to the roller, so apply to it a piece of twill tape across the raw edge to reinforce it and keep it from ravelling.

If the selvage edge has any tendency to draw up, trim it off. To be sure that the fabric for the roller shade is absolutely grain-perfect, pull a crosswise thread and cut it true along the thread. The heavier drapery fabric or chintz from which roller shades are usually made should never be torn because this distorts the grain or "dimensional stability," as they call it in the home decorating field.

Set up your iron and ironing board and get out your pressing gauge (Fig. XIII-3). If I never used this little device for anything else than pressing in curtain hems, it would be worth the investment for this purpose alone. The hems are so much more accurate and less work when first pressed in. Placing the straight side of the gauge under the hem edge, turn the fabric over as far as the ¼" mark and press. Continue for the length of the side edge, pressing in a straight ¼" turn. Now, turn the folded edge over the straight side of the gauge to the 1" mark and press in a 1" hem down the entire side. Press the hem into the opposite side length the same way, Then, stitch the two side hems.

To make a simple casing hem at the bottom edge for the stick to slip through, turn up the ½" seam allowance on the pressing hem gauge to the ½" line and press. Turn the folded edge up wide enough to accommodate the stick and press over the straight edge of the gauge the entire distance of the hem. Stitch the hem and insert the stick. Staple the

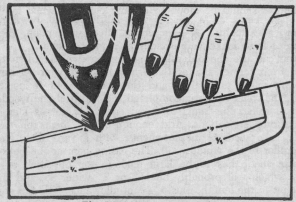

Fig. XIII-3   Pressing Gauge

top of the shade to the roller. Press your shade and hang it up.

If you want to make a fancy scalloped edge to hang below the stick, it has to be calculated as double the width of this edge plus the width of the casing. At the same time, remember, when finished, this wider hem is a part of the over-all length of roller shade, not added to it. So, let us say the decorative hem will be 4″. Turn back 4″ plus 2″, wrong side out. In other words, a 72″ shade has to have 6″ added for a fancy hem. Find the center of the width and place a pin. Lay the edge of the *see-thru scalloper* on the folded fabric at this center line and draw around the largest-size scallop, with chalk, repeating the design to the edge of the fabric. Begin again at the center and mark scallops to the other side. Stitch around scallops carefully, with two stitches across the joinings of each. Cut out the scallops, snip the curve at the outer edges, turn and press. Now, press and stitch the side hems, making a casing for the stick, and blind-stitch finish outside scallop ends. Upholstery fringe might be added to this edge for decoration.

▶ *Sewing Your Curtains*

Sheer curtains may be made of nylon or dacron or fiber glass, ninon, from marquisette, scrim, voile, dotted Swiss, organdy or batiste; and for more formal treatment from thin silks or synthetics, often containing threads of gold, embroidered, flocked or screen-printed. They may be tucked, tiered, ruffled, shirred, decoratively stitched and trimmed with braid or fringe.

Fixtures should be mounted so that curtains, when hung, will cover the window frame. There are three correct lengths for curtains: to the window sill, to the lower edge of the apron (the part of the window casing below the sill), or to the floor. The fixture may have been placed at the top of the window casing or anywhere between there and the ceiling.

For measuring curtain material: measure the length from the top of the rod down to wherever you wish the curtain to come. For width, measure from the outer edge of the fixture brackets, adding the length a rod may curve inward on both sides (this curve is called a return). Your roll-up yardstick measures a return exactly. The hem and heading widths have to be added to the length measurement. Several widths of fabric may have to be sewn together to make curtains full enough. With some fabrics as much as 1″ per yard may have to be allowed for shrinkage. With sheer fabrics it is often much prettier to use double hems so this amount should be added to the rest. Very sheer fabrics usually look best made three times the width. In other words, three lengths of fabric are added together. If fabric is stiffer and less sheer, two or two-and-a-half times the width is enough.

Use mercerized thread and a size 14 needle for anything made of natural fibers. But, sew synthetic fabrics with synthetic thread and a size 11 needle.

With sheer glass curtains, use a double side hem of 1¼″ width and press over the hem pressing gauge in the same way you did the roller shade hems. A top hem is frequently made with a casing for the rod to go through, but it is sewn straight like the side hems. The bottom hem is made 4″ to 6″ deep and doubled, if very sheer.

Criss-cross curtains. White or very light-colored criss-cross curtains are so lovely to look at but such a chore to launder, as they must be kept absolutely clean. Here are my directions for making them so they are put together at the heading with *Dot snappers* (Fig. XIII-4) to make them easier to take care of:

Ours were made for a 77″ window, and the following measurements of fabric are given accordingly; but measure yours for your own. From a 10½-yard length to 39″ permanent-finish organdy cut 4 widths, each 89″ long. Lay aside the remaining 22″ piece to be used for tiebacks and heading ruffle. With the help of the marks on your cutting board and your see-thru ruler measure

off 18½" from the edge. Lay two widths of fabric over
the cutting board and pin down at the first edge crosswise
and lengthwise mark. Use a yardstick and mark a chalk
line down the length, 18½" from one edge. You will have to
shift the fabric once to the other end of the board to finish
through the entire length. Use the narrow hemmer or
hemstitch attachment or setting on your machine and stitch
straight along this line on both pieces, laying aside each
18½" strip for ruffling.

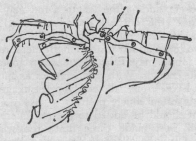

Fig. XIII-4

Join each remaining 20½" strip to each full width, basting
a ½" seam along the selvages. (If you are covering a wider
window, add widths of fabric according to the 2-to-1 ratio.)
Hemstitch along this seam and cut through the center of the
hemstitching to form a picoted edge. Turn under the remaining selvage edge and stitch. Hemstitch ½" from the
edge, then cut through to form a picot finish here.

Ruffles. Every 6" mark off lines on each of the two 18½"
strips and hemstitch through them to make 6" wide ruffling.
Join into one continuous strip with picoted seams. Measure
and cut off 64" to use for the ruffling on the top casing
edge. Set the ruffler attachment on your sewing machine
for the scant ruffle, allowing approximately once and half
again for fullness. Ruffle the remaining 6" strip and apply
along the picoted edge of the length and lower edge of
each curtain. (Take care that two pieces face each other
right side out.) On the 22" strip which runs from selvage
to selvage, picot a row ½" from outside edge. Then, mark
and picot into 6" strips from selvage to selvage for heading
ruffles. There will be a 4" strip left over which will be used
for tiebacks. Join the 6" strips with picot seams, and ruffle
on the ruffler as before.

Casing and heading. Press a ¼″ turn on the raw edge, and stitch. Cut off a 64″ strip of cotton twill tape and apply it along the right side of one folded edge. With Dot snapper pliers apply the "ring" and "socket" half of Dot snappers all the way across, according to the package instructions. Place them about 4″ apart, through organdy and tape, with "socket" facing out on the tape which is on the wrong side of the heading piece. This is the half of the curtain which crosses *over* the other half. After the top halves of the snappers have all been applied, bring the opposite folded edge over the "ring" parts and stitch it across the taped edge, which makes the casing. Pin the casing ruffle along the seam edge of the casing, on the right side of the band, placed so the heading of the ruffle will further conceal the "ring" of the snappers, and stitch together. Turn the upper edge of the top curtain half to the wrong side and press a ¼″ turn. Pin this fold under the ruffle of the casing, along the heading line, and stitch.

Press a ¼″ turn toward the right side on the upper edge of the under curtain and press over the hem pressing gauge as always. Pin a second 64″ piece of twill tape along this folded edge and stitch on the right side. Apply the "stud" side of the Dot snappers along the edge with the "stud" out on the tape side, spaced so each one matches the corresponding "socket" on the top curtain.

Snap the under curtain to the top curtain and thread the rod through the casing. Only one rod is needed and the two curtains may be unsnapped and washed separately much more easily.

Tie Backs. Cut the tie-back strip in two, leaving each piece 19½″ x 4″. Turn under each short side ¼″ and stitch a 4″ strip of twill tape along the folded edge, stitching down both sides of the tape. Apply corresponding sides of Dot snappers to each end. Fold in half lengthwise, stitch, turn and press.

I have these criss-cross curtains at the top of my bedroom windows now. But, what if you had to deal with the problem of my windows pictured in Fig. XIII-5A? One long window is right next to one short window, in a long narrow room. After much searching through decorating magazines and wandering around department store display rooms, I finally found the solution and here it is:

Café curtains. My furnishings are quaint, so café curtains to match the dust ruffle on my bed are appropriate at the

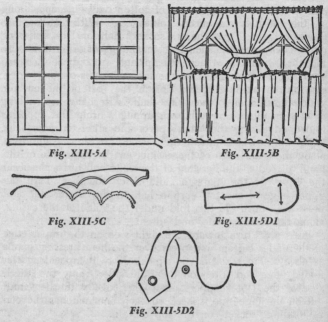

Fig. XIII-5A   Fig. XIII-5B

Fig. XIII-5C   Fig. XIII-5D1

Fig. XIII-5D2

bottom half of the windows (Fig. XIII-5B). A brass café rod was mounted a little above the half-way point across both windows. With floor-length cafés all across, the camouflage is complete, and you'd never have known if I had not told you the two windows are not alike. Moreover, the treatment lends width to the room.

I used Dot snappers on my café curtains, too, but this time decorative pearl Dots to snap the fabric loops together around the café rod. Another nice way to trim would have been to use size 30 buttons covered in chintz against plain colored loops. Make bound buttonholes with the bound buttonhole maker or machine-stitched buttonholes at the center of each loop.

Chintz is about 36″ wide and I made 5″ scallops with 1¼″ loop spacing between each one. It's easier to make the loops separately and sew them on at the space line than to plan them all at once; also it saves fabric. There are six scallops and seven loops to each width of fabric. To the length of your curtains add 4½″ for the top hem and 2¾″

for the lower hem. Cut a strip of stiffening (please use the very best washable crinoline) 4″ wide and as long as the width of the curtain, minus 2½″ which is allowance for side hems. Draw the scalloped outline on the stiffening with chalk and the help of your see-thru ruler. Measure off the amount for each scallop and loop space between and use the edge of a cup or saucer to get a good curve. On the wrong side of the curtain, 4½″ below the top, pin marked stiffening between the side hem allowances. Using hem pressing gauge, turn and press a ¼″ fold and 1″ hems down both sides and stitch them in. Turn the top hem back, right sides together, along the top edges of the stiffening. Stitch around the scallops with a smaller stitch than usual and cut around shaping ¼″ from stitching. Slash the seam towards the stitching every ½″ (Fig. XIII-5C). Turn the hem right side out, shape the curve, and press. Stitch or hand hem.

My loops were made with three-corner points, but you might shape yours round with the help of your see-thru scalloper, or make them some other shape according to your fancy (Fig. XIII-5D1). Make a pattern the size indicated here with the aid of your see-thru ruler. Cut two pieces of fabric for each loop and place them right sides together. Leave the bottom end open and, allowing ¼″ seams, stitch from the narrow end all around. Trim the seams to about ¹⁄₁₆″ and turn the loop inside out with a bodkin. Use a point turner to poke the pointed corners, then shape and press. Turn in and close the end edges, stitching them neatly. Stitch this end of loop to the wrong side of the curtain at the space between curves (Fig. XIII-5D2). In this way, make and apply as many loops as required to finish the top of the curtains. Apply the decorative top of Dot snapper at the center point of a loop, fit it around the rod and mark where the other snapper half belongs. Allow the loop to hang gracefully and not too tightly to the rod. Attach the other half of the snapper over the mark. Be sure snappers are applied on all loops the same way.

Of course, you can hang scalloped café curtains without adding the loops between the curves. I made some striped denim cafés for a friend's shore cottage, and punched large eyelets through the top of the narrow space between scallops with my two-way eyelet pliers. We hung them on the rod with thick cotton cord through each eyelet and tied a sailor's knot. Then we made cushions for her "ice-cream-

Fig. XIII-6 Organdy Shower Curtain

parlor" metal-framed chairs that were laced together around the boxed edge with the same large eyelets and heavy cord. There was enough denim left over for place mats. We made a ship-shaped pocket at the corner of each mat to hold a napkin and keep it from blowing away.

Organdy shower curtain (Fig. XIII-6). I am going to tell you how to make an organdy shower curtain! Sounds utterly unpractical? With its clear plastic lining, long enough to keep inside the tub while showering, it is as sensible as any other, and oh so glamorous!

Shower curtains are a standard size, so I can give you the amount of material required: 10 yards of permanent finished organdy; 6 yards of 36" vinyl plastic for lining (if you find 72" width, get 3 yards); 2 yards of 1" dress belting; 2 yards of "buck shot" weighting; 1 spool of nylon elastic thread; 1 duo-purpose eyelet pliers kit and an extra package of large eyelets; 1 package decorative Dot snappers.

If the plastic is 36" wide, cut into two equal pieces and flat-seam them together. Fold the edge over the belting for a casing, and stitch. Using eyelet pliers, apply large eyelets, 6" apart, through the belting, all across the heading. Make a ¾" hem at bottom and run a strip of "buck shot" weighting through it, fastening each end with a few stitches.

Now cut the organdy in three 2½-yard lengths, and seam them together at selvage edges. Make a 1" hem down both outside edges and across the bottom. Cut remaining organdy into 4" strips crosswise for ruffles. Finish the edges of the ruffles as on criss-cross curtain. Flat-seam them together or picot the seams. Shirr-stitch the top of the ruffle with three rows of nylon elastic thread about 1" from edge. Stitch the shirred pieces, three tiers deep, at the bottom of the organdy curtain and stitch one ruffle at the top. Gather the top of the curtain to the size of the eyelet heading on the plastic piece and stitch it together. About 8" apart on each side of organdy curtain apply two decorative Dot snapper tops toward the bottom on the side hem edges. Apply the other halves of the snappers on plastic so the two curtains snap together.

▶ *Making Draperies*

No matter what room you are sewing for, your decor may be formal or it may be informal. The type of fabric you chose for draperies in a formal room must be appropriate, such as: velvet or velveteen, taffeta, satin, brocade, moiré, brocatelle, silk, wool or nylon fabric which could be threaded, spattered, etched, figured, or embossed with metallics or other luxurious effects. Formal drapery is often teamed with elaborate matching valances. Your draperies may be trimmed with silk braid, fringe, or other edgings. They may be straight or draped in swags or cascades, all of which you can learn to do at home.

For less formal draperies you might use linen, chintz, cotton homespun, corduroy, denim, sailcloth, polished cotton, monk's cloth, wool felt, or burlap. Informal draperies should be made very simply. If valances are used they should be on straight, simple lines.

When estimating drapery yardage, allow for the length from the top-of-window fixture, plus hems and heading, and the amount necessary to cover the width of the space. Over-curtains or draperies of medium weight fabrics require a fullness of 2 to 2½ times the width. Also, if you select a large one-way design, or plaid, allow one full length of the motif for each additional length required for draperies. Some home decorating fabrics such as chintz and cotton are only 36" wide. Most synthetics and blends are 40", 48", or 54"; the average is 48". There are a few 60" drapery fabrics, and wool felt is usually 72" wide. There is a special type of inexpensive homespun in several popular weaves that is up to 10 feet wide.

Drapery fabric must have true dimensional stability. It must hang from the fixtures in straight, graceful folds. Pull a thread to guide you, and cut on the straight crosswise grain; never tear, for you are likely to distort the grain. Then you will have to pull it back in shape again to make it fall correctly. Also, that is why you should invest in good quality merchandise for such a large project.

Draperies are made unlined or lined and interlined, depending upon whether a fabric has a right and wrong side and whether it is formal or informal. Interlining is often done to give a more luxurious appearance, or for insulation. If draperies are lined, the lining fabric is often a firmly-woven cotton sateen in a neutral color. However, if you wish to line for insulation, Milium-insulated drapery lining materials act as a radiant heat barrier, cut air-conditioning or heating bills by helping maintain even room temperatures, and almost eliminate light filtration which fades draperies or other fabrics in a room.

I hope to have set you dreaming about all the possibilities of making beautiful drapery treatments for your home. I've told you that there are instruction booklets available at sewing centers, notion counters and drapery fabric departments, as well as paper patterns, which will help you learn how to make the specific pieces you are planning. So, let's spend the remaining space left in this chapter on some special ideas and hints I have found useful.

Fig. XIII-7

One of the hard tasks in making draperies is having to measure and count off spacings for pinch-pleat clusters. Now there is a 4"-wide ready-pleated drapery stiffening as easy to use as the narrower one for pleating garments.

The one thing you must keep in mind at all times is that most draperies are made in pairs, with right and left panels facing each other at the center. Fig. XIII-7A gives yardage measurement charts for various widths of material.

Chart For 36" Wide Material

WINDOW WIDTH	FABRIC WIDTHS NEEDED
26" TO 32"	2 WIDTHS
33" TO 50"	3 WIDTHS
51" TO 68"	4 WIDTHS
69" TO 85"	5 WIDTHS
86" TO 104"	6 WIDTHS
105" TO 122"	7 WIDTHS
123" TO 140"	8 WIDTHS
141" TO 158"	9 WIDTHS

Chart For 45"-To 48" Wide Material

WINDOW WIDTH	FABRIC WIDTHS NEEDED
26" TO 43"	2 WIDTHS
44" TO 66"	3 WIDTHS
67" TO 91"	4 WIDTHS
92" TO 116"	5 WIDTHS
117" TO 141"	6 WIDTHS
142" TO 165"	7 WIDTHS
166" TO 189"	8 WIDTHS

Fig. XIII-7A

TO JOIN WIDTHS AND SET HEMS

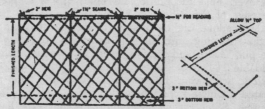

Fig. XIII-7B

TO CUT CRINOLINE

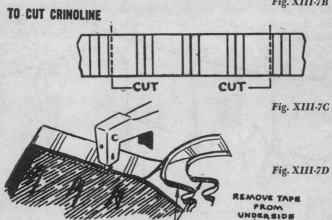

—CUT— CUT—

Fig. XIII-7C

Fig. XIII-7D

REMOVE TAPE
FROM
UNDERSIDE

Clip and cut off the selvages, and join the panels until each half is the right width, matching plaids, stripes or patterns, if any (Fig. XIII-7B). The chart tells you how many spaces and pleats you need for each half of the drapery. Cut the first end, which comes at the front edge of each half of the drapery, 4" before the first set of pleats

(Fig. XIII-7C). Measure off the necessary amount according to the chart and cut two pieces the same.

With your hem pressing gauge, turn and press a ¼" turn and then a 1¼" turn for each side hem. Beginning at the last hem crease, place the right side of the fabric top raw edge ½" over the long edge of the crinoline stiffening, untaped side of the crinoline facing up. Remove the holding tapes as you sew, and stretch out the crinoline to its full length (Fig XIII-7D). Continue stitching the crinoline flat across the top of the drapery fabric until you reach the hem crease of the other side hem. Cut off any crinoline left over. Fold the fabric and lightly press to crease over the edge of the stiffening. Then turn under the full width of the heading. Lightly press in the second fold. At the ends of the stiffening, turn the side hems inward together, even, and pin. Then stitch the full length of both side hems. Make a double 3" hem at the bottom edge.

Now, with your fingers, fold the fabric into the pre-pleated crinoline folds where they come, and pin the pleats together. Stitch the pleats in vertically along the back edge, letting the width of presser foot ride over the thickness

Fig. XIII-7E   *Fig. XIII-7F*

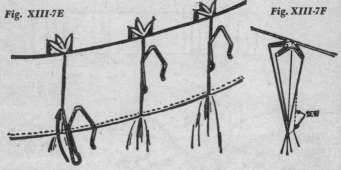

(Fig. XIII-7E). When the stitching has reached the bottom of the pleats at the edge of the stiffening, stitch horizontally across, back-tacking at the beginning and end of the stitching. Finish the top of each set of pleats by pulling the center folds together with invisible hand stitches. This makes the finest-looking custom drapery heading without a row of stitching to mar the top (Fig. XIII-7F). Weight the bottom edges, if desired.

This new ready-pleated stiffening will also make a completely new "butterfly" pleat for an enchanting bedroom decor, with a combination of a country garden printed sateen and contrasting plain-colored heading. It looks as though a bevy of butterflies has breezed in from outdoors and taken up residence in your room. Dot snappers keep the butterflies in flight formation while performing the double duty of holding the fabric to surfaces for easy removal when laundering (Fig. XIII-8).

Fig. XIII-8

Butterfly heading for valance. Centering the pleating clusters properly at both ends, cut a strip of pleated stiffening the length of the valance board. Pull off the holding tapes. With a see-thru ruler and chalk, mark a vertical line through the center crease of each pleat cluster.

Cut a piece of plain-colored sateen the width of the valance board plus an allowance for a 1½″ hem, and same length as the flat stiffening. Cut another piece of printed sateen, 5″ wide, the same length. Lay the right sides of the two fabric pieces together and the strip of stiffening on top of the floral sateen piece, all even at one edge. Pin the three pieces together with a pin running vertical on the marked line at the center of each pleat cluster. Now, using 20 stitches to the inch, seam ½″ from the top edge to within ⅛″ of the first center line. Make two diagonal stitches, turn and stitch parallel with the vertical mark to within ¼″ of end of stiffening. Stitch two stitches across the line and turn, stitching upwards ⅛″ from the other side of the mark to within ¼″ of the edge, turn on two diagonal stitches and continue across the top to the next set of pleats. Repeat until all pleats are finished. With Dot snapper pliers, attach "ring" and "socket" half of the snappers at the center of each space between the pleat clusters. Push the ring through the crinoline side and take up only the printed sateen thickness of fabric. Turn the raw edge of sateen over the crinoline and stitch them together. Make the 1½" hem in the bottom of the plain sateen with the help of the hem pressing gauge.

Now slash on the center marked line on each set of pleats, taking care not to cut into the stitching. Trim away the excess stiffening and fabric at the edges and corners. Use your point turner to turn points squarely to the right side. Press lightly and form a pleat cluster at the base of the slash. Match the last two creases together and stitch down behind them to the end of the crinoline. Then stitch across, back-tacking at the beginning and end of the stitched line. The slash will form into a little "revere" which exposes the color of the print and forms the butterfly effect. Cut a piece of twill tape the length of the valance board. Pin it to the edge of the pleated covering where the Dot snappers come, and mark on the tape where the other half of the snapper must be applied. When all the snappers have been applied to the tape, staple it to the valance board at the point where the heading will go. This makes the heading completely washable when it has to be taken down.

There are so many beautiful suggestions for making bedspreads in those little instruction books you can get in the drapery departments in shops, that almost any could be made to match your butterfly-headed draperies.

▶ Making a Bed Headboard

How would you like to have a glamorous button-tufted headboard (Fig. XIII-9)? If you have a handyman around the house you don't have to dash out to buy the headboard, either. It really does not take much of a carpenter to make this simple headboard. Make it the width of a bed frame to which it may be attached. Mine was made for a single bed 41" wide, 23" deep at center and 2½" thick. Cut a piece of ¼" plywood 41" x 36". From one long edge at center, cut out an area 13" x 33". This leaves 4" x 13" each side (Fig. XIII-10A). On these two sides nail two sturdy lumber support two-by-four's, 36" long. Complete the frame across the bottom and top with two-by-four's, 33" long.

Fig. XIII-9 Button Tufted
Headboard Cover

Fig. XIII-10A

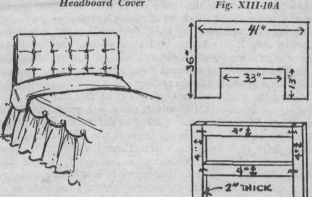

Fig. XIII-10B

This gives the whole frame 2¼″ thickness around the edges (Fig. XIII-10B).

Cover the whole headboard frame, including the supports, in muslin; then the legs should be covered up with solid color sateen 2″ past the joining. After the button-tufted headboard cover is adjusted, the height of the headboard is determined and two holes are drilled through the wood supports and metal bed frame. Fasten them together securely with large 2″ stove bolts.

▶ *Slip Cover for Headboard*

The tufted slip cover may be made from the same fabric as the bedspread and draperies, if you have sufficient material; or it could be made of a harmonizing fabric if you prefer to use some individual decorating theme. The slip cover which looks sleek is one made of a plain-color sateen. The cover fits over the headboard much better and has a more professional look if it is made with a lining of preshrunk muslin (or perhaps an old sheet). For clarity, I will refer to "sateen" for the outside of the slip cover and "muslin" for its lining.

Cut two pieces of sateen 42″ x 25″. Cut two pieces of muslin the same size. (It is safer, of course, to first cut a pattern out of newspaper, over your headboard, to get the proper measurements you need; the measurements given here are a guide for your own work.) With blue tailor's chalk mark off a 1″ seam allowance all around the edges on one muslin piece. Now mark off the remaining area inside the seam into 5″ squares. Lay the sateen piece right side down. Smooth over it two layers (batts) of cotton wadding. Place the muslin piece (with its marked side out) over the batting. Pin all thicknesses of material together around the edges and stitch on the seam allowance line.

Count the places where markings cross and end, and cover that many buttons in the sateen print, following the simple directions on the "no-tool" package. These new buttons are especially good for upholstery because the tab-fastened back keeps them from popping apart. Thread a curved mattress needle (Fig. XIII-11) with double heavy-duty thread and wax it (on beeswax) for further strength. Sew the buttons over the markings, pulling the thread as tight as possible so as to make the batting puff up between the buttons.

Make 18 yards of bias cording from the printed sateen. Stitch the necessary amount of cording around all edges of the batted piece. The second piece of muslin lines the other piece of plain-colored sateen (which becomes the back of the slip cover). Mark off a 1″ seam allowance on the muslin. Apply the cording on the sateen side and stitch around the marked line. Cut a boxing strip of sateen 3½″ wide and long enough to go up one side, across the top and down the other side of the covering. Stitch the boxing at the cording edge on both the tufted and plain piece, leaving the bottom edge free. Now, pull the cover over the headboard frame and check for fit. If the cover fits properly, trim all the seam allowances to ½″. Cut two 3½″ widths of sateen, muslin, and buckram, 35″ long, for lapped boxing at the bottom edge of

Fig. XIII-11   Fig. XIII-12

the slip cover. Sandwich buckram strips between the sateen and muslin. Sew together all around, making two stiffened strips. Finish both ends with a 1" turn-in. Apply Dot snappers so the two pieces snap together. Center and stitch one strip at the bottom of both the tufted and plain bottom edges of the cover. When the tufted slip cover is fitted over the wooden headboard, snap it together between the legs (Figure XIII-12).

▶ Slip-Covering Furniture

Furniture has so many shapes and proportions—there are so many different kinds of pieces that can be slip-covered or re-upholstered at home that it is difficult to find patterns for more than a limited number of standard shapes and sizes. In the spring a homemaker's fancy turns to thoughts of how to cover that faded but otherwise perfectly good sofa or that chair that just doesn't blend into a room. If you would begin with a pattern for something with straight lines, you would learn to understand how to measure and shape a more intricate piece of furniture without a pattern. The underlying principles of slip-covering furniture are all the same. Here, again, you can find good booklets on how to make slip covers in the upholstery departments of most fabric shops and at sewing centers. Also, the Superintendent of Documents, U. S. Government Printing Office, Washington 25, D. C., will send you (upon your written request) a list of booklets on how to repair furniture, upholstery, etc. You might also write to the Home Economics Department or Extension Department of your State Agricultural College, and ask for the same information from that source. The booklets are all helpful in their instructions, they are often free, and sometimes cost just a few cents.

The home sewer can do a good job of camouflaging dejected, old misfit pieces of furniture with smart slip covers.

▶ Needlepoint Hand Work

If you have a fine, old chair frame that is an heirloom, you may enjoy making a needlepoint seat or back for it. This medieval pastime has become a very modern, smart, and popular one today, due to the sudden fashion for needlepoint handbags. I've discovered it is so easy to do while watching television, particularly if you choose a light background color for your handiwork. This helped to revive my interest in it which was dimmed by my first efforts at learning it, some years ago. Then, I didn't like the way the yarn wore thin and uneven when it was pulled through the coarse canvas. But, the wonderful new nylon tapestry yarn pulls through so evenly that every stitch is perfect and lovely and smooth-looking. It comes in a beautiful range of decorator colors. It's completely practical to use white or pastel backgrounds in this yarn because it cleans perfectly and is moth- and mildew-proof.

There is no reason to consider needlepoint as only suitable for antique or traditional furniture. Many excellent designs are completely appropriate for modern and contemporary pieces. Some furniture manufacturers now sell their pieces in a muslin undercovering only, so that you can make your own needlepoint coverings. When you are choosing a chair or other piece to cover, you will probably be wiser to get one with a slip seat or stretched seat, rather than with a cushion or all-upholstered arms and back. That doesn't mean that you cannot cover this more intricate type piece, simply that it takes more work to accomplish such a project.

There are many needlepoint stitches, but the two popular ones are *petit point* and *gros point*. All needlepoint stitches are some variation of the simple half cross stitch, even though the size of the stitch and mesh are not the same. Needlepoint canvas is made in France by the same factory where it was invented in 1865. It is woven of a semi-stiff, coarse, cotton thread in a double-stranded mesh. When you look at a piece, examine the weave and be sure it is perfectly even and uniform. There are 10 meshes to the inch.

Gros point is done with a dull pointed needle over the two close-together threads in both directions, through the large mesh holes only. That means 10 stitches to the inch, or 100 stitches to a square inch. Petit point is done over every thread, so that there are four petit point stitches to every gros point stitch. Of course, gros point is much the easiest to do. Today, most of the needlepoint pieces have their designs already worked by expert needlewomen in Madeira. You just have to fill in the background. Some have all petit point centers, some have part petit point and part gros point, some have all gros point centers.

Quick point is done on rugs where the canvas is very coarse with large meshes, 5 to the inch. The design is colored on the meshes, and you make both design and background with thick rug yarn.

I know of a woman who made a whole coat in needlepoint. She bought the plain canvas by the yard and designed her own motif. Men have made themselves needlepoint vests. During the last few years, the making of beautiful needlepoint handbags has been the fashion to lead women back to this old-time hand art.

Many home furnishings can be made in needlepoint. So many old-fashioned bell-pulls have been bought that I decided to ask what they were being used for in this day of the servantless home. I discovered that they are being turned into handsome coverings for valance boards as well as corner decorative effects to hide unsightly water pipes. A lovely touch in a guest room is a needlepoint luggage rack. Many large pieces are made into fireplace screens. One of the very newest needlepoint pillow designs is a replica of our national emblem with the bald eagle. There are musical motifs made into piano bench covers, as well as interesting hassock and footstool cover designs. There are wall hangings, throw pillows, and telephone book covers, also many needlepoint pictures to frame. For an antique-furnished home, you might practice your first needlepoint on an old-fashioned motto in the style of the old "sampler."

Measuring for needlepoint (Fig. XIII-13): Let's take a chair for an example. Measure the surface to be covered from edge to edge in both width and length directions. Allow 1" extra to turn in on all sides when mounting. For "slip-seat"

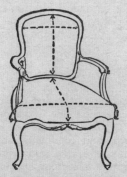

Fig. XIII-13   Measuring Chair for Needlepoint

furniture, allow 2″ all around. If your chair, with the added amount for mounting, measures 19″ x 23″ the standard 23″ x 23″ canvas would not be large enough. This is canvas size from edge to edge. You would have to get a 21″ x 30″ piece, probably.

The ready-worked designs come in a vast array: every flower and fruit imaginable, leaves, scenes, combinations of flowers and birds, or butterflies, musical themes, medallions, and scrolls. Be sure the design you choose is in proportion to the article it will cover. If you make a back and seat, they may be had proportioned as a set. You can also get several all-over patterns by the yard. Or, you can buy the canvas by the yard, get some graph paper (10 squares to the inch), draw your own design and thus express your own taste.

There are three basic needlepoint stitches. The choice of stitch depends upon the ultimate use of the article being made. For something that gets no wear, use the simple *half cross*, the easiest to learn. An example would be a small picture or pillow top. The other two are the continental (or Gobelin) stitch, and the basket weave stitch.

Before you start, cut the hank of needlepoint yarn at both ends so that you will be working with a strand no longer than 18″. The only time you need to know the petit point stitch is when filling in around the edge of petit point centers. Then, you have to split the four-ply yarn into two strands of two-ply thickness. You will need a finer dull-pointed needle for this petit point stitching.

Half cross stitch (Fig. XIII-14): This stitch crosses over from upper left of first mesh to lower right of second mesh diagonally below. The needle under the canvas is put through the next mesh above the one it just went through, and the whole process is repeated. The stitch on the right side is diagonally left to right, the one on the wrong side is short and up and down.

Continental stitch (Fig. XIII-15A): This stitch crosses over from lower right, diagonally across to upper left and then the needle is crossed diagonally under two sets of threads to the next mesh to the left of the first one used on the lower row. The stitch on the right side is diagonally left to right. On the wrong side it looks the same but longer.

Both the half cross and continental stitches are worked most successfully always in the same direction. If worked back and forth, the rows look ridgy and un-uniform.

With both these stitches the canvas may become distorted

Fig. XIII-14　Half-Cross Stitch

Fig. XIII-15A　Continental Stitch

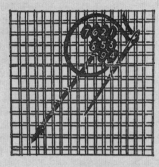

Fig. XIII-15B
Basket-weave Stitch

SKEINS REQUIRED

Canvas Size	Skeins Needed Continental Stitch	Skeins Needed Half Cross Stitch
8x10	3	2
9x11	4	3
9x12	4	3
10 x 12	4	3
10½x13	4	3
12x12	5	4
13x13	6	5
12x14	6	5
12x15	6	5
13x15	7	6
15x15	8	6
16x16	9	7
15x18	9	7
18x18	10	8
21x21	15	11
18x24	14	11
23x23	17	13

Fig. XIII-15C　Estimate Chart

on the bias; but don't worry, it will straighten out in the blocking which is done when the work is finished.

Basketweave stitch (Fig. XIII-15B): This takes up more yarn but it does not distort the canvas to the same degree as either of the others. Of course, this distortion is easily remedied when the needlepoint is wet, then tacked to a board straight and allowed to dry. The basketweave stitch begins on the diagonal with one stitch at the corner of the canvas. Follow the diagram shown here and you will see that where the other two stitches came side by side, these diagonally-placed stitches begin between the ones of the last row. You can never use any of these stitches on the same piece of needlepoint.

Continental and basketweave stitches are best for something that is being given hard wear. But, they both take a lot more yarn than the half cross. See the estimate chart in Fig. XIII-15C.

Of course, it takes time to finish a set of lovely fruit design dining room chair seats of hand-worked needlepoint. Perhaps the old upholstery wears too hopelessly thin and you need a quick replacement. Or, perhaps you haven't the time or energy to tackle real needlepoint, yet. There are loomed needlepoint replacement squares with foam rubber backing that are so easy to put on at home. They come in black, red, green, wine and beige, in several sizes.

You can re-upholster four slip-seat dining room chairs within a matter of two or three hours. First, measure your chair seat from front to back at center, and from side to side. If it measures 15½" x 17, for instance, the 20" x 20" size would turn under 1½" on each side one way, and 2" on each side the other way. The slip-seat has to be unscrewed to remove it from the frame. Turn the chair upside down and remove the screws that fasten the seat to the frame (Fig. XIII-16A). Carefully remove all staples or tacks which fasten the old seat cover to avoid ripping the old fabric, if possible. Check to see how the old covering was folded around the corners so you can fold the new same way.

Place the old cover on the wrong side of the replacement cover and draw around it with tailor's chalk, after you have centered the design as you wish it to come on the right side. Keep the grain line running straight both ways and cut with heavy shears. The seat part to be covered will have some padding on it. Lay it, padded side down, on the new covering, again taking care to center the design (Fig. XIII-16B).

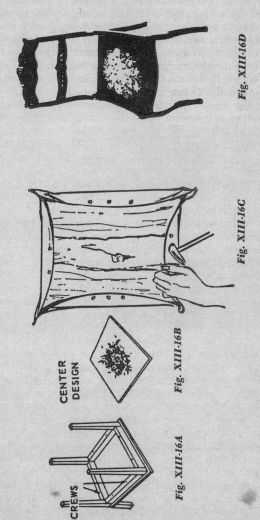

CENTER
DESIGN

SCREWS

Fig. XIII-16A

Fig. XIII-16B

Fig. XIII-16C

Fig. XIII-16D

Beginning at the middle of each side of the new covering, pull it up to fit snugly around the edge of the seat, and tack the center on grain. This keeps the fabric straight while you work toward the corners (Fig. XIII-16C). Now, from each side of the center, tack every 2" up to within about 3" of the corners. Because the replacement seat cover has been padded with a shallow layer of foam rubber, you may peel some of the foam away from the corner edges. You learned how to cut mitered corners in sewing. Follow the same process here but do not cut too far. Turn in the edges and manipulate the excess fullness so as to make the fabric lie flat at the corners. Slip the seat back into the frame, replace and secure the screws, and your chair will look like new (Fig. XIII-16D).